The Five Labours of Europe

A Europe That Will Make Us Grow

Philippe-Emmanuel Partsch

106 West 32nd Street, Suite 144 New York, NY, 10001, USA
www.concurrences.com
book@concurrences.com

First Printing, May 2024
978-1-939007-37-7 (Paperback)
Library of Congress Control Number: 2024937471

Cover Design: Yves Buliard, www.yvesbuliard.fr
Book Design and Layout implementation: Nord Compo

Concurrences Books

Tributes

James F. Rill, *P. Lugard, J. Taladay (eds.), Forthcoming 2024*

Eleanor M. Fox – Antitrust Ambassador to the World, *2021*

Herbert Hovenkamp – The Dean of American Antitrust Law, *2021*

Frédéric Jenny – Standing Up for Convergence and Relevance in Antitrust, (Vol. I & II), *2019 & 2021*

Albert Foer – A Consumer Voice in the Antitrust Arena, *2020*

Richard Whish – Taking Competition Law Outside the Box, *2020*

Douglas H. Ginsburg – An Antitrust Professor on the Bench (Vol. I & II), *2018 & 2020*

Wang Xiaoye – The Pioneer of Competition Law in China, *A. Emch, W. Ng (eds.), 2019*

Ian S. Forrester – A Scot without Borders (Vol. I & II), *A. Komninos (eds.), 2015*

William E. Kovacic – An Antitrust Tribute (Vol. I & II), *2013 & 2014*

Practical Books

The DMA and more – Future application and margin of manoeuvre for national jurisdictions, *G. Muscolo & A. Massolo (eds.), Forthcoming 2024*

AI & Competition Policy, *A. Abbott, T. Schrepel (eds.), Forthcoming 2024*

State Aid & National Enforcement, *J. Derenne, D. Jouve, C. Lemaire, F. Martucci (eds.), Forthcoming 2024*

The 2023 U.S. Merger Guidelines: A Review, *Sean Sullivan (ed.), 2024*

Competition Inspections in 25 Jurisdictions 2nd Edition – A Practitioner's Guide, *N. Jalabert-Doury (ed.), 2024*

EU Antitrust Enforcement – Law, Economics, History, Policy & Practice, *Wouter P. J. Wils, 2024*

The EU Foreign Subsidies Regulation, *Andreas Reindl, Isabelle Van Damme, 2024*

Compendium of Antitrust Damages Action – International Chamber of Commerce (ICC) – 2nd edition, *J.W.H. Denton AO, F. Brunet, S. Williams, C. Inthavisay (eds.), 2023*

Pharmaceutical Antitrust: An Analysis of US and EU Law, *M. Thill-Tayara, G. Gordon (eds.), 2023*

Innovation Paradox in Merger Control, *G. Gurkaynak, 2023*

Antitrust and the Digital Economy, *Y. Katsoulacos (ed.), 2023 (in collaboration with CRESSE)*

Judicial Review of Competition Cases, *D. Ginsburg, T. Eicke (eds.), 2023*

Competition Law Treatment of Joint Ventures, *B. Bleicher, N. Campbell, A. Hamilton, N. Hukkinen, A. Khan, A. Mordaunt (eds.), 2022 (in collaboration with the IBA)*

Information Exchange & Related Risks, *Z. Marosi, M. Soares (eds.), 2022 (in collaboration with the IBA)*

Rulemaking Authority of the US Federal Trade Commission, *D. Crane (ed.), 2022*

The International Competition Network at Twenty, *D. Anderson & P. Lugard (eds.), 2022*

Competition Case Law Digest – 5th Edition, *F. Jenny, N. Charbit (eds.), 2022*

Competition Inspections in 21 Jurisdictions – A Practitioner's Guide, *N. Jalabert-Doury (ed.), 2022*

Perspectives on Antitrust Compliance, *A. Riley, A. Stephan, A. Tubbs (eds.), 2022 (in collaboration with the ICC)*

Turkish Competition Law, *G. Gürkaynak, 2021*

Competition Law – Climate Change & Environmental Sustainability, *S. Holmes, D. Middelschulte, M. Snoep (eds.), 2021*

Merger Control in Latin America – A Jurisdictional Guide, *P. Burnier da Silveira, P. Sittenfeld (eds.), 2020*

Competition Inspections under EU Law – A Practitioner's Guide, *N. Jalabert-Doury, 2020*

Gun Jumping in Merger Control – A Jurisdictional Guide, *C. Hatton, Y. Comtois, A. Hamilton (eds.), 2019 (in collaboration with the IBA)*

Choice – A New Standard for Competition Analysis? *P. Nihoul (ed.), 2016*

PhD Theses

The Economics of Digital Markets – Essays in Theoretical and Empirical Industrial Organization, *E. Arnoud-Joufray, Forthcoming 2024*

Abuse of Platform Power, *F. Bostoen, 2023*

Reform of Chinese State-Owned Enterprises, *X. Bai, 2023*

Competition & Regulation in Network Industries – Essays in Industrial Organization, *J-M. Zogheib, 2021*

The Role of Media Pluralism in the Enforcement of EU Competition Law, *K. Bania, 2019*

Buyer Power, *I. Herrera Anchustegui, 2017*

General Interest

Why Competition? Voices from the Antitrust Community and Beyond, *D. Crane, D. Gerard, R. Tritell (eds.), Forthcoming 2024*

Global Dictionary of Competition Law, *D. Healey, W. Kovacic, R. Whish (eds.), Forthcoming 2024*

Great Antitrust Enforcers, *W. E. Kovacic, 2023*

Competition – How to Speak Like an Expert, *E. Combe , 2023*

Women and Antitrust – Voices from the Field (Vol I & II), *E. Kurgonaite & K. Nordlander, 2020*

e-Book versions available for **Concurrences+** subscribers

Quo Vadis Europa?

The new collection title "Quo Vadis Europa?" encapsulates the essence of this publishing initiative. *Quo Vadis* means both *Where are you going?* and *What do you want?* Books of this collection aim to answer these two pivotal questions: "Where is Europe heading?" and "What do we want for our Europe?" The works we intend to publish in this new collection will be dedicated to answer these interrogations, to shape and question European dynamics in all their aspects.

The collection will address a wide array of topics critical to understanding European dynamics, including but not limited to European sovereignty and autonomy, security strategies highlighted by the war in Ukraine, economic strategies notably through technological competitiveness, risks of shortages of raw materials, the green deal, health policy, taxation, and the preservation of social values within Europe .These subjects are at the forefront of European discourse, reflecting the complex and multifaceted nature of the continent's challenges and opportunities.

We are committed to providing a platform for contemporary thinkers to share their ideas, fostering a dialogue that is crucial for the future of our modern democracies and economies. The "Quo Vadis Europa?" collection is designed to be comprehensive, covering a broad spectrum of themes and approaches, from politics and economics to security, the environment, and technology. Each book in this collection will be the product of thorough contemplation and rigorous research, offering unique insights into the Europe of both today and tomorrow.

We are convinced that "Quo Vadis Europa?" will become an invaluable source of knowledge and insight, and that this collection will help to fuel debate and stimulate reflection on Europe in a constantly changing world.

Nicolas Charbit, Sébastien Gachot, Maevy Lakrouf

The views expressed in this essay are those of the author and not of the local authorities and institutions of which he belongs. He can be contacted on Linkedin and at the following address: philem.partsch@gmail.com.

Overview

Foreword

It's a paradox that makes you smile. Europe, the nymph carried off by Zeus incarnate as a white bull, means "wide-eyed". And yet, we are so short-sighted when it comes to European integration! On the one hand, we underestimate what it brings us in terms of lower costs. On the other, we do not demand enough of it, given its untapped potential… and the current situation.

Is this indulgence still justified? Our loss of technological, economic, financial and even educational momentum is dramatic. Poverty is growing despite social transfers. Public finances are showing alarming imbalances in some Member States, our demography is nosediving, and our ecosystem is suffering. Geopolitical tensions are multiplying.

In all areas, the signs are clearly amber. We need to do more than just halt the decline of our economy and save our social democracy. We also need to develop a more eco-responsible economy and a defence system that is less dependent on the goodwill of the United States.

However, our destiny remains in our own hands. Europe, which made it possible for us to get back on our feet after the Second World War, can help us – citizens, businesses and Member States alike – to develop further because it has a number of major assets at its fingertips. Provided we play them right.

Without transferring new competences to the European Union or making major sacrifices the prosperity of the 27 Member States, the wages, the employment rates and social justice can be substantially improved. By consolidating the foundations will our democracies be able to negotiate the transition towards eco-responsibility and the strengthening of our external security.

Prosperity, development and solidarity, eco-responsibility, democracy and internal freedoms; the triptych generosity, stability, security vis-à-vis third countries. How can Europe contribute to these five Labours (after all, it is not much compared to the twelve inflicted on Hercules, his quasi nephew[1])?

This is the main thrust of this essay, which draws on years of diverse professional experience of European integration, both inside and outside the institutions. One of the common threads is that, being neither a state nor a superstate, and having to do what a state is not capable of doing alone, the European Union (EU) benefits from giving priority to certain specific types of intervention.

This book is also an opportunity to provide an overview of the Union's priorities and policies, to highlight some of the key elements for our quality of life as well as our children's, to reflect on the ways in which economic and social policies are being pursued today, to revisit some of the concepts in these areas as well as the relationship between the EU, the Member States and the public.

I do not know or have the answers to everything. My aim is to ask questions, lay the foundations for further fruitful – let us hope so – discussion and debate, to open up new perspectives, while remaining realistic and pragmatic. There is much to question, reconsider and reinvent. The current upheavals and disruptions are an invitation to do so.

With the European elections just a few months away, readers will also find in these pages concrete measures, specific objectives, a roadmap and an approach for the future. The next European Commission, Parliament and Council are free to draw inspiration from them.

Europe, lend us your sense of vision and action.

---

1 Hercules is the result of another of Zeus' extramarital romances.

Introduction

Europe: A Still Enviable Lifestyle

Europe is a great place to live – more so than in many other parts of the world, even rich ones. Think of the quality of life, the prosperity, the social justice, the democracy, human rights and freedoms, the environmental record, the generosity.

Numbers are not everything, but they do provide a first glimpse. Let us take a look at the most significant ones.

Quality of life? Nine Member States in the 20 countries with the highest happiness index,[2] 6 in the top 10, the top 2 places. Half of the world's top 26 countries in terms of human development. The 5 most advanced countries in the world in terms of gender equality, one of the highest life expectancies (81 years,[3] compared with 78.6 years in the United States, where it is falling[4]), 5 of the 10 best cities for eating well, a high level of safety (homicide rate and percentage of people in prison, respectively 7 and 10 times lower than in the United States), the two most pleasant cities to live in (Vienna and Copenhagen), and 2 others in the top 10. In comparison, people feel happy in mind and body in Europe where they live and travel in safety.

In economic terms, Europe has the world's second-largest GDP, behind the USA[5] and just ahead of China, is one of the world's

---

2 The same score applies to the Human Development Index (HDI), which takes into account life expectancy, length of schooling and gross national income per capita.

3 Eurostat, *Key figures on Europe – 2021 edition*, Luxembourg, Publications Office of the European Union, 2021, p. 15; however, Covid has reduced life expectancy to 80.1 years, Eurostat, *Key figures on Europe – 2023 edition*, Luxembourg, Publications Office of the European Union, 2023, p. 16.).

4 According to the latest statistics, it has even fallen to 76.1 years, the same level as in 1996 (*La Croix*, 31 August 2022).

5 In 2020, €13,306 billion compared with €13,923 billion in 2019 (a decrease attributable to the pandemic) (*Key figures on Europe*, 2021), €14,400 billion in 2021 (*Key figures on Europe – 2022 edition*, Luxembourg, Publications Office of the European Union, 2022, p. 34), €15,800 billion in 2022 (*Key figures on Europe*, 2023, p. 34). GDP in 2020 is just under three quarters of US GDP ($15,192 billion compared with $20,936 billion).

biggest trading powers (second-largest exporter, behind China), is the world's biggest investor as well as attracting investment, with 8 countries in the top 20 on the competitiveness index. Even the unemployment rate is historically low: before and after the pandemic (6.2%[6]). Since then, it has continued to fall (5.9% in December 2023, despite the war in Ukraine!). Europe remains one of the richest regions in the world, and still boasts a degree of economic dynamism. Contrary to popular belief, Europe is not just a population of spoilt consumers.

In social terms, we have the highest level of welfare spending[7] and the most redistributive society.[8] We are a long way from being the second stereotype of a neoliberal Europe strangling public services. Moreover, public services are expressly recognised at a European level, and the Member States remain largely free to create and scale them.[9]

Scores on the rule of law are generally very good, with two of the top three places in the world.

The European Union (EU) is also a world economic powerhouse with the lowest *energy intensity* (ratio of energy consumed to GDP). The USA has a more mediocre performance of between 30 and 45%. On average, a European emits less than half of the CO_2 and consumes six times less water than an American. In this area, we are both more efficient and more sober.

---

6 This is the lowest rate since its measurement began in January 2000 (Communiqué from the Statistical Office of the EU, published on 30 January 2020, *Europe Daily Bulletin* ("*EDB*") 12415 of 31 January 2020, p. 20). After rising to 7.5% in April 2021, it fell back to 6.2% in March 2022.

7 On average, social spending is 10 points higher than in the United States, at 30.3% of GDP, with a range from 35.2% (France) to 15% (Ireland). That said, such a score should be interpreted with caution. It may be a sign of a weak economy (but is not necessarily so), with high unemployment and the need for high transfer spending to help the poorest. A strong economy, especially if it provides a majority of high value-added jobs, will require less transfer or redistribution spending, without necessarily being less social.

8 Income inequality in the EU is, on average, lower than in other OECD countries (*OECD Economic Surveys: European Union*, June 2018, Executive Summary, p. 2).

9 On services of general economic interest (SGEIs), *see* below, Title I, Ch. 2, E.

The EU is the most generous region *vis-à-vis the rest of the world*: it provides more than half of the world's official development assistance[10] (we will come back to this later[11]), or 0.48% of the GDP of the 27… but is eclipsed by the USA, a more modest contributor (0.2% of its GDP), which "sells" its achievements better.

The Role of European Integration ukin This Overall Success

Europe brings us a series of advantages, in our everyday daily lives, starting with goods and services that we would not find at home or that are more expensive, the freedom to come and go in large groups and to settle in 26 other Member States, without the need to convert our money in most of them. I know three people who owe their lives to a specialist doctor practising in another Member State.

The explanation? A country cannot excel at everything. A pool of 445 million people offers more varied, high-quality goods and services than a population of 1, 10 or 100 million – especially when it has as many different languages, cultures, histories and educational backgrounds as the Member States of the EU.

Someone wanted to build, using wood, a project designed for a concrete framework. The first floor had an overhang that posed a technical challenge for a timber structure… After an international competition, the right company was found in Slovenia, where the timber industry is of the highest quality. The project went ahead without a hitch.

At a conference I was giving on Brexit, I was surprised to see a charming acquaintance active in the motoring world. She told me that most spare parts for vintage sports cars are made in the UK. Brexit would make them more expensive and more difficult to ship. Another

10 *EDB* 12376 of 26 November 2019, p. 4.

11 *See* below, in the Introduction, "Comparative Cost of the EU and Aid to Developing Countries".

participant was worried because he produces animal medicines. Few companies outside the UK are capable of manufacturing the containers.

Luxembourg has reintroduced a tram recently. It is changing the lives of residents and commuters alike: improved mobility, less pollution. The project is very European: Spanish trains, a French project manager, a loan from the European Investment Bank (EIB), the EU's economic development bank, whose current loans to the European economy represent almost two years of French budget revenue[12] (€550 billion compared with €300 billion).

We have become so accustomed to these advantages that we think they are normal. However, they are not. Just ask the British, who have recently discovered/rediscovered border controls, shortages and raging inflation, post-Brexit.

We are also sometimes unaware that one aspect of our quality of life is due to Europe, whose action/role is often discreet, indirect and underground. Unlike the Post Office, the European Union does not have an office in every locality. Like the Electric Fairy, it is elusive and immaterial. A light superstructure, focusing on the design, it acts mainly through national and regional administrations. The result is an image deficit[13] that suits the Member States. They fear being sidelined. Like Anastasia and Drizella, they like to keep Cinderella-Europe in the attic.

We also sometimes dismiss Europe's usefulness, or even act in bad faith. Could Emmanuel Macron have implemented his "whatever it takes" policy in the fight against Covid-19 without the backing of the European Central Bank (ECB) and Germany? Before the euro,

---

12 On the European Investment Bank (EIB), *see* below, in particular Title II, Ch. 1., B.

13 Europe is rarely represented or depicted, apart from Plantu who, in his caricatures, draws her as an ethereal, ethereal, empathetic young woman, half-vestal, half-sympathetic young sovereign.

such a declaration would have led to the immediate devaluation of the French franc. Europe protects us against external shocks far more than we realise. Just ask the British again.

Europe has increased the purchasing power of its population, increased the protection of its workers and facilitated their free movement. It has helped to strengthen democracies (think of the Mediterranean countries), human rights and the peaceful coexistence of different communities within the Member States.

The construction of Europe has therefore acted as an Archimedean lever in economic, social and democratic terms. It has enabled much of the continent to rise from the ashes after two world wars, while consolidating its fundamental values and preserving its diversity.

The Contribution of European Integration to This Overall Success: A Few Figures

According to various studies, *the increased prosperity resulting from European integration is estimated at between 9 and 12.5%.* Without the EU, the 27 Member States would have a GDP of around €14,529/€14,077 billion instead of €15,837 billion. This is a significant surplus given the reduced resources deployed. The budget of the EU is around 1% of the GDP of the 27 Member States (slightly more in 2022, €170.6 billion, or 1.07%). The *multiplier effect of European integration, its leverage effect, would therefore be between 7.7 and 10.6 if we compare the European budget to the GDP gain achieved.* In other words, Europe costs each inhabitant €380 a year for an additional income of €2,917–€3,925.

European integration is giving us a lot in return for very little. We are back to the light superstructure. The EU is not a 28th state or a superstate. By comparison, the EU budget is between 30 and 60 times smaller in relative terms than that of the Member States (see figure 1), on average 50 times smaller. In addition, the EU has a low level of operating expenditure (6% of the European budget).

Comparative Cost of the EU and Aid to Developing Countries

The European budget should also be compared with the combined development aid of the Member States and the EU: €165 billion versus €70.2 billion.[14] *We are therefore allocating the equivalent of almost half the EU budget to Developing World countries.*[15]

Putting these figures together raises a number of questions:[16] do we care enough about our common interests? The reactions to these two figures are also intriguing. Development aid is considered insufficient, with a target of 0.7% of GDP seen as a minimum. On the other hand, there is no question of increasing the Community budget, even though the latter seems to be bearing more fruit than aid to certain third countries.

European Integration: An Archimedean Lever for All Member States

All Member States benefit from Europe. Europe is not a zero-sum game where one country wins at the expense of another. It increases the size of the cake for each national economy, contrary to a third common misconception.

In this respect, the overall return to a Member State from its membership of the EU is far greater than its contribution to the European budget.

14 In 2021.

15 To be exact, development aid is equivalent to 42.5% of the Community budget (0.48% compared with 1.17% of the GDP of the EU27).

16 Especially if we take into account the much lower cost of living in developing countries: in relative terms, are not we allocating more resources to these countries than to European integration?

On the one hand, a Member State receives a proportion of the European budget directly, through the allocation of European funds. Depending on the case, this is greater than, equal to or less than its contribution (the richest Member States contribute more to the Community budget than they benefit from directly).

On the other hand, and above all, as explained above, the surplus wealth that a national economy derives from its participation in the EU is, in any case, out of all proportion to its possible net contribution (the difference between the contribution and the part of the European budget to which it is entitled), taking into account the leverage effect of 7.7 to 9.4 mentioned above.

For example, after five short years of Brexit, the UK would have already lost a sum equivalent to 47 years' net contribution to European integration! That is a "deleverage" effect of 9.4%, in the high range of the leverage of EU membership mentioned above. QED! Brexit is the best proof of the EU's usefulness and profitability. Yes, the EU is bankable.

Irrespective of the Member States' shared values, their attachment to democracy and a certain solidarity, the EU is therefore a rational marriage.

Europe's Contribution Underestimated or Even Denied

As for the rest, national grumblings about Europe costing too much or other Member States benefiting from it make us smile. We are quick to see the splinter in our neighbour's eye, but less quick to see the beam in our own.

France does not like to be reminded that some of its farmers, not just the more marginal ones, have benefited since 1957 from the Common

Agricultural Policy[17] (CAP), which for a long time consumed three quarters of the European budget. The Germans underplay that they are ideally placed at the centre of the single market to serve it with their powerful industry. Italy pays little heed to the money paid to the Mezzogiorno since 1957. The Netherlands criticises spendthrift Member States, but downplays the revenue they receive from the port of Rotterdam, the main collection point for European customs duties on products from third countries.[18] The Belgians criticise the Eurocrats for being overpaid and adding to the cost of living in Brussels. They do not realise what a boon these few thousand civil servants are as they only pay a fraction of their salaries. Without them, Brussels would be toothless, a victim of bickering between Flemish and French speakers.[19]

A Success That Respects Diversity at the Same Time

What's more, such global success has not come at the cost of our specific national, or even regional and local, characteristics.

Linguistic diversity has been preserved and is expressly protected. The Member States have not been dismantled. They also remain free to set the level of public services offered to the population and, correlatively, the level of taxation to fund them. People's expectations of the state may still differ from one country to another. Public spending varies by more than double, as can be seen in figure 1 below. While in 2021 it represented 25% of GDP in Ireland, it reached 59% in France. Social protection spending represents between 15% and 36% of GDP, with an average of 30.1%. Such variations in the role

17 On the Common Agricultural Policy (CAP), *see* below, Title III, Ch. 2.

18 As Jean Quatremer, a journalist at *Libération* specialising in European issues, pointed out, he himself forgot that Rotterdam's de facto monopoly owed a great deal to the Le Havre CGT.

19 P. Deglume, "Un quart de l'économie bruxelloise est liée à l'Europe", *L'Echo*, 25–26 September 2021, pp. 1 and 4.

of the state and the public sector[20] are both the result of and driven by different mentalities. This being the case, to say that Europe is neoliberal or that it wants to standardise everything is complete nonsense.

Another guarantor of diversity is… the EU's cumbersome decision-making process: proposals from the European Commission, trialogue with the European Parliament and the Council, the two co-legislators, majority requirements in terms of states and population.

20 Property can be either private or public in Europe and cannot be discriminated against on the basis of whether it belongs to the private or public sector (principle of neutrality of the property regime). This is another element of European diversity.

Figure 1. Government revenue and expenditure, 2022[1]
(% of GDP)

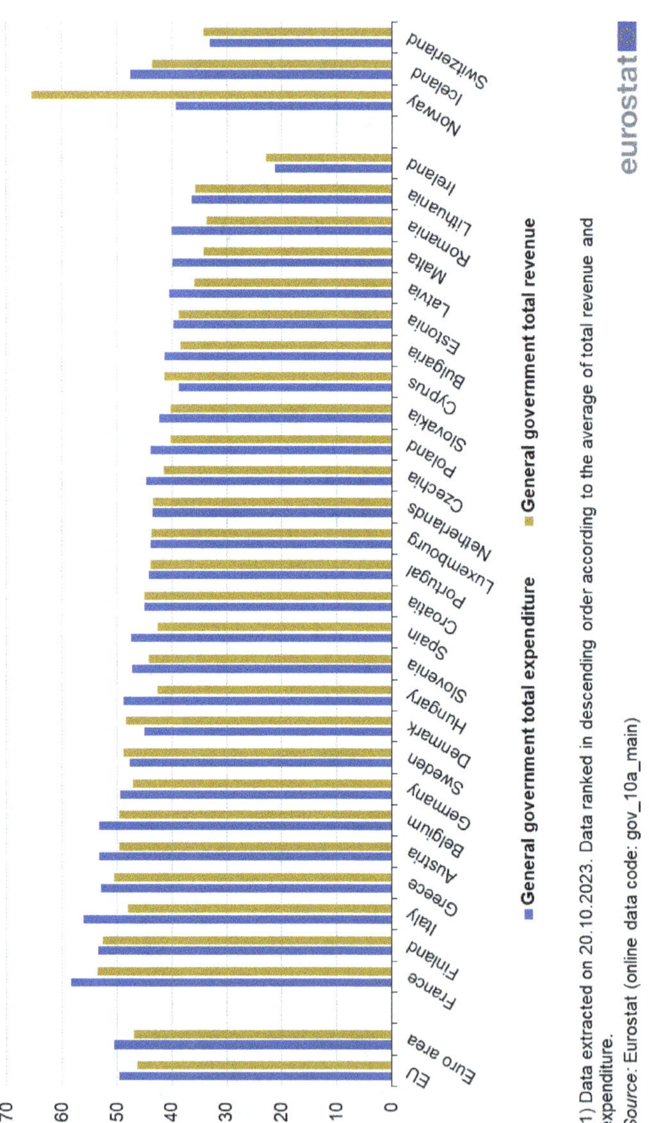

The allocation of public expenditure also differs significantly from one Member State to another (social protection, education, police, etc.). This is a logical consequence of maintaining Member States' autonomy in political, economic, social and societal matters.

Europe simply requires Member States not to live beyond their means and to ensure a balance between their income – in other words, tax revenues – and expenditure (principles of budgetary responsibility and sustainability of public finances).[21] For the rest, they have carte blanche, provided they respect certain important principles, such as freedom of movement, the (relative) ban on State aid,[22] and the framework of Economic and Monetary Union (EMU). Europe lives up to its motto: "United in diversity". Remarkably, we have managed to maintain this trait in a Europe enlarged to 27 and therefore, by definition, increasingly diverse. It is a real tour de force.

Once again, we see the outline of a light, almost imperceptible structure, which must be neither cumbersome nor intrusive, not just for the Member States, but also for citizens and businesses. Nor should it have unlimited powers.

The European project brings us a great deal (starting with a 27-fold increase in space and increased prosperity) *while taking away little*, above all *from* the Member States, *at a lower cost and with a smaller footprint*.

But is this the reason why the EU, so disembodied, rational, minimalist and complex, does not arouse unbridled attachment and affection? The nymph Europe has become more like Juno,[23] precious but unexciting, rather than Venus.

21 On this question, *see* below, Title I, Ch. 2, devoted to the public sector.

22 On these issues, *see* below, Title I, Ch. 1, on the internal market.

23 An unusual development since, in mythology, the nymph Europa has an affair with Zeus, the husband of Hera, and therefore of Juno.

A Balance Sheet in Jeopardy?

This positive balance sheet should not obscure the fact that we are running out of steam, showing weaknesses and even signs of decline. Europe is in a rut. The elation and dynamism that characterised its abduction in the founding myth are long gone.

So let us take another look at some numbers and figures, as we would after a medical check-up or blood test. An individual may feel fit, but excessive blood pressure can lead to kidney and/or cardiovascular problems. In the same way, human society must take into account any deterioration in certain essential elements that could jeopardise its future, its equilibrium and its quality of life. Watch out for the silent killers of prosperity, harmony and happiness. They are at work in Europe today, more than we might think.

First of all, for several years now (2010), the USA has had a higher GDP than us, with a population that was 40% lower before Brexit (325 million compared with 514 million) and 25% lower after (332 million compared with 448.4 million). Per capita income is therefore much higher and the gap is only widening. The difference in purchasing power (40% in 2017) continues to grow. In absolute terms, the gap is more brutal. In 2021, GDP per capita in the USA was €58,584.20 compared with €28,095.61 in the EU, a difference that is more than double. China is now on our heels in terms of GDP, albeit with a much larger population.

In 2011, Europe still accounted for 30% of the 500 largest companies in the world[24] (147 to be exact). By 2020, this share had fallen to less than 20% (93 companies), a decline of more than a third. This is a severe decline, even if we take into account the losses linked to Brexit (17 UK companies). This is exacerbated by the fact that European companies

24 J.-C. Defraigne and P. Nouveau, *Introduction à l'économie européenne*, New Leuven, De Boeck, 3rd ed., 2022, p. 539.

have fallen down the rankings to the advantage of American and Chinese companies.[25] They have also fallen back in the ranking of the largest market capitalisations, with American companies occupying 8 of the top 10 places, and 67 of the top 100. And to think that these figures predate the emergence of artificial intelligence.

The pace of growth has been slower in Europe than in the United States (and even more so in China) over the last twenty years or so, and we are progressively producing less wealth and added value than these countries, as figure 2[26] shows. The European decline is clear and contrasts with the resilience of the United States compared with China. Moreover, real GDP growth over the last 23 years in the other two blocs has exceeded that of Europe by more than 50%.

Figure 2.

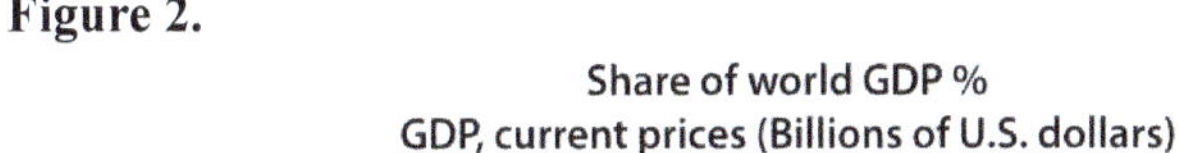

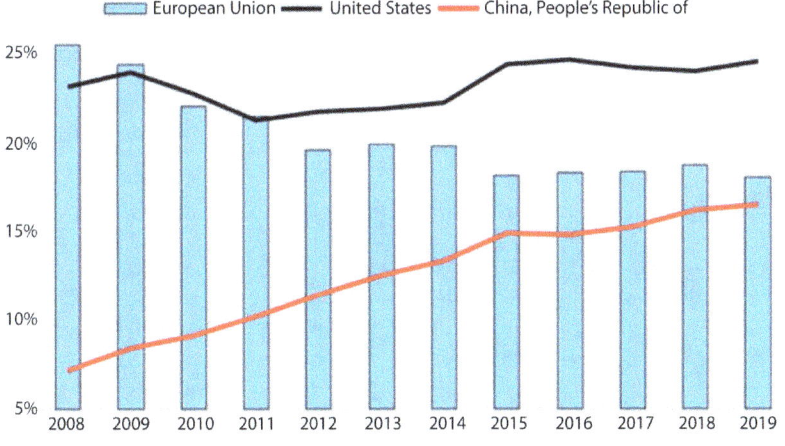

25 The leading European company is 16th in Kantar's top 100 largest global companies of 2019, and only 3 European companies feature in the top 25.

26 N. Goetzmann, "For a new European growth strategy: The EU and Globalisation", 16 January 2022, Schuman Papers and Interviews, *Schuman Papers* no. 619, Website of Foundation Robert Schuman.

A Key Indicator: Labour Productivity

One figure epitomises this decline: *labour productivity*[27] (as well as overall productivity of the factors of production), i.e. the added value that, on average, one worker is capable of producing in a given period of time. In Europe, it was only 70% of that in the United States in 2014.[28][29] Each hour worked in Europe was therefore 30% less productive in the creation of wealth than an hour worked in the US 9 years ago. Today, the gap has widened to around 34–38%, as can be seen in figure 3[30] below (the USA is fourth from the left, with the EU27 just inside the OECD average in the centre). If we add to this a higher number of working hours per person in the USA, the difference in per capita income becomes clear.

27 And, more broadly, of all factors of production.

28 J.-C. Defraigne and P. Nouveau, *Introduction à l'économie européenne*, New Leuven, De Boeck, 2nd ed., 2017, p. 155.

29 More and more observers are realising that productivity gains need to be made. *See* for example J.-Y. Huwart, "Relever la productivité devrait être l'objectif n° 1 du plan de relance belge", *L'Echo*, 9 January 2021.

30 Comparison of labour productivity between countries (from *OECD Compendium of Productivity Indicators*, 2021).

Figure 3.

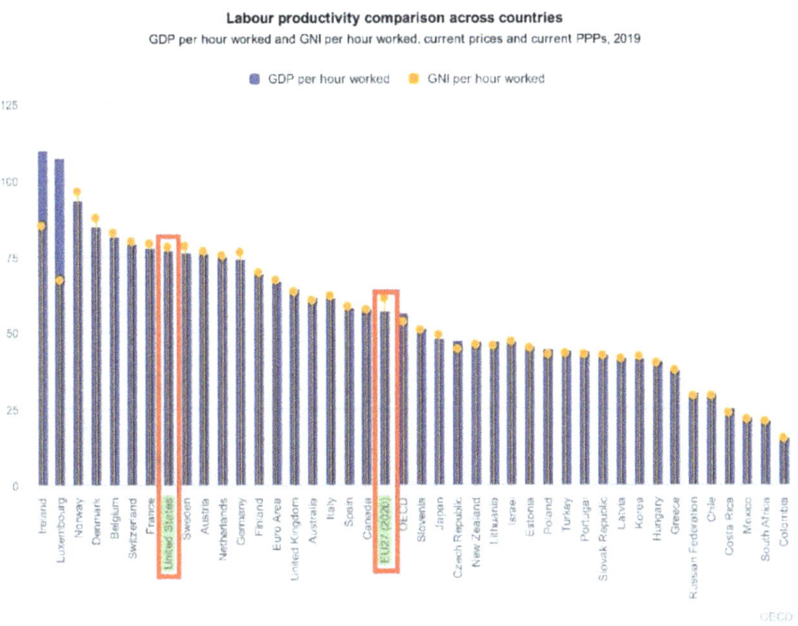

More generally – and this is all the more worrying – the EU27 has been losing ground to the first half of the OECD's most advanced countries over the last two decades, as figure 4[31] shows:

31 This relates to the gap with the top half of OECD countries in terms of productivity per hour worked (minus 13%) (figure from the OECD library).

Figure 4.

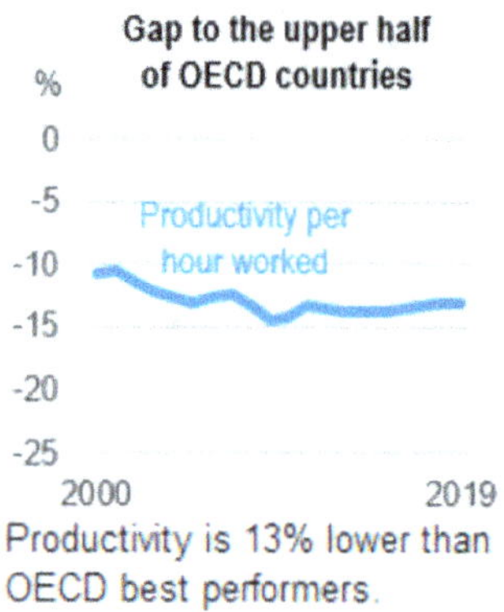

Work Productivity: An Essential Parameter for Quality of Life Too

Labour productivity, and more broadly total factor productivity,[32] are essential barometers of the efficiency and health of an economy. They also have a major impact on society.

Firstly, wages are a direct function of labour productivity. An employer cannot pay a worker more than the value he produces, bearing in mind that they also have to cover other production costs (equipment, administrative and management costs, financial resources made available). For this reason, a compulsory minimum wage that is too high is an unemployment trap. It will discourage an employer from taking on a person, often with little training, whose productivity has not yet matched these costs.[33]

32 Since labour productivity is easier to measure than total factor productivity (TFP), it is generally the latter that is referred to.

33 On this subject, *see* below, Title II, Ch. 2.

Secondly, high labour productivity makes it possible to reduce working hours. This opens up the option of part-time work, with direct implications on the quality of life, work-life balance, combining two careers within a couple or even a family, etc.

Finally, high labour productivity often goes hand in hand with stimulating, innovative work and a supportive environment.

It therefore contributes to the overall quality of life in a society. Countries with a high happiness index often have high labour productivity,[34] while countries that are losing momentum, depressed or suffering from social tensions have lower labour productivity.

In this respect, the EU is in the middle between the USA, where it lags behind in terms of technology and productivity, and the emerging countries, where labour costs are lower. The corollary is a lower level of wages in Europe than in the United States and, for Member States with particularly low labour productivity, the need to make their populations work long, poorly paid hours. To give an example, "the steps that create the most value are not in assembly. They are upstream, in R&D and product design, and downstream, in sales, marketing, distribution and after-sales services. These are very labour-intensive steps".[35]

In fact, as we shall see, we have not invested enough since 2000, particularly in research and development and innovation (R&D&I). As a result, we are plateauing and losing ground to more dynamic economies and societies. The gloom is spreading, as the following symptoms attest.

34 Four of the eight happiest countries are among the eight most productive countries in the world: Denmark (second happiest, fifth most productive), Switzerland (twice fourth), Sweden (seventh and eighth) and Norway (eighth and third).

35 E. Combe, *Chroniques (décalées) d'un économiste*, Paris, Concurrences, 2022, p. 24 (in French).

Social and Societal Ills

Our social model, of which we are so proud, is failing. 21.6% of the population, or 96.5 million people, were at risk of poverty or social exclusion in the EU in 2022.[36] More than the entire population of Germany! Although the situation has improved from a peak of almost 25% in 2012, it is still far from satisfactory. What's more, the target of lifting 20 million people out of the risk of poverty by 2020 has been missed by a wide margin, with only 41% (8.2 million people) having achieved it. A time bomb for our democracies.

We are also having fewer children. The Old Continent is turning into an ageing continent.[37] This is probably a sign of reduced confidence in the future, an effect of the rise in the cost of housing over the last twenty years, combined with relatively stagnant wages, an excessively high youth unemployment rate[38] and insufficient support for families, particularly couples with two full-time jobs.

In short, there is relatively less wealth and dynamism, more poverty despite high social protection spending and substantial public debt in some Member States, fewer children and an ageing population, as figure 5 shows. So there are serious problems in our societies, especially in certain Member States (because the results are relatively mixed from one country to another). We have fallen asleep and are shrinking.

---

36 *Key figures on Europe*, 2023, p. 27.

37 The average age is 43, compared with 30 worldwide (E. Le Boucher, "À chaque crise, l'Europe décroche", *Les Echos*, 29–30 January 2021, p. 11); the fertility rate has fallen to 1.53 births per woman (*Key figures on Europe*, 2023, p. 12).

38 The youth unemployment rate, which is more than double the average rate, is an indicator to be taken with a grain of salt because it includes students. That is why I prefer to refer to the youth unemployment ratio, which is about the same as the average unemployment rate.

Figure 5.

A laughing Europe

Life expectancy at birth

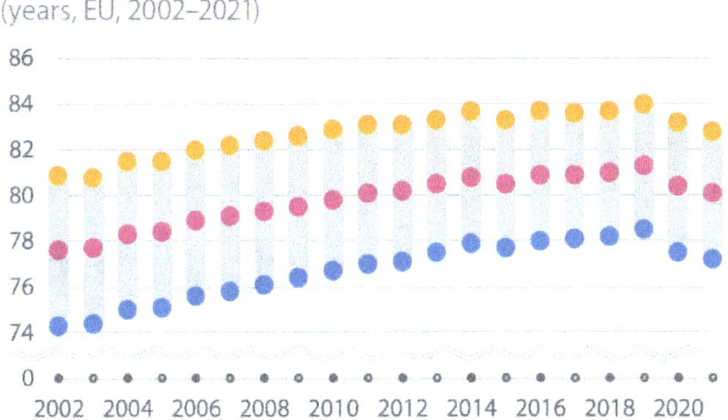

Public spending on social protection (% of GDP)

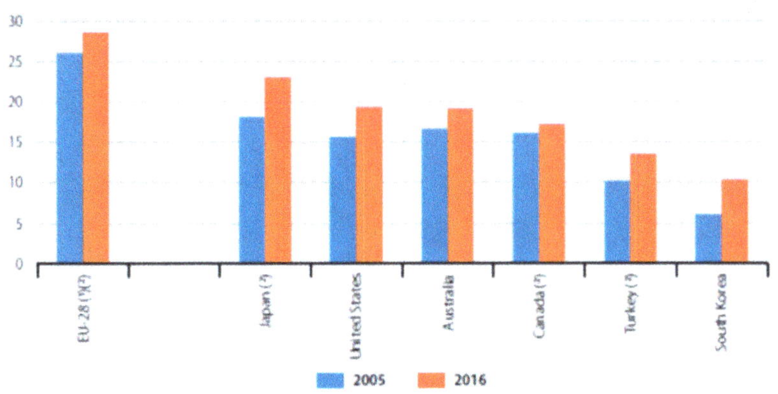

A laughing Europe

International trade in goods with non-member countries (billion EUR, EU, 2002-2020)

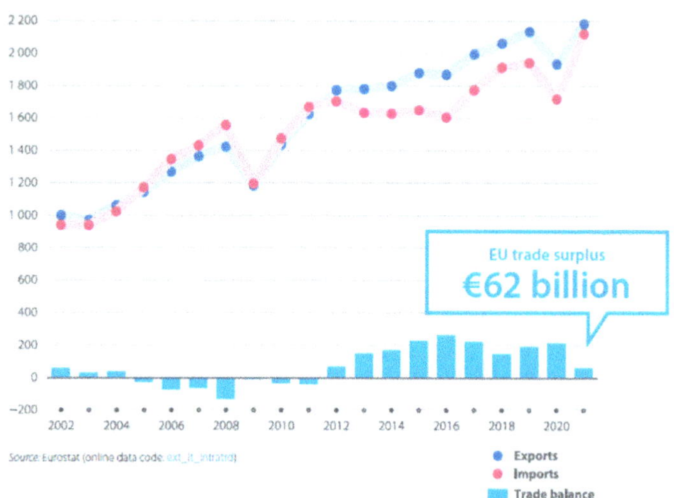

Top 10 partners for EU international trade in goods
(% share of total, EU, 2020)

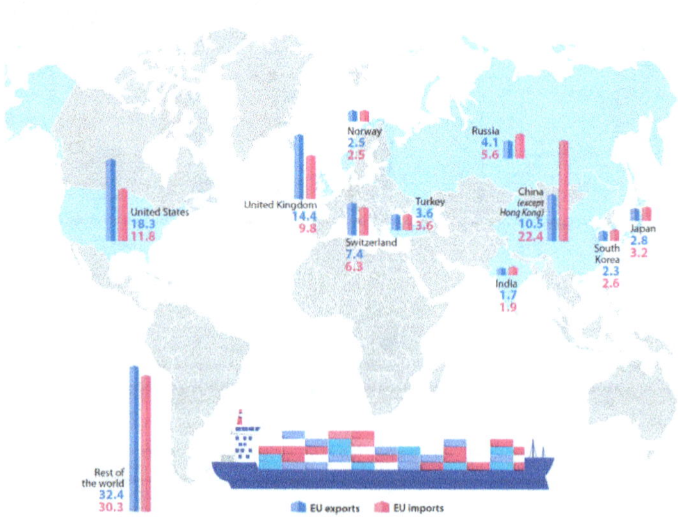

A Europe in tears

Fertility rate (live births per woman, 2020)

Gross expenditure on research and development, 2005 and 2015

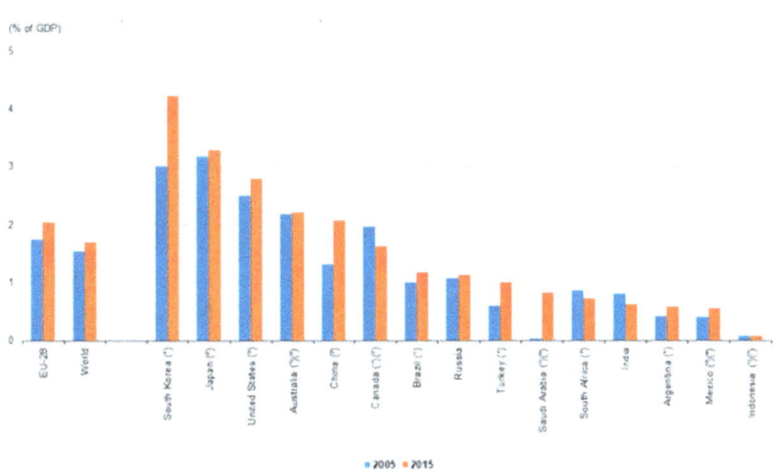

Europe: Heading for a Better Place

An initial surge in growth, investment and employment took place under the impetus of the Juncker European Commission[39] (2014–2019) and the plan of the same name.[40]

We can do much better. These improvements can not only be continued, but also extended to other, non-economic emergencies. They must also be made more tangible for the public.

Europe's potential is still largely underexploited, as we will show through five major areas outlined in the foreword:

- Prosperity
- Development, solidarity and inclusiveness
- Eco-responsibility
- Freedoms, strengthened rule of law and democracy
- With regard to third countries, generosity, stability and security.

Without sacrifice, without pain, without obsessive austerity, it is possible with the current instruments to increase the GDP of the 27 by 12.5% by 2030 to make our societies more socially just, our democracies more solid or even more developed, our economy greener and our external security stronger. This involves unleashing the energy and innovation of businesses and citizens, having greater ambition in the public sector, improving the interaction between the market and public authorities, increasing investment, placing more trust in people and businesses, and encouraging resourcefulness and ingenuity.

---

39 In fact, the Juncker Commission's programme was entitled "Growth, Innovation, Employment".

40 With €21 billion alone, including €16 billion in the form of guarantees, the plan has mobilised more than €500 billion in private investment. A public boost with a substantial leverage effect. We will come back to this (*see* Title II, Ch. 1, D).

TITLE I

EUROPE AND PROSPERITY

Europe and the Two Horns of Plenty

In the 16th century, when it dominated the world, Europe was depicted as sovereign with a wealth of attributes.[41] These included two horns of plenty.

Today, the first benefit of European integration is the single market (Chapter 1). This can be a powerful engine of prosperity if it is not hampered by national protectionism and if it is appropriately, even intelligently, regulated by the EU and the Member States. Under these conditions, businesses and citizens will be able to deploy their talents and grow much more than they can today, including in non-economic spheres. Contrary to a fourth misconception, a large, efficient market means that more qualitative projects (social, ecological, etc.) can be pursued.

---

41 Cesare Ripa, *Iconologia*, 1593.

Another aspect of our societies that Europe can help to advance is more surprising: the public sector. Public management, particularly at state level, could become a second cornucopia (Chapter 2).

Not only must the public sphere not strangle the engine of this large market, but it can also give it extra power, like a turbo… and/or a well-tuned booster. Given that the public sector manages around half of the wealth produced in the EU,[42] any improvement in this area will have a considerable impact on overall prosperity.

In addition, synergies between this large market and the public sector can have a multiplier effect. Contrary to fifth belief, the market economy and public initiative are not necessarily opposed to each other.

In my view, the public sector can become a much more powerful instrument of prosperity than it has been in the past. On the one hand, given the scarcity of labour and the growing level of employment in the EU, it no longer has to maintain artificial jobs. On the other hand, in view of the social, energy-related, environmental and military challenges as well as the emergence of the rest of the world, it must become even more efficient and effective.

Priorities are changing. From playing a defensive role, the public sector must become forward-thinking. The "evil" market is no longer its adversary but an ally. They will operate in tandem. Our current intellectual approach in this area will have to evolve.

Let us look at how the EU can boost these two engines and optimise their interaction.

---

42 In 2021, general government spending in the EU27 represented an average of 51.6% of GDP (source: Eurostat, extracted on 8 July 2022).

Chapter 1

Completing the Single Market

Introduction: A Large Single Market, Remarkably Compact and… Under-Exploited

1. A Single Market

As the difficult Brexit negotiations have reminded us, the European single market is THE major asset shared by the Member States, their populations and their businesses.

After Brexit, the internal market is now a borderless area of 447 million inhabitants, in which people, primarily as economic operators (including commercial companies), goods, services and capital move freely.

Or should be. As we shall see, there are still too many obstacles and they are on the rise.

General Benefits

By addressing a larger demand in a larger market, companies can produce more varied and sophisticated goods and services at lower cost (economies of scale). For example, it is now easier to develop medicines in Europe. It is also possible to mobilise more material, human and financial resources for investment and production. A large market means we can produce more, better, cheaper and faster. It also means we can think bigger. This imperative, which underpinned the construction of Europe,[43] is even more relevant today. China and its billion-and-a-half-strong population frighten even the USA.

Benefits for Consumers

People have access to more goods and services at lower prices.

Admittedly, life is still too expensive. But don't we have more purchasing power than we did 40 years ago?

I lived in a family where there was only one car for six people, a black and white television set... no subscription to a package of foreign TV programmes. We only went on holiday once a year and went to restaurants two or three times a year. I flew for the first time when I was 17. At that time, I only had pocket money of the equivalent of €12.5/month. But we weren't destitute; a lot of people lived like that. Most of the boys wore shorts until they were 15 or 16. My father nearly choked when I bought a polo shirt at the age of 17 that cost €90 and that I'm still wearing, decades later... to my wife's dismay.

Today, a range of goods and services are now commonly available, whereas 40 years ago they were considered luxuries, such as restaurants

43 Even before the First World War, the United States had overtaken the European countries in competitiveness thanks to its large market. Without an integrated market, Europeans would not have been able to recover after the Second World War, to have a high-performance industry and to offer living conditions and a sufficiently high level of remuneration to their population to turn them away from the temptation of communism.

and travel. Technological advances have enabled the creation of new goods. And how easy it is to communicate! A phone call to another Member State costs no more than a domestic call. Not to mention Skype and WhatsApp. If you could see the prices in the 1970s or 1980s for a local call within a country!

This development did not happen overnight/with a magic wand. In particular, it stems from the single European market and an undistorted competition regime,[44] which must above all preserve this innovative process, and of proactive measures such as the ban on roaming, aimed at creating a single area for phone calls.

Other Benefits for Businesses

European companies can also export to all the Member States of the EU without paying customs duties. Since Trump threatened to tax imports, this advantage has become more tangible: we are less exposed to changes in the policies of third countries as a result of intra-EU trade. The figures speak for themselves. While the EU and the USA each account for 12–15% of international trade, China accounts for 30%. It is therefore more vulnerable to protectionist threats.

We stand to gain far more from deepening the internal market than from concluding a free trade agreement with one or more third countries. What's more, we can do so without having to give up some of our own ideas (hormone-free meat, etc.). We are back to a European construction that brings us much (and could bring us even more) without giving away much. Optimising the internal market will become all the more crucial as world trade may well suffer from geopolitical tensions and production may have to be relocated to Europe. If we want to limit inflationary pressures, which are already strong, we will no longer be able to afford the luxury of protectionist frictions that make trade within the EU even more expensive.

---

44 *See* Title I, Ch. 1, D, 2.

Internal Market and External Dimension

Thanks to this large domestic market, some[45] European companies are acquiring the critical mass to export to third countries, bringing in additional revenue for the European economy. IKEA, for example, is making impressive inroads in India. Once again, this leverage role.

The EU27 is one of the world's biggest exporting powers, with a positive trade balance (i.e. exports exceed imports),[46] a fact that is often overlooked. We therefore have a clear interest in world trade and the liberalisation of trade with third countries. Europe's free trade policy is not naïveté, contrary to popular opinion. The media focus too much on European companies falling victim to competition from third countries. They do not put these losses into perspective with the gains made by other European companies through the opening up of third-country markets. For example, France was very concerned about a free trade agreement with South Korea. Yet its car manufacturers have in the end benefited from this agreement.

The opportunity presented by the single market is an asset when negotiating free trade agreements. Together, the Member States obtain more favourable terms than if they had to negotiate on their own with a third country, especially if that third country is large. Just ask the British, who are now in such a weak position in their discussions with the United States, India and even Australia.

The single market and European trade policy make it easier to export our products and services to the rest of the world. These can become international standards, benchmarks, must-haves. This is the case for

---

45 On the reasons for this restriction, *see* the section on European SMEs (Title I, Ch. 1, A, 1).

46 In 2020, the European trade balance in goods generated a surplus for the ninth year running. This amounted to €218 billion on total exports of €1,932 billion (a total representing around 15% of European GDP). The services trade balance also showed a surplus of €60 billion (compared with a record of €131 billion in 2018) on total exports of €867 billion, for at least the tenth year running. Exports of goods and services to third countries therefore represent more than 20% of European GDP, and the surplus more than 2%.

fashion and luxury goods, in particular, but not only. We will come back to this later. We must not underestimate what Europe represents in terms of quality of life and refinement for a number of third countries. This brand image can be further exploited.

Europe and Direct Investment in the Rest of the World

A large single market is also a lever/source of leverage which, as the benefits gradually accumulate, facilitates *direct investment* in the rest of the world. This refers to the control of companies abroad, a guarantee of recurrent income for the European economy (dividends, royalties, interest, etc.). The EU remains the largest direct investor in the world, well ahead of the USA (70% of the EU level).[47]

So Europe is not just the world's largest mass of affluent consumers, to which it is often likened. It remains a major centre for the creation and control of wealth. Europe is an economic power in trade, industry, finance and agriculture.[48] We must be aware of these assets, preserve them and develop them, particularly as part of a global strategy.

Direct Investment in the EU

The EU also attracts the most direct investment in the world. Both Western and Eastern Europe are in demand. One of the EU's assets in this respect is its stability. We will have to see if the war in Ukraine does anything to undermine this.

Direct investment in Europe is invaluable. In the short term, they guarantee more jobs and economic activity, a bit like the Wimbledon tennis tournament. This event takes place in London; the setting is

47 This is probably the result of centuries of European domination, which American leadership since 1918 has yet to make up for.

48 *See* below, Title III, Ch. 2.

English, but the players are foreign. There are hardly any British players left, and even fewer who are hopeful of winning (apart from the Scotsman Andy Murray a few years ago). The event does, however, generate economic activity in and around Wimbledon.

In the longer term, direct investment brings Europe into contact with new technologies and knowledge that we have not yet mastered, thereby improving our level of competitiveness. Economies that are open to foreign investment are more likely to adapt to technological progress and move up the productivity ladder. Once again, this is a key concept. Foreign direct investment can therefore be a spur, a source of stimulating competition, especially for the best European companies.[49]

This is why it is important to attract and retain third-country operators, which means respecting the rule of law with regard to them. This implies a certain degree of access to the European market, subject to certain conditions, the benefit of certain rights and the possibility of liquidating the investment and repatriating the proceeds to the third country of origin, even if this can cause some grumbling. The exit option is necessary to attract further foreign direct investment. During the 2017 French presidential election, no candidate dared to point out that Whirlpool, which had closed a factory in Amiens, was an American group and had the right to reorganise its subsidiaries.

However, we must retain control of part of the production chain. We must not abandon certain sensitive and/or strategic sectors to companies from third countries. Hence the introduction of a European framework for screening such investments in 2019.[50]

49 In a similar vein, *see* P. Aghion, C. Antonin and S. Bunel, *Le pouvoir la destruction créatrice*, Paris, Odile Jacob, 2020, p. 83.

50 However, it is to be feared that this will give rise to protectionist abuses, given the (excessive) room for manoeuvre left to the Member States. The market's sanction will come in a second phase. Those Member States that have gone too far will be shunned by international investors; the prosperity gap will continue to widen in favour of the more liberal Member States.

Demonstrating the Benefits of the Single Market Through the Absurd: The United Kingdom After Brexit

The UK used to be one of the most dynamic economies in the EU, with above-average growth, low unemployment, inflation, public debt and public deficit relatively contained.

Six years after Brexit, the UK has been hit hard by international crises (Covid, war in Ukraine) and is finding it very difficult to deal with them (it is now on the brink of recession and, unlike most EU Member States, is not experiencing a recovery). Its currency has depreciated, contributing to inflation on the demand side (higher import prices). The departure of large numbers of EU nationals and barriers to immigration have fuelled inflation on the supply side, with businesses short of labour. Today, the UK is facing record inflation of 11.1%. Exceptionally for this country, the summer of 2022 was rocked by mass demonstrations against the rising cost of living. Public debt is growing. The Conservative Party was forced to raise taxes. Investment is at a standstill and the productivity gap is widening. Liz Truss's mini-budget forced the Bank of England to intervene in a panic to save British pension funds, precipitated the sacrifice of the unfortunate finance minister, and ended with the pitiful and express resignation of the Prime Minister after only 45 days in power. Almost simultaneously, the London financial centre lost its leadership in Europe.

Trade negotiations with third countries, even friendly ones, are stalling, as they refuse to offer the UK conditions as favourable as when it was part of the European club. Trade in goods and services with the EU is falling, with customs formalities discouraging many British companies from exporting to the Continent. Conversely, it is becoming more difficult and less attractive for companies from the Member States to do business in the United Kingdom.

The result: shortages, even of basic necessities, and some bizarre situations, too! Germans living in the UK were courted by the government because their German driving licences allowed them to drive lorries, the transport sector having been profoundly disrupted by Brexit. With the departure of Polish workers, there was no longer enough manpower to kill turkeys at Christmas, so orders had to be placed *… in Poland. The ultimate humiliation: the United Kingdom, which based part of its glory – notably its colonial empire and victory over Napoleon – on its good relations with the financial markets, has been "punished" by them and called to order by the International Monetary Fund in September 2022.

Thanks, Boris, for all your claptrap about the economic benefits that Brexit would bring.

"You can tell happiness by the noise it makes when it leaves."[51] The benefits of the single market are intangible, while the disadvantages of leaving are painful and long-lasting (we now speak of "Bregret"). The British example also shows the extent to which belonging to the single market helps to attenuate the violence of external shocks, and protects… for a time, at least.

However, the EU has no reason to celebrate Brexit. It is a lose-lose event because, like all the other Member states, the UK was helping to make the cake bigger for everyone.

51 L. Robequain, "Le vrai coût du Brexit", *Les Echos*, 13 February 2023.

2. A Large Market… in a Small Area

In Asia, the major centres are nine hours by plane from each other. The United States is more than twice the size of Europe and has around a third less population, as already mentioned and as evidenced by figure 6 below.

Figure 6. US-EU territory comparison (carried out using the https://www.thetruesize.com/ tool)

In these times of energy and environmental challenges, the compactness of the territory and the high population density are major advantages. As already mentioned, a European emits two to three times fewer tonnes of carbon than an American and, for the same amount of wealth produced, uses 30 to 40% less energy. This brings us back to the energy intensity rate.[52] Yet, Europe can still substantially improve its performance in this area!

52 *See* above, Introduction, "Europe: A still an enviable lifestyle".

Europe's compactness is all the more important given that energy accounts for the bulk of its imports.[53] If we become more self-sufficient and energy-efficient, thanks in particular to *technical progress* – a factor as fundamental as labour productivity, as we shall see – our quality of life will only improve.

These are also facts to be opposed to the advocates of negative growth. The compactness of the European territory and our present and future energy intensity scores make it possible to envisage an increase in our economic activity.

3. A Large Market That Is Clearly Under-Efficient

Although we are a MICROCONTINENT and, in absolute terms, it is easier for us to create wealth, there is 30 to 40% less economic exchange between EU Member States than within the USA. At the same time, as already mentioned, our per capita standard of living is 40% lower than that of an American.[54] Despite vastly superior energy efficiency, our productivity is 35% lower. These figures suggest that there is still a great deal of friction and waste in the internal market, 30 years after the launch of the single market.

Barriers remain. European companies are constrained in supplying goods and services throughout the EU.

One of the consequences is that innovations conceived in Europe are launched in other parts of the world.

A good example is *Spotify*, the music application. This company, listed on the New York Stock Exchange, was founded by young Swedes.

---

53 These lines were written before the invasion of Ukraine. They are even more relevant today, when rising energy costs have pushed the eurozone's traditionally positive trade balance into the red.

54 *See* above, Introduction, "A balance sheet in jeopardy?"

Why in the United States? Given the strictly national organisation of music copyright in Europe, they realised that it was impossible to put their idea into practice there.[55] The project for a European system of copyright and exploitation licences was abandoned following vigorous opposition from national collective management societies, such as GEMA[56] in Germany and SACEM[57] in France.[58] Each Member State has kept its piece of the pie… and the United States is reaping the rewards. Look for the mistake.

Is it not also interesting that most of the Covid vaccines were developed by European researchers, but within the framework of companies in third countries?

4. A Large Market That Is Increasingly Under-Efficient

Not only is the single market not moving forward, it is actually moving backwards, contrary to a seventh common misconception.

A Weak Single Market in Services

The services market *accounts for only a quarter of intra-Community transactions, even though services now account for three quarters of European GDP*. By comparison, European companies export services outside the EU more easily than they export goods.[59] In fact, the global services market is growing faster than the intra-Community market.

55 G. Verhofstadt, *Le mal européen*, Paris, Plon, 2016, pp. 189–190.

56 Gesellschaft für musikalische Aufführungs- und mechanische Vervielfältigungsrechte (GEMA).

57 Société des auteurs, compositeurs et éditeurs de musique (SACEM).

58 Defraigne and Nouveau, 3rd ed., p. 298.

59 Non-EU service exports account for 75% of intra-EU service exports, while non-EU goods exports account for 70% of intra-EU goods exports (*see* Communication from the Commission, "Long term action plan for better implementation and enforcement of single market rules", COM(2020) 94 final, 10 March 2020).

European services companies are lagging substantially behind their US counterparts in terms of productivity (once again, this key performance criterion) and competitiveness.[60] Europe's technological deficit in the most promising services is significant. For example, the digital economy accounted for 5% of GDP in Europe compared with 8% in the USA[61] in 2015, and the digitalisation of the economy in Europe is estimated to be 60% of the level achieved by the US economy.[62]

The digital market is even said to be suffering from "fragmentation and barriers that do not exist in the physical single market".[63] It is easier for a European company to market digital solutions in Indonesia (with a population of nearly 300 million) than within the EU!

What a failure! While the founding states managed to relaunch trade in goods between themselves barely 12 years after the end of the Second World War, they have been unable to complete the services market in the first 22 years of the 21st century. If there is one sign that European integration is in a bad way, it is this one, because it touches on the EU's core business and on what should be a project of common interest.

Protectionism Has the Wind in Its Sails

Since 2008, Member States have increased the number of barriers to intra-Community trade. The European Commission has lacked political courage. Bringing a complaint against a Member State before the Commission has become an exploit. What's more, the Commission has brought too few legal actions against these abusive practices.

60 Productivity gap in 2010: 30% (Defraigne and Nouveau, 2nd ed., p. 153); competitiveness gap in 2018: 50% (Defraigne and Nouveau, 3rd ed., p. 240).

61 Defraigne and Nouveau, 2nd ed., p. 311.

62 Ibid., p. 308.

63 Communication from the Commission, "A Digital Single Market Strategy for Europe", COM(2015) 192 final, 6 May 2015, p. 3, cited by Defraigne and Nouveau, 3rd ed., p. 295.

A real-life example: in the case of life insurance, France requires the contract to provide a series of details, but only those prescribed by French law and in the order in which they are set out. Any foreign contract that provides more information or adopts a different presentation will be declared null and void. The Commission has raised no objection to this.

A number of directives that are essential for the progress of the internal market are not applied in practice, or have not even been transposed into law in some Member States. For example, in 2019, ten years after the transposition deadline expired, a number of Member States had not brought their legislation into line with the Services Directive.[64] The Energy Directive, adopted in 2007, provided for the establishment of a single energy market by 2014. In 2022, more than 50% of cross-border electricity lines are not open to competition, whereas 70% should have been by 1 January 2020.[65] A number of Member States have also obstructed the objective agreed at a European Council in 2014 of achieving interconnection of at least 10% of their installed electricity production capacity by 2020.[66]

In general, the effective application of internal market legislation raises questions. Member States and their administrations often speculate about the absence of penalties or, at the very least, about the slowness of procedures. This discourages many victims. When the Court of Justice of the European Union (CJEU) finally issues a ruling, the damage has been done. National markets have been closed to foreign companies. They will not get them back.

64 Ibid., p. 291.

65 Ibid., p. 281.

66 F. Simon, "Les États membres se braquent contre l'objectif d'interconnexion des réseaux électriques", *Euractiv*, 12 December 2017.

Making use of the freedom of movement is beginning to be viewed with suspicion. Problem situations that may involve two or more Member States are subject to increasing controls, both fiscal and administrative.

Let us now look at how we can close these loopholes and put an end to these backward steps.

In my view, given the urgency of the situation, priority should be given to a number of major measures to liberalise and complete the internal market that are likely to produce significant and rapid progress (A). In order to sustain and build on this progress, we also need to work on sustainable/long-term improvements to the general framework, especially in relation to six areas of the internal market (B). There is also the question of the method or methods to be advocated by the EU to achieve its objectives (C). Given the strengths, specific features and constraints of the EU, a policy of structural or modern supply-side measures (which, however, also includes measures to improve purchasing power) seems particularly appropriate. Finally, a few words will be said about two policies that at first sight may appear technical but which are not always clearly understood, but which are essential to the proper functioning of the single market: the common commercial policy and the competition policy (D).

Two new elements may help to accept the ideas expressed below. On the one hand, the reluctance of the Member States to create the single market in services and to complete the internal market was probably linked to the fear of seeing unemployment rise (again). Today, this scourge is on the wane, with the European economy facing the opposite problem of a shortage of labour. On the other hand, the current challenges (catching up on technology, the social divide, the energy and environmental transition, increased international competition, geopolitical tensions and the need for a European military defence) require considerable financial resources.

A. A Single Market to Be Completed and Liberalised

The creative potential needs to be released as quickly as possible. We need to put the focus in the right place and determine the most effective lever for action.[67]

1. Towards A Barrier-Free Playing Field, Particularly for SMEs: Mutual Recognition of Goods and Services

The name is technical, but the reality it covers is more tangible. The aim is to ensure the free marketing of goods and services within the EU as soon as they are legally produced in a Member State. In other words, a Czech product or service will be worth the same as a French or German product or service: it will have access to the entire single market as long as it meets Czech requirements, even in the absence of a harmonisation directive.

Current Situation

To date, mutual recognition is not automatic, far from it.

Economic activities are governed either by European harmonisation texts or by national provisions. Where the former are lacking, Member States may restrict the import of goods or services legally produced in another Member State for "good reasons" that are officially non-protectionist: public health, consumer protection, environmental protection, effective tax controls, etc.

67 Strategy against noma, a gangrene that necroses the faces of children in the poorest countries, recommended by B. Piccard, *Réaliste : soyons logiques autant qu'écologiques*, Paris, Stock, 2021, p. 24.

This is the traditional approach, known in European jargon as the *Cassis de Dijon* jurisprudence for goods. Moreover, the freedoms of services and capital are even less automatic.[68] In particular, Member States can hinder trade in these areas through national professional qualifications. They have increased the number of such qualifications since the deadline for transposing the Services Directive in 2006, and have even refrained from notifying most of them in advance, in flagrant disregard of their obligations.[69]

The consequence is that companies from other Member States have to comply with the rules of the host country in addition to those of their Member State of origin. This discourages them from exporting, especially small and medium-sized enterprises (SMEs) and operators seeking to market their products in several host Member States, because for each export market, the rules will by definition change, fragmenting the internal market. What's more, the system is extremely complex and opaque.

In Favour of a Genuine General Principle of Mutual Recognition

Forty-five years after the *Cassis de Dijon* ruling, 30 years after the launch of the single market, we can no longer be satisfied with this approach of attempting to reconcile conflicting options; nor with the European Commission's marginal improvements, which leave most of the fundamental problems unresolved. We need a breakthrough in our approach. We need to drastically reduce national trade filters. In my opinion, we need to move[70] radically.

68 However, this is not yet the case for services and financial products, where the approach is even less favourable to freedom of movement.

69 Defraigne and Nouveau, 3rd ed., p. 290.

70 Do we use many goods and instruments that have not changed in the last 40 years? Asking this question begs the question of whether the *Cassis de Dijon* case law is still relevant today, or whether the parallel case law on the freedom to provide services, freedom of establishment and free movement of capital is more in the background.

Firstly, there has been progress in the convergence between us. We can trust each other more. What's more, with national education budgets across the EU and modern means of information and communication, citizens are better able to determine what they can and cannot buy from other Member States. As we shall see on several occasions, *the EU's paternalism is outdated.* It is as if the ideas of the 1980s were set in stone. The construction of Europe, which was previously an innovative project, has in some respects become a museum. Is the ultimate ambition of consumer law to keep consumers on permanent assistance?[71] As we shall see, a more fruitful and rewarding alternative is to educate consumers.

This statement may be a little strong, but the domestic market is like the Augias Stables, in which layers of waste have gradually accumulated. What did Hercules do? Unlike the European Commission, he did not become bogged down in patiently removing it. He created large openings in the stables, diverted two rivers and completed one of his most famous projects in one day.

In this respect, it is "sufficient" to proclaim the principle of mutual recognition of goods and services legally produced in a Member State, *even if the sector has not been harmonised at European level.*

In this way, the internal market in services will become a reality. Most of the barriers to trade in goods that remain or have been reintroduced since 2008 will also fall.

Let us put our trust in entrepreneurs and consumers… Let us decorate European society. Let us take the lid off at a time when we need growth, when new technologies make it easier to take initiatives, when consumers are more autonomous. Let us get rid of self-righteousness

71 In our view, consumer measures should generally be coupled with consumer education and be degressive or even temporary. Once again, it is essential to grow the population.

and the weight of censorship. The European economy is comparable to American society on the eve of the emergence of rock and roll: stuck, stale, mothballed…

No Restrictions Without Prior Authorisation from the European Commission

A Member State wishing to introduce a restriction would have to notify it to the European Commission. As long as the Commission has not given its green light (or at least an opinion) within a reasonable period of time (two months), the measure cannot be implemented.

Why, in fact, should it be the customer wishing to obtain products and services from another Member State, or the company wishing to export them, who has to endure a lengthy trial in order to remove such obstacles? Or wait for a hypothetical reaction from the European Commission, which may also be slow?[72]

The requirement for a reasoned notification to the Commission will discourage a series of market partitioning measures. As already mentioned, these have flourished since the 2008 crisis.

This notification procedure should be public and allow interested parties to submit comments. Appeals against the Commission's decision should be open to the courts. These debates will raise questions about the need for unilateral restrictions by Member States and the possibility of alternatives that are less detrimental to intra-Community trade.

All it takes is a few articles in a European regulation. It can be drawn up and adopted quickly. Cost to the community: zero. Another equally effective option would be a ruling by the CJEU proclaiming generalised mutual recognition.

72 Investigation of the case, approaches to the Member State, pre-litigation procedure and then litigation before the CJEU, second procedure before the CJEU in the event of refusal to comply.

Immediate Gains in Economic Dynamism

- Products and services that are more varied, more innovative, cheaper, better quality and in greater quantity.
- A stronger European industry in the broadest sense, with higher productivity.
- Many more exporting SMEs in the EU.
- The setting in motion of a positive dynamic that will go far beyond an intensification of trade between Member States, more incentives for entrepreneurship, more prosperous businesses.
- Very rapid net growth in the GDP of the 27.

A Playground Finally Open to SMEs

In 2015, there were more than 23 million businesses in the EU28, compared with 4 million in the United States.

SMEs are also much more numerous in Europe than in the USA; *99.8% of businesses in Europe are SMEs with fewer than 250 employees*, and 93.5% are micro-businesses (with fewer than 10 employees).[73] The EU average is less than six employees per company in the real economy (i.e. other than the financial sector).

European SMEs are also growing less quickly than their American counterparts[74]... probably due to the incomplete/fragmented internal market.

73 *Key figures on Europe*, 2023, p. 50.

74 By the same token, the renewal rate for listed companies is much higher in the United States. There are significantly more listed companies in the US that are less than 30 years old.

In 2015, only 8% of Europe's 21 million SMEs were involved in intra-Community trade. While this percentage has almost doubled in 3 years (15%), which bodes well for the future, the participation of SMEs in intra-Community trade remains marginal. What is *a single market in which 84.32% of companies do not participate?*

Below a critical threshold, small businesses have lower productivity:[75] while they represent only 0.2% of businesses in Europe, businesses with more than 250 employees employed 35.7% of workers in the non-financial sector and produced 47.5% of value added in 2020.[76]

Figure 7 below[77] confirms the low productivity of micro-businesses (fewer than 10 employees) and, to a lesser extent, small businesses (10–49).[78]

75 "Their small size (89% of Walloon companies employ fewer than 20 people) does not allow them to generate scale effects or invest sufficiently. The question of size is particularly critical, since overall, the added value per job in Belgium varies from €55,000 for companies with fewer than 10 employees to €94,000 for companies with more than 250 employees" (extract from the report commissioned by the Walloon government, quoted in *L'Echo*, 9 January 2021, p. 3).

76 *Key figures on Europe*, 2023, p. 50.

77 Which concerns the size-class structure of companies in the non-financial business economy..

78 *Key figures on Europe*, 2023, p. 50.

Figure 7.

Enterprise size class structure of the non-financial business economy

(%, share for each enterprise size class, EU, 2019)

Furthermore, the propensity to develop an innovative activity seems to increase with the size of the company,[79] as the following figure 8 shows.[80] This is corroborated by figures from the European Patent Office (EPO), according to which, in 2021, 75% of patents were filed by large companies, 20% by SMEs or individual inventors and 5% by universities and public research institutes.[81]

79 Even if the most disruptive innovations come from micro-businesses and the academic world.

80 Eurostat, *Key figures on European business – 2022 edition*, Luxembourg, Publications Office of the European Union, 2022, p. 20.

81 That said, it would seem that the most significant innovations are proportionately more likely to come from SMEs than from large companies.

Figure 8.

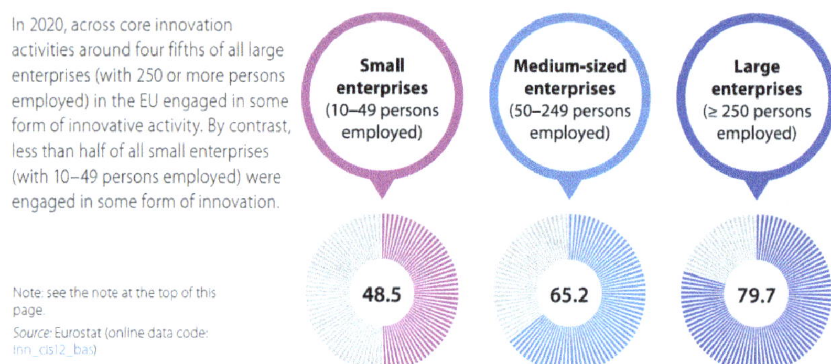

This brings us back to the key concept of productivity. Its weakness prevents micro-businesses, and even certain SMEs, from participating in intra-Community trade. Indeed, "it is only beyond a certain productivity threshold that a domestic company is able to export its production",[82] as figure 9[83] shows:

Figure 9.

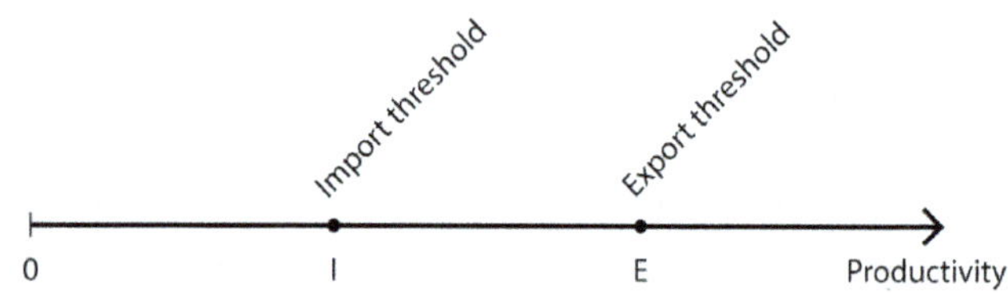

Figure 13.7 Ability to import and export as a function of a company's level of productivity
Source: Authors' diagram

82 Aghion et al., p. 324.
83 Aghion et al., p. 324.

This factor partly explains why the productivity of the European economy is lower than that of the US economy.[84]

A more integrated market, with fewer barriers to access other Member States, would facilitate the growth of SMEs. There are a lot of (very) small businesses because the single market has not yet been completed, so they don't have access to it and can't grow. Why are there more large companies in the USA? Because their market is more integrated. This brings us back to Spotify.

The generalisation of mutual recognition should therefore make it easier for SMEs to take part in intra-Community trade.

Medium-Term Gains (i): More Self-Financing

In the USA, a good idea can make you rich. It is likely to appeal to 350 million consumers.

A large effective market offers another medium-term advantage in addition to greater productivity: *self-financing capacity*. If a company succeeds in America, it accumulates reserves that enable it to face up to more difficult times, to invest, to grow… and to last. The life expectancy and prosperity of mature companies (over 26 years old) are greater in the United States than in France, as shown in the following figure 10 comparing the share of employment according to the age of establishments.[85]

84 "In 2018, only around one in ten EU companies analysed big data, while only one in four used cloud computing services" (Communication from the Commission, "A New Industrial Strategy for Europe", COM(2020) 102 final, 10 March 2020).

85 Taken from Aghion et al., p. 97.

Figure 10.

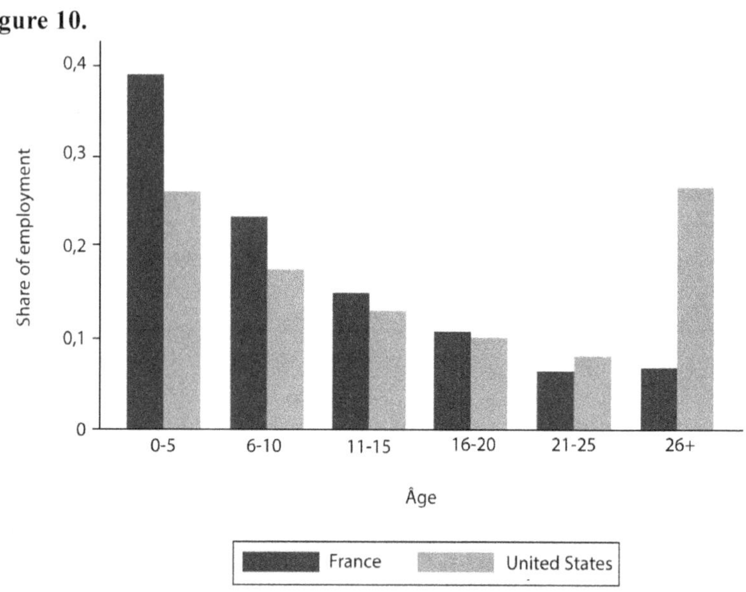

Figure 4.7. Share of employment by length of establishment.
Source: Aghion, Bergeaud; Boppart and Bunel (2018).

The example takes us back to the world of music. Why is the English group Depeche Mode still around? Right from the start, they were very successful in the United States. As a result, they built up a fan base that is much more impressive than that of other groups whose success was limited to Europe. This base has helped them through periods of lesser inspiration… with all that this can often imply in terms of excess for a rock or pop band.

By being able to export thanks to the mutual recognition of goods and services, European companies will win new markets, increase their margins and build up reserves. These reserves will facilitate investment, particularly in research and development, as we shall now see. This will be particularly the case for SMEs, whose access to financing from banks or financial markets is difficult.

Medium-Term Gains (ii): More Investment in R&D&I

One of the reasons for Europe's stagnation is that, for more than 20 years, the USA and a number of Asian countries have been investing much more (particularly in research and development and innovation – R&D&I). The technological gap is widening, and we are in danger of being left behind. There is not a single *Apple*, Google, Amazon, Facebook... in Europe. And yet we had Nokia and Ericsson in the 1990s. Our electric and hybrid cars are less efficient than their American and Asian competitors.

The EU is losing ground in key areas. When it comes to 5G, we have fallen behind the USA and China. There is no major European player in voice assistance. The connected speaker war has begun between the USA, China and South Korea... without Europe.[86] There is no latest-generation European fighter aircraft, but there is an American fighter... and a Chinese fighter. And what about artificial intelligence?

The rankings in the Global Innovation Index 2021 are clear: first Switzerland, second Sweden, third the United States, fourth the United Kingdom, fifth the Republic of Korea. That's just one EU Member State, and a medium-sized one at that.

The composition of investment in research and development in Europe is also revealing: the share of/investment by companies and the private sector is lower than in other parts of the world, as figure 11 shows.[87]

86 M. Courtecuisse, "La guerre des enceintes connectées a commencé... sans l'Europe", *Les Echos*, 23 August 2018.

87 OECD, *OECD Economic Surveys: European Union 2021*, Paris, OECD Publishing 2021, p. 11.

Figure 11.

Figure 2. Investment in R&D is low

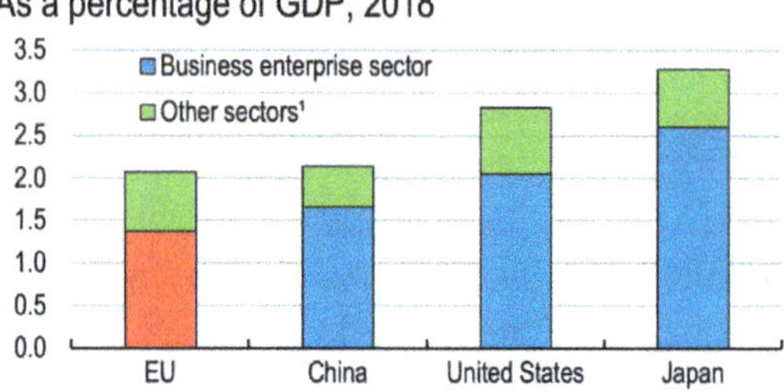

It seems that the smaller number of innovative SMEs in Europe can be explained by weaker financing capacity. This comes back to the lack of productivity and even size of SMEs in Europe, their high infant mortality rate, their lower self-financing capacity (see once again the counter-example of Depeche Mode), in short the incompleteness of the internal market. This reduces the prospects of a return on investment in R&D&I,[88] which discourages such projects: since the horizon is neither vast nor clear, why embark on a long-term adventure? Expanding a market increases income and therefore the incentives for innovation.[89]

Possible Accompanying Measures for Mutual Recognition

At the very least, mutual recognition could be accompanied by flanking measures (as long as they do not lead to it becoming devoid of substance). Properly designed, they could even enhance the expected economic dynamism.

88 *See*, by analogy, O. Blanchard, D. Cohen and D. Johnson, *Macroéconomie*, Montreuil, Pearson, 6th ed., 2016, p. 82.

89 *See* Aghion et al., p. 204.

One of these measures would be to harmonise *information rather* than regulations on the content and quality of products and services. This would indicate whether there is European harmonisation of the regulation of the product or service concerned and, especially if not, what the main characteristics of the product or service offered are. Consumers would be able to make informed decisions.

Alternatively, we could consider minimum requirements for access to and exercise of economic activities by natural persons and companies. These would apply to activities and professions in sectors that remain unregulated. They would form *a minimum common base applicable to operators.*

This could even improve the quality of business organisation and processes, their reliability, integrity and eco-responsibility. It could have a positive impact on the quality of the products and services offered; ultimately increase the productivity of economic operators in the EU (once again) and facilitate their growth, whether internal (self-financing, business development) or external (mergers, acquisitions, etc.).

As regards the latter point, better comparability and greater familiarity of potential investors with the characteristics of companies would overcome the reluctance of third-party investors. One of the major problems in financing SMEs, which represent the overwhelming majority of European businesses, is the lack of reliable information about them (the so-called information asymmetry problem). This type of measure could also make it easier for economic operators to prepare for technological change.

This framework should be horizontal in scope and cover only what is strictly necessary, especially as it would apply mainly to the smallest companies.

As far as consumers are concerned, we could think about *educating them about the internal market*, along the lines of what is being increasingly advocated for financial services.[90] Since the internal market is a facility made available to consumers, we might as well ensure that they are able to use it under the right conditions. This would reduce the need for consumer protection rules that are generally paternalistic and disempowering. We need to help people grow, particularly in their role as consumers.

In the event of proven abuses by economic operators from certain Member States, targeted measures could be taken by the host Member State subject to notification to the European Commission and as part of an organised procedure. These would be more proportionate than unilateral restrictions on imports applying to goods and services from all EU Member States, including those that do not pose a problem. We need to reverse the logic, so to speak, and make restrictions the exception, the last resort. Restrictions on intra-Community trade in goods and services must be limited.

Completing the Single Market Is Vital for the European Social Democratic Model

We will not be able to preserve our generous social security and redistribution system and our diversity in the long term without considerable financial resources and therefore economic dynamism.

The generosity and complexity of our system must be supported by a strong, simple and identifiable economic basis. Let us complete the single market immediately by introducing virtually unconditional recognition of goods and services. Let us capitalise on its compactness.

We do not have much choice: our public authorities have been living beyond their means and are not in a position to finance the various challenges we are facing and will face in the near future. It is illusory

90 On this subject, *see* below, Title I, Ch. 1, B, 3.

to think that our populations will accept living in poorer conditions than they have up to now. Why should they resign themselves to decline?

The removal of every conceivable obstacle to intra-Community trade will be a welcome breath of fresh air for European citizens and businesses. It will also send a clear message to the rest of the world: Europe has decided to move forward and make use of one of its strengths, without being aggressive or imperialistic.

2. A Large Playing Field Where the Rules Are Better Respected

Towards a More Effective Crackdown on Protectionist Measures

The major enlargement of 2004 has probably reduced the power of the European institutions, and in particular the Commission as guardian of the Treaties, vis-à-vis the Member States. The number of Member States has risen from 15 to 27. The number of staff at the European Commission, especially those assigned to hunting down breaches of European law, has not increased accordingly, while the average level of compliance with European law has deteriorated. The effectiveness of European law has suffered as a result.

The European Commission must intervene much more decisively with Member States that hinder trade and/or fail to transpose directives correctly. In particular, it should bring more infringement proceedings and make use of its increased powers with regard to state aid.

There is also a need to improve judicial protection of the rights that economic operators and citizens derive from the internal market. This raises the question of whether litigation relating to the internal market should not give rise to harmonisation of certain procedural and substantive rules (along the lines of what has been done for liability actions for breach of competition law). Should we go one step further and entrust this litigation to specialised national courts, or even to courts that include judges from other countries or members of the European courts? Should this litigation be transferred to a European court?

The possibilities for compensating companies and individuals who are victims of protectionist measures are limited, if not theoretical. While the European Commission can impose dissuasive or even terrifying fines on companies for breaching competition law, the same cannot be said of Member States when they fail to comply with European law. At most, they are liable to fines for persistent infringement and, in very rare cases, to an obligation to compensate individuals or companies that have suffered damage. Sanctions and possibilities for compensation should be strengthened. However, it is unlikely that the Member States will agree to pass texts along these lines within the Council.

There is, however, a simple solution to the problem of non-transposition of directives, which probably does not require the adoption of a text on the subject. The directive would be accompanied by an annexed regulation that would apply by default when the transposition deadline expires in inactive Member States.

Need for a Change of Mindset, Mainly on the Part of Member States

In addition to the European institutions mobilising the legal arsenal at their disposal, we need to tackle a cancer eating away at European integration: the cynicism of the Member States and the drift towards intergovernmentalism. The EU has become a cheese that each Member State is trying to gnaw away at. Under the guise of major projects, the reality is quite different: de-Europeanisation is underway. A series of policies are being renationalised (the Common Agricultural Policy) or steered by certain capitals solely to further national interests. There is a loss of a sense of Community interest and of the will to take integration further.

3. For a Great Playground, Not a Morgue: Towards a Recalibration of European Regulations

Europe's co-legislators, the European Parliament and the Council, must bear in mind that SMEs are now the norm. As a result, European rules must be drawn up with them in mind, rather than simply granting them derogations. There needs to be a Copernican revolution in this respect.

This requires a rethink of the European institutions. They tend to look at things in global terms, preferring to deal with large companies and to design the rules around them.

SMEs and micro-businesses have been left out of the European venture. This is probably one of the reasons for Euroscepticism: "small businessmen" – an expression of disdain – feel as neglected as workers in industries undergoing restructuring or regions undergoing conversion. Europe must help them grow.

Harmonisation of national rules to create undistorted conditions of competition (the famous "level playing field") must not lead to regulations that only large companies can put up with. Otherwise, on the pretext of fair competition, we will be reducing competition to a few giants and dismantling the European economic fabric, creating a vast field of ruins ("level dying field").

The idea of an "SME filter" to identify proposals that could be barriers to SMEs, suggested by Commissioner Breton, is a good first step.[91]

91 *EDB* 12422 of 11 February 2020, p. 13; along the same lines, *see* "*Think small first*" (*EDB* 12429 of 20 February 2020, p. 11).

However, we need to go further and reverse the logic. Such proposals should only be derogations in European regulations and directives applying only to large companies.

4. Towards a Positive Dynamic with Unsuspected Cascade Potential

In our view, the broad enshrinement of the principle of mutual recognition, possibly coupled with a few organisational rules applicable to any economic operator, a more determined fight against protectionism and the moderation of standards by the European authorities should intensify economic activity in Europe and encourage the participation of SMEs in intra-Community trade.

Eventually, their average size will increase, they will make productivity gains, they will be able to pay their staff better, they will increase their self-financing capacity (cf. the Depeche Mode syndrome mentioned above), they will invest more in research and development, and they will be in a position to attract external capital more easily or even be floated on the stock exchange. The result will be a greater production of wealth, higher wages (which is essential if we are to bridge the social divide),[92] a denser fabric of medium-sized businesses and a new dynamic of innovation and investment.

In our view, the growth of SMEs and their rise up the economic ladder are essential parameters for the success and vitality of the internal market. In this respect, one objective could be to double the average size of SMEs in Europe within five years. A substantial

92 The possibility of creating start-ups and growing SMEs is a key way of ensuring that the social ladder works. If those who have little to lose are encouraged to take risks in order to gain a lot, there will be more renewal and enlargement of the affluent categories.

fabric of companies employing between 500 and 3,000 people each could be an exceptional asset for the European economy and society.

Beyond that, the emergence of new giants, greater renewal among large companies, an increase in the market capitalisation of European companies, progress in the world's top 500 firms, strengthened financial markets, an improvement in the employment rate and salaries as well as in the morale of the population will be the positive spin-offs of the policy outlined above.

Liberalisation and completion of the internal market should boost the GDP of the 27 Member States by around 5%, or €800 billion a year, in just a few years. A precious windfall for reducing our R&D&I deficit, turning Europe's economy green and laying the foundations for a common defence.

Objections may be raised that the growth of SMEs will kill off their DNA. An SME can keep its soul while growing. It can undertake more ambitious projects under better conditions and aim for a higher quality without giving up its identity. Let us not idealise life in a small business. *Small is not always beautiful*, contrary to the eighth common misconception. Let us not demonise those who are growing.

Personally, I joined a firm of around a hundred lawyers after ten wonderful years at the European Court of Justice. The firm now has grown to 400 lawyers and over 1,200 staff with support functions and ancillary activities. The greater comfort (at the start I felt like I had joined a countryside pharmacy) and the constant improvement in quality have enabled us to attract prestigious clients and undertake ambitious projects under better conditions. At the same time, we have preserved the firm's traditions and the quality of relationships within our teams, which have kept their human scale, perpetuating the lawyer's expertise and passing it on to younger generations.

In addition, products and services are becoming more sophisticated, requiring more expertise, both in terms of quality and quantity, and more financial and technological resources. The collective dimension of production is likely to intensify, particularly under the influence of artificial intelligence. We must have an internal market in a state that allows the European economy to undergo this transformation.

We need to put our trust in businesses and the public, unleash the potential of our researchers, bet on an open society where as many people and businesses as possible take the initiative and display healthy ambition. We need to regain our appetite, our desire to move forward. The sources and forces of progress are here.

5. A Great Playground Despite Linguistic Diversity

Europe is the Switzerland of the world in the sense that the single market has not crushed national identities. As already mentioned, diversity, particularly linguistic diversity, is protected by the European treaties.

From an economic point of view, however, this comes at a price, as it tends to keep markets fragmented. A product or service offered in a foreign language is generally considered, for the same price, to cost 7% more than the same item presented in the customer's own language. As a result, *consumers* will prefer to buy at a higher price in their own Member State. As a corollary, there is a linguistic barrier to export for *suppliers*, especially the smaller ones.[93] Many SMEs are reluctant to export for this reason in particular.

93 Whose products and services are not well-known enough to overcome this barrier.

Linguistic diversity is an objective handicap compared to the United States in terms of the level of integration of the single market.[94] It must therefore be overcome.

Linguistic diversity is also a source of additional difficulties in the digitalisation of Europe. If we do not tackle this head-on, the gap with other economic blocs will only grow.

Solutions?

Today there are powerful voice translators and translation applications, such as Google Translate and DeepL.

The market for language applications could be further developed in Europe. All the more so as it would not undermine linguistic diversity. We would be squaring the circle: facilitating exchanges while respecting linguistic and cultural particularities, thanks to the leverage of technical progress.

Is this not an area where the EU could give a helping hand? A European agency[95] such as the Translation Centre could be involved. One of its missions is to implement the strategic framework for multilingualism. There could also be an initiative involving the industry's driving forces under the[96] industrial policy to encourage the production of applications tailored to Europe's specific characteristics.

Applications can also accelerate the emergence of a genuine European political society, by making it easier for people to get involved in European debates.[97]

---

94 For example, it delayed the creation of the Community patent by more than 10 years.

95 European agencies are bodies set up by the European institutions to develop expertise or exercise certain powers in a specific area. These include the European Supervisory Authorities in the banking, financial markets and insurance sectors.

96 On industrial policy, *see* below, Title I, Ch. 1, B, 2.

97 On this point, *see* below, Title IV, Ch. 2.

Beyond Solutions, Potential

Not only would we increase trade within the EU, but we would also be able to export our multilingual solutions.

We are in fact a laboratory for a number of multilingual states or regions such as India or African countries. If we manage to develop a viable solution for almost 500 million people speaking 20 or 30 different languages, it could be offered to other large multicultural communities. This brings us back to the external dimension and the idea of a standard.[98]

B. A Single Market to Be Strengthened and Improved Over the Long Term: Six Priorities

How Can the Dynamic Proposed Above Be Consolidated and Sustained?

Without claiming to be exhaustive, let us look at six European policies whose success is, in my view, crucial to extending and building on the benefits of the completion and improvements to the single market advocated above. These are: (1) R&D&I, the mother of much progress; (2) re-industrialisation, another guarantee of prosperity and a more inclusive society; (3) financial services policy, both a complementary driver of prosperity and a key player in financing the ecological transition; (4) mobility and training of people; (5 and 6) transport and energy policies.

98 *See* above, Ch. 1, "Introduction", under 1.

1. A Framework Conducive to R&D&I

But Where Are the European Products and Services of Tomorrow?

This morning, you glanced at your iPhone or even your iPad. You've turned on the television screen, which is probably Japanese or South Korean. Maybe you put on some Nike, Asics or UQ (Swiss brand) shoes for a jog, with your connected watch... Apple again. Before leaving, you drove past your American, Japanese or South Korean electric, hybrid or plug-in hybrid car. Or you preferred to watch an episode on Netflix while riding your indoor bike.

The meal has probably taken you back to Europe, or even to your immediate neighbourhood. The same goes for your clothes. But if you've tried to communicate, Facebook, Instagram and TikTok will take you out of Europe again. The same applies to Amazon orders.

What have we created in the last 20 years that has changed our daily lives?

Traditional activities are also being carried out with more and more products and services from third countries. Fans of racing bikes will think of prestigious names, often Italian: Bianchi, Campagnolo, Colnago, Pinarello. These brands still exist, but their products are often expensive. They are equalled or even surpassed in comfort and/or performance by... American bikes. Companies such as Cannondale and Works make one-piece carbon frames, without reinforcement or welding, weighing less than a kilo and at "reasonable" prices. Peloton Interactive has turned indoor cycling into a fun and social activity. And yet cycling is more of a European pastime than an American one.

A Persistent Lack of R&D&I

For 20 years, investment in R&D&I has been too low in Europe.

At the beginning of the 2000s, the USA was devoting 2.8% of its GDP to investment in R&D&I[99] compared with 2.1% for the EU15,[100] i.e. one third more. The 3% target set in 2000 to make Europe the leading knowledge-based economy has never been reached. With enlargement, the rate has even fallen, with the new Member States often investing less in R&D&I, probably due to a lack of resources.

In passing, we would stress the usefulness of mechanisms for monitoring the achievement of targets set at European level. Budgetary discipline in terms of public debt and deficit, organised around the Stability Pact and the European Semester,[101] may be relative, but it nonetheless makes it possible to achieve results in terms of balancing public finances that are less catastrophic than those observed in the area of R&D&I investment.

Since the financial crisis (2008), Europe's investment gap with other economic blocs has widened still further, to €200 billion a year.[102] Just imagine the size of this gap: more than the annual European budget, 1.33% of European GDP! For example, in 2016, R&D spending in the EU stagnated at 2.03%, compared with 4.23% in South Korea, 3.29% in Japan and 2.75% in the USA.

The backwardness accumulated over a generation is frightening. The tangible results are there for all to see: the omnipresence of third-country products and services, especially in innovative areas. And we are only at the beginning of the wave of artificial intelligence with ChatGPT. If you do not invest, you will stagnate and then go

99 *EIB Investment Report 2019/2020: accelerating Europe's transformation – Key findings*, p. 8.

100 Defraigne and Nouveau, 3rd ed., p. 372.

101 *See* below, Title I, Ch. 2.

102 Verhofstadt, p. 20.

backwards. Those who do not shape the future are condemned to its consequences. It is true that investment in R&D&I in Europe is picking up (2.19% in 2019; 2.31% in 2020), but this is not enough to halt the decline, as the following figure 12[103] shows.[104]

Figure 12.

Gross domestic expenditure on R&D, 2010 - 2020
(%, relative to GDP)

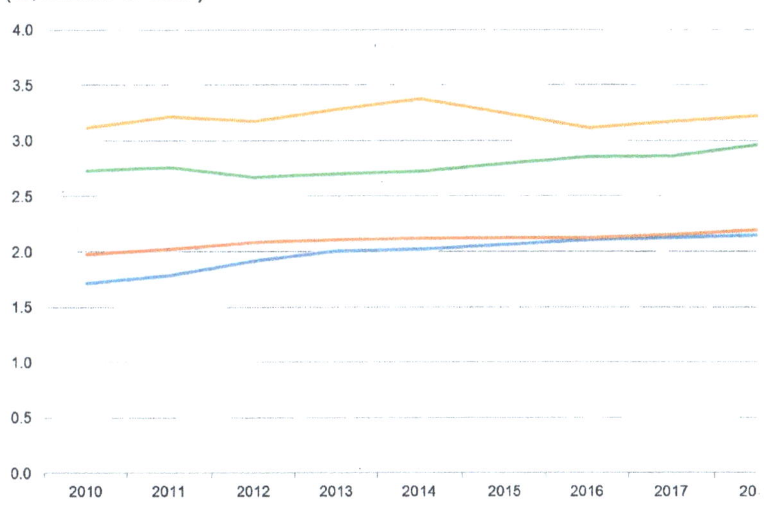

(¹) 2008, 2013 and 2018: break in series
(²) Excludes most or all capital expenditure, definition differs: 2010-2020
(³) 2020: provisional
(⁴) 2010: estimates
Source: Eurostat (online data code: rd_e_gerdtot) and OECD database

103 Eurostat, R&D.

104 And with good reason: the budget fell in 2021 (2.27%), then again in 2022 (2.23%), while at the same time the United States reached 3.5%, Japan 3.3%, South Korea 4.5% and China 2.4% (see *EDB* n° 13353 of February 20, 2024).

The Crucial Importance of Completing the Internal Market for Scientific and Technological Progress

As has already been pointed out, the deficit in business R&D&I in Europe is particularly high, because of the incomplete nature of the internal market and the resulting negative effects.

The negative spiral threatening the European economy is largely due to:[105] *an incomplete single market, protectionism, inadequate business productivity, deficiencies in R&D&I and hence in technical progress. With its social and societal consequences: falling living standards, unemployment, job insecurity, lack of hope for a better future, a shrinking population.*

Scientific and technological progress improves labour productivity and pay. It is also an essential factor in prosperity, dynamism, optimism and confidence. It is also crucial to the achievement of all the quality policies (environmental protection, energy efficiency, resource management, healthy and high-quality agriculture, a more inclusive society, health, work-life balance, etc.) that we want to pursue. Let us add to that European security (cutting-edge military industry). *A greener, energy-self-sufficient and safer Europe requires a Europe that is at the cutting edge scientifically and technologically. R&D&I is also the best guarantee of sustainable growth,*[106] one of the objectives of European integration.

The margins generated will also enable us to deal with the social consequences of certain technological developments such as artificial intelligence and digitalisation.

105 Other deteriorating factors include the downgrading of the European financial sector. On this point, *see* below, Title I, Ch. 1, B, 3.

106 On the key role of technical progress in sustainable growth, *see* in particular M. Burda and C. Wyplosz, *Macroéconomie : une perspective européenne*, Brussels, De Boeck, 6th ed., 2014, p. 82 ; E. Phelps, *La prospérité de masse*, Paris, Odile Jacob, 2017.

It is revealing that the five Member States that feature in the top ten of the Global Innovation Index 2021 are among the most prosperous and those where individuals are particularly happy: Sweden, the Netherlands, Finland, Denmark and Germany. Four of the world's top five happiest countries[107] are also in the top five for the highest number of patent applications per capita at the European Patent Office.

It is no coincidence that the Europe depicted as sovereign in the 16th century included scientific books and instruments among its attributes!

Aggravating Factors

There is an urgent need for action, because technological innovation is galloping ahead, requiring ever greater investment, as we have seen with bicycles.

Yet another revolution – Industry 4.0 (automation, the Internet of Things and artificial intelligence) – is underway. Who would have thought five years ago that we would no longer be manufacturing diesel-powered cars, or even internal combustion engines, in less than 15 years' time? Our way of life is going to change profoundly over the next few years, particularly in view of the challenges we face in terms of the environment and energy. The pandemic has only accelerated the process,[108] with videoconferencing, teleworking and ordering goods and services over the internet. In this respect, the United States is likely to widen the gap with Europe.[109]

With Brexit, we have lost many scientists,[110] two world-renowned universities and an economy that is more focused on new technologies;

107 Finland (first and fifth respectively), Denmark (second and third), Switzerland (fourth and first) and the Netherlands (fourth and fifth).

108 *See* "Innovations: c'est la lutte finale !", *Le Point*, 10 December 2020, pp. 62–68; N. Baverez, "En attendant le retour des Années folles", *Le Point*, 4 March 2021, pp. 12–13.

109 These lines were written before ChatGPT appeared.

110 In the EU, 19% of scientists came from the United Kingdom, which accounted for just 13% of the European population. In comparison, with the same population, France accounts for only 10% of European scientists (source: Eurostat).

in this respect, the UK is closer to the USA than to the Continent. For example, it has three times more start-ups and companies with growth potential in relative terms than the EU27.[111] As already mentioned, it is also one of the four most innovative countries in the world.

A Few Areas for Improvement

The deepening of the internal market advocated above should lead to an increase in private sector investment in R&D&I in the medium term. This is because, on the one hand, it will improve the prospects of profitability, which then strengthens the incentive to innovate. On the other hand, the increase in productivity and even in the range and size of companies that it will bring about will enable them to invest more in R&D&I.

In addition to the cross-cutting measures proposed above, more specific R&D&I actions can be developed. As we shall see, they are also part of a structural/modern supply policy (see below, under C).

We need to work on all the links in the chain, even if some initiatives will only produce effects in the long term. In what follows, I will focus on a few measures that are likely to have the most immediate positive effects.

(i) Facilitating the Filing of Patents

Access to legal protection for inventions should be made easier. The EU now accounts for only 20% of patent applications worldwide, compared with 30% a decade ago,[112] a reduction of one third, as figure 13 shows.

111 The gap between the EU and the USA in this area is 1 to 4 (*EIB Investment Report 2019/2020*, p. 9).

112 *EDB* 12495 of 29 May 2020; in the same vein, the European Patent Office notes in 2021 that the share of patents from European countries (in general, not limited to those from the EU) continues to fall (from 50% in 2013 to 44% in 2021).

Figure 13.

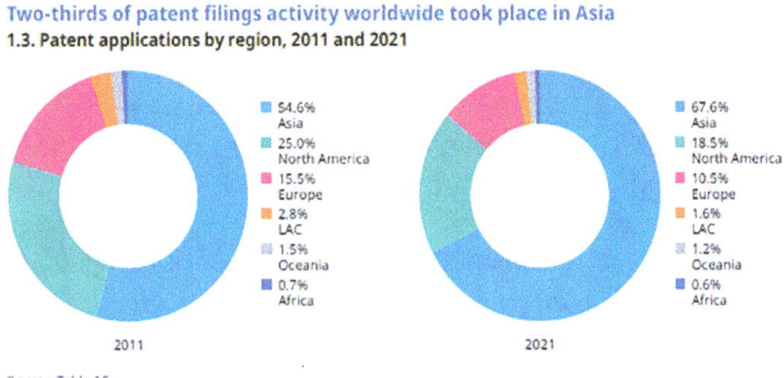

Source: Table A5.

The latest ranking of companies applying for European patents is instructive, with those from non-EU countries occupying the top places, as figure 14 shows[113]:

Figure 14.

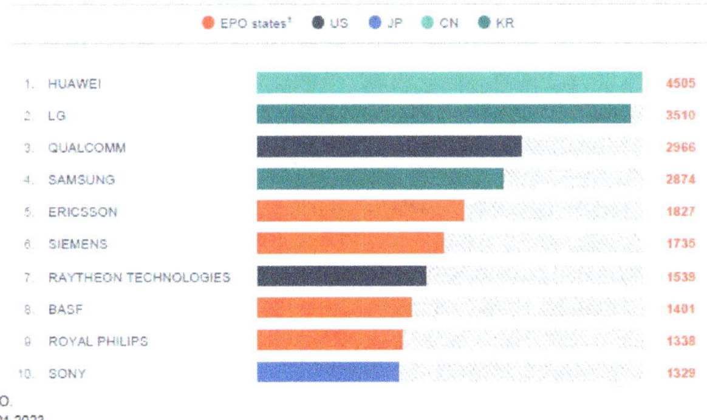

Source: EPO.
Status: 30.01.2023.

[1] This is the ranking of the main consolidated applicants at the EPO in 2022 (first-named applicant principle). It is based on European patent applications filed with the EPO, which include direct European applications and international (PCT) applications that entered the European phase during the reporting period.

[2] Country of residence of the headquarters.

[3] EPO states: the 39 member states of the European Patent Organisation, which includes the 27 states of the EU.

---

113 Ranking of largest applicants at the EPO in 2022. Source: EPO website.

The filing procedure must be less costly, if not quicker. The cost of *obtaining and keeping patents in Europe is prohibitive (almost four times more expensive than in the USA*). The loss of potential patents is greater in that, given the imperfections of the single market, the prospects of a return on investment are both more uncertain and weaker, as has already been pointed out.

As a result, *the cost of patents in Europe should not only be brought down to US levels, but should become substantially lower. In the current state of the single market, it should be divided by 10.*

To paraphrase Abraham Lincoln, "the patent system must add the fuel of incentives to the fire of genius".[114]

In order to accelerate the transition to a more eco-responsible economy, and given the tendency of existing companies to favour innovations in existing technologies (known as path dependence in economic jargon), to the detriment of breakthrough technologies that are much cleaner, *the cost of filing eco-responsible patents should be reduced by 20.*

This is certainly a matter for the Member States, but the EU could invite them to develop *a tax system favourable to intellectual property*. This was the option taken by the Nordic countries 20–30 years ago, and it has proved effective. Again, taxation could be further reduced for intellectual property rights protecting clean technologies.

Given the current inefficiencies of the single market, a tax rebate could be granted while structural improvements take effect. If the single market is not sufficiently buoyant, the incentive to innovate can be fiscally stimulated. This applies even more to eco-responsible inventions.

114 The original quote being "The patent system… added the fuel of interest to the fire of genius, in the discovery and production of new and useful things." *See* Aghion et al., p. 107.

(ii) More Funding

In 2020, the European Commission has reaffirmed the objective set in 2000 of investing 3% of GDP in R&D&I.

In my opinion, given the deficit accumulated over a generation, the 27 Member States and the EU must make a greater effort to invest in this area, probably 4% or even 5% over a number of years, or €640 to €800 billion a year.

Where can this additional funding come from?

The first two answers that come to mind are, on the one hand, the completion and liberalisation of the single market, which will enable and encourage companies to invest more in R&D&I, both in relative terms (three quarters of investment in R&D&I as in the United States instead of two thirds) and in absolute terms, because their prospects for outlets and earnings will increase; on the other hand, the growth that will result from this and will provide more resources for the Member States and the EU to invest more in R&D&I as well. Hopefully, they will be able to resist incentives to further increase non-productive public spending.

However, this room for manoeuvre on the part of the business community and the public sector will only exist in a few years' time: the time it will take for the structural measures/modern supply-side policies mentioned above to take effect.[115] What additional funding is possible in the meantime?

The Financial System in General?

Is this due to the preponderance of banks in the European financial system, the lack of former entrepreneurs in the system, or a certain degree of risk aversion in European society? The fact remains that

115 On this question, *see* below. Title I, Ch. 1, C.

inventors, start-ups and promising young companies are encountering financing difficulties both at the launch of their project and as the company grows.

In this respect, the pan-European Scale-up Initiative, launched in 2022 by the European Investment Fund (EIF) to provide European funding for innovative companies that have succeeded in growing, is to be welcomed. However, an ecosystem needs to be put in place and this will take time. Other sources of funding need to be found.

Towards a Framework That Encourages Private Investment?

We could think of (collective) investment vehicles for R&D&I. In recent years, the EU has created such vehicles to promote the incubation of promising businesses, investment in sustainable infrastructure and social entrepreneurship. In these cases, neither the EU nor the Member States make financial resources available to the entrepreneurs, not even in the form of guarantees. They simply create the right framework to attract investors.

As things stand, these so-called labelled EU funds are failures, as they are penalised by an overly cumbersome legal regime. However, the success of both retail investment funds (undertaking for collective investment in transferable securities – UCITS) and alternative investment funds (AIFs) augurs well for the future of certain labelled funds, provided they make a few improvements.[116]

However, such players are driven by the prospect of profitability. To overcome the current imperfections of the single market, a favourable tax regime should be considered. The tax incentive should be stronger for investments in clean innovations.

116 One wonders whether such a vehicle might not also help to absorb some of the current excess liquidity without destroying financial resources, as a rise in interest rates indiscriminately does. This liquidity would be invested over the long term to make the European economy more innovative. While not a panacea, such an initiative would be likely to reduce the pressure on the European Central Bank (ECB), which is confronted with inflationary pressures. It would be part of a panoply of various measures to combat rising prices while seeking to avoid recession.

More Public Funding?

The public authorities could give a boost in the meantime and go beyond 0.625% of the GDP of the 27. Provided their budgetary situation allows them to do so.

More State Aid and Other National Public Funding?

In principle, I am not calling for more subsidies for businesses. They are costly for the public authorities and, ultimately, for the public, they harm competition and business dynamism, and they are not necessarily effective.[117] The days when Jacques Chirac could say that the way for a minister to solve a problem was to give a subsidy are over. Economic policy must evolve.

In terms of R&D&I, however, the problem is partly different.

In particular, basic research would require public funding, both because of a lack of interest from the private sector (too many risks) and because the dissemination of discoveries and inventions in this field would be more favourable to the economy at large than the privatisation of their fruits. In addition, it would appear that there is a fundamental tendency for the market to under-invest in R&D&I (which constitutes a market failure that justifies public intervention). According to economic theory, companies do not integrate the positive spin-offs of innovations for society as a whole into their R&D&I decisions.

As a result, permanent public funding would be more justified for R&D&I than in other areas. It would also be particularly crucial to maintain this funding during a downturn, as it is the first area of expenditure that many companies cut back on.

117 On the disadvantages or even the harmful nature in principle of aid to companies, *see* below. Title I, Ch. 1, C.

Secondly, in view of the path dependence, which leads to a preference for improving existing technologies rather than exploring new, generally cleaner ones, it is all the more justified that the public authorities should fund research into the latter,[118] in light of today's demand for a more eco-responsible economy.

Provided that they comply with European rules, State aid (i.e. funding from Member States in favour of certain companies) for R&D&I is possible. Various categories of aid are available. For the reasons explained above, R&D&I enjoys a fairly high profile in this area. This will be even more marked in the case of SMEs and collective projects involving at least two Member States (Important Projects of Common European Interest – IPCEI), which aim to promote innovation in strategic industrial areas of the future.

Once again, a more favourable regime (higher rate of eligibility of costs) could be devised for R&D&I or IPCEI relating to clean technologies.

These considerations raise the question of the optimal level of public authority contribution to research and, by extension, its importance in relation to other public spending, particularly social protection spending. Underlying this is the question of the priorities of the public budget and the conditions for striking a balance between certain public investments and social spending.

The current geopolitical context and the driving role of this type of innovation also argue in favour of funding defence research into products and services with potential civilian applications or derivatives. The American and Israeli successes in this area argue in favour of a type of *military Keynesianism*.

118 Aghion et al., pp. 218–230.

More European Public Funding?

Research has become the third largest item in the European budget after the Common Agricultural Policy and cohesion policy, with around €10–15 billion per year (€13.5 billion in 2022), i.e. one fifteenth/one tenth of the European budget or around 0.1% of European GDP. Its share of the European budget quadrupled between 1985 and 2002.

Community spending also includes space policy (€2.2 billion), where investment has a leverage effect of 6 on general economic activity, part of European strategic investments (€4.9 billion) and security and defence policy (€1.2 billion). In fact, the innovations generated by the latter can give rise to civilian applications.

There are also partnerships between the EU and Member States, such as Joint Undertakings.[119] For example, supercomputers are funded in equal parts at European and national level.[120] EuroHPC is responsible for the purchase of these machines, which significantly increase the computing capacity of businesses and universities, essential for the development of new products in particular.

The current Community R&D&I budget remains largely insufficient given the major deficit in R&D&I. The question therefore arises as to whether its share of the Community budget should not be increased, for example at the expense of the CAP or even cohesion policy, which could be rationalised, made more dynamic and improved.[121]

---

119 The EU can set up joint undertakings (generally between the EU, industry-led associations and other partners) to ensure the successful implementation of EU research and technological development programmes in particular. There is, for example, a joint undertaking responsible for purchasing supercomputers, infrastructures that multiply the computing capacities of industry and research institutes, EuroHPC.

120 *EDB* 11936 of 11 January 2018.

121 *See* below, Title II, Ch. 1.

Public Seed Funding, a Lever for Private Investment

Other forms of funding, partly public, should also be tapped into, as they have a much better multiplier effect than subsidies.

Let us turn our attention to the European Investment Bank (EIB), the European development bank whose shareholders are the Member States, and its specialised subsidiary, the European Investment Fund (EIF). These have shown their ability to catalyse private investment. For example, under the Juncker Plan[122] between 2015 and 2020, they have attracted more than €500 billion, mostly from the private sector, starting with €21 billion from the public sector, which includes €16 billion in the form of guarantees. This mode of intervention is particularly interesting given its high multiplier coefficient (around 25) and the fact that the public support did not give rise to immediate disbursement, since it was granted in the form of guarantees. In fact, guarantees only give rise to public expenditure in the event of borrower default.

The Juncker Plan has a successor, the InvestEU programme (2021–2027). The initial objective was to mobilise €650 billion of additional investment in the EU in cutting-edge technology sectors (particularly digitalisation) from an initial guarantee of €38 billion. This was increased by €5.6 billion through the European Recovery Plan,[123] to €43.6 billion.

At least €6.6 billion of the EU guarantee will be allocated to research, innovation and digitisation, which should generate at least €100 billion in investment, or 0.8% of European GDP per year.

More generally, experience shows that public investment, especially in this area, encourages private sector investment.[124] In addition, the

122 *Ibid.*

123 *See* below, Title I, Ch. 2, D.

124 On the correlation between the amounts committed to university research and private R&D investment, *see* Defraigne and Nouveau, 3rd ed., p. 374.

involvement of the private sector in R&D funding at a later stage should encourage the search for commercially exploitable results.[125] This approach is also likely to reduce the gap between the worlds of research and business.[126]

(iii) Research, Entrepreneurship and Market Interaction

When it comes to basic research, Europe remains a benchmark. Most of the vaccines against Covid-19 were developed by European researchers.

However, too little of our scientific research has been translated into patents and practical applications.

The entrepreneurial spirit in the world of research needs to be given greater prominence. One way of bridging the gap between laboratories and markets is to take into account, in the evaluation of researchers (or at least some of them), not only their publications in quality journals, but also the patents filed and the economic projects developed or made possible by their work.

One idea would be, without reducing the scientific quality of European researchers, to make them more complete or, at least, to encourage different profiles.[127] To draw an analogy with other fields, tennis players and footballers are more versatile today than they were in the 1970s and 1980s. The same applies to actors, comedians and opera singers. Their range has expanded substantially. The former now sing and dance, and are even capable of physical prowess. Conversely, the acting skills of the latter have improved. Similarly, more entrepreneurial education for scientists would be welcome.

---

125 On the American example, *see* ibid.

126 On this point, *see* below, (iii).

127 An alternative or, better still, a complementary measure would be the emergence of councils and specialised agents to deal with these issues.

There could also be portals and forums where researchers could present their projects, with a view to attracting entrepreneurs and investors (bringing together supply and demand for projects, improving information); platforms where research requests and projects could be brought together, calls for projects, innovation prizes; broadcasts where researchers could present their projects to professional investors or even the general public (crowdfunding). Anything that can bring a research activity closer to the market should be tried.

(iv) Towards a Genuine European Research Area (ERA)

We need to work towards the emergence and strengthening of a network of world-class research centres. The need is all the more pressing given that, following Brexit, we have lost two of the world's most prestigious universities.

This will require the emergence of centres based on a culture of excellence, with the resources, autonomy and critical size to match. In this respect, the pooling of skills, resources and infrastructure at the Université Paris-Saclay is a step in the right direction.

These centres should preferably be cross-border or at least interconnected. Alongside transport, energy, spatial planning and economic, social and territorial cohesion, R&D&I is one of the areas where we need to think more "European" and global, in terms of an articulated whole rather than a simple juxtaposition of national policies, institutions and achievements. The European Research Area,[128] which is still in the making, is a key element in this process.

(v) Promoting Science and Technology Courses

Interest in science, technology and research needs to be further stimulated. The prestige of these sectors varies from one Member

128 On this point, *see* in particular the Communication of the Commission, "A new ERA for Research and Innovation", COM(2020) 628 final, 30 September 2020.

State to another. While the German chancellor attends industry fairs, the French president runs a marathon at the Salon de l'Agriculture. It is not uncommon to see scientists in German fiction. On the other hand, in French series.[129]

As the technological and economic barriers to innovation in the broadest sense come down, we need to promote a scientific culture[130] AND innovative entrepreneurship.[131] This means setting up edutainment and science parks, like the Cité des Sciences et de l'Industrie, 3D printing, modelling and model-making laboratories where inventors of all ages can test out their ideas and associations for teenagers interested in science and technology. Such facilities are made available by certain incubators and innovation clusters. They should be included in school visits.[132] Science and mathematics teaching must be restored and improved in secondary schools, and universities and research centres must be enabled to pursue ambitious research programmes and retain high-level researchers,[133][134] as already mentioned.[135]

Once again – and this is one of the main themes of the essay, along with technical and scientific progress, productivity, an open economy, moderation in standards, and giving priority to financial techniques over traditional subsidies, in particular – *education and the adaptation of training to the realities of the internal market and to the society of today and tomorrow are fundamental to enabling the population and businesses to grow.*

---

129 On France's inadequate capacity to train scientists, *see* J. de Larosière, *40 ans d'égarements économiques : quelques idées pour en sortir*, Paris, Odile Jacob, 2021, p. 46.

130 On the risk of scientific downgrading, *see* in particular A. Landier and D. Thesmar, "Science : la France doit se ressaisir", *Les Echos*, 18–19 December 2020, p. 11.

131 *See* above, (iii).

132 The EU has a role to play here, given its competences in the area of human development. On this point, *see* below, Title I, Ch. 1, B, 4.

133 Landier and Thesmar, p. 11.

134 On the "brain drain", *see* in particular J. Attali, "Nous devons faire plus pour retenir nos talents", *Les Echos*, 19–20 March 2021, p. 13.

135 *See* above, (iii), developments relating to the European Research Area.

(vi) Miscellaneous

It should be remembered that the fact that the European economy remains open to the world (direct investment in the EU) and one of the main players in world trade is likely to help it to absorb technical progress more quickly.[136]

We can also expect an ambitious industrial policy (see next section), focused on improving the competitiveness of the European economy, to have a positive effect on R&D&I.[137]

2. A Dynamic, Eco-Responsible Industrial Policy That Respects Competition Law and Is Well-Informed

Benefits of Reindustrialisation

Re-industrializing Europe is important, not least for social reasons. Indeed, industrial activity generates higher value-added jobs and greater productivity (again, this crucial notion), resulting in higher salaries and higher GDP per capita.

One of the reasons for the widening gap between "northern" and "southern" countries is that the former are often the most industrialised,[138] Plus, industry generates twice as many indirect jobs as the service sector.

The moment an economy stops any industrial activity, it innovates less and gradually loses technological control over the production sites. Like technical progress, industry is therefore also a factor in sustainable growth.

136 *See* above, Title I, Ch. 1, "Introduction".

137 *EDB* 12417 of 4 February 2020.

138 This is how France has lost 2.5 million industrial jobs since 1974. *See* the excellent essay by J.-P. Clamadieu, Chairman of the Board of Engie, L'Europe, avenir de l'industrie française, Le cherche midi, 2022, p. 19.

Reindustrialisation can also mean creating companies in innovative sectors and/or in the green economy. It is essential to preserve Europe's autonomy in a number of critical areas, as the pandemic has highlighted, with the manufacture of masks, respirators and vaccines. It also plays an important role in the emergence of a European defence.

EU Industrial Policy Responsibilities

The EU's mission, together with the Member States, is to develop *the most favourable framework possible for the development of the European economy in order to guarantee its competitiveness while respecting the principle of an open economy with free competition.*

The emphasis is on the quality of the playing field offered to businesses. The EU must allow access to markets for new entrants (cf. the concept of the "open economy"), create the right conditions for economic activity, particularly industrial activity, and then allow operators to take the initiative and assume their responsibilities. This healthy emulation between a plurality or even a multitude of operators is likely to generate a vigorous economic fabric and activity.

The philosophy is in line with what I advocate in general and differs profoundly from subsidies, for example in the Common Agricultural Policy.

This new approach, which consumes less public money and generates more jobs, prosperity and sustainable growth, has been applied in particular in the cultural and creative industry sectors (e.g. fashion). There have also been similar initiatives in the tourism sector, which is extremely important for southern countries. One idea is to promote quality tourism, particularly with a view to sustainable development that respects the regions that the tourists visit.

A New Strategy

In some respects, the industrial policy strategy initiated by Commissioner Thierry Breton is in line with this approach. For example, the European Alliance for Clean Hydrogen brings together the public, private and research sectors to create a market. There is also the European Alliance for Batteries and the European Alliance for Semiconductors, a key technology sector.

These initiatives are not only synergies between all the driving forces, but also attempts to create conditions conducive to the development of economic activity. In short, they are general frameworks for the reindustrialisation[139] of Europe in the broadest sense, rather than one-off support for one or more specific companies.

Reindustrialisation and Eco-Responsibility

Reindustrialisation will not be at the expense of the ecosystem. The growth we seek will be clean. The environmental dimension is systematically integrated into all European policies. For example, the European initiative for the battery industry seeks to guarantee the recovery of used batteries.[140] The hydrogen that Europe is seeking to promote is green. The European Investment Bank is also financing more and more environmentally friendly projects.

Industry is ready to go green. Improvements in the energy and environmental performance of industrial manufacturing processes and products can be substantial. Too many technologies still in use are inefficient compared to the possibilities they offer. Just think of blast furnaces that could use cleaner energy and recover some of it, dishwashers and

139 It is worth noting that the situation in the Member States varies. While Germany has maintained or even slightly increased the share of industry in its GDP (which has grown considerably) between 1998 and 2018 (24% instead of 23.5%), France has suffered a loss of almost 25% (13% instead of 17%), which is indicative of a problem of competitiveness (on these points, *see* Larosière, pp. 83–90).

140 D. Perrotte, "Bruxelles veut imposer des batteries électriques 'propres'", *Les Echos*, 11–12 December 2020, p. 36.

car washes that could dry clean, air conditioning systems, etc. The Solar Impulse foundation launched by Bertrand Piccard has labelled nearly 1,500 new processes or products that are environmentally friendly in just a few years.[141]

Industrial Policy and Competition Law

In order to reindustrialise in line with the principle of an open market economy, distortions of competition must be avoided, particularly in the form of subsidies to certain companies or even certain sectors.

In addition, we need to have a certain number of European operators to ensure sustainable emulation and dynamism. The Japanese example is instructive in this respect. Having set the conditions for the development of the car industry, the Japanese government has ensured that there is keen competition between a small number of manufacturers: Honda, Toyota, Mazda, Mitsubishi, Nissan, Datsun, Suzuki, Subaru, etc.[142] This is also a healthy diversification of risks by the public authorities, a concept that should be pushed further.

That said, European state aid law offers a degree of flexibility by authorising certain types of aid provided that they meet a real need and offer more advantages than disadvantages. For example, the European Commission has authorised two major projects of common interest[143] to support research and innovation in the battery value chain.[144] The IPCEI instrument has also been used by 16 Member States to develop production capacity in the field of electronic chips.[145]

141 Piccard, p. 149. *See* the list at <www.solarimpulse.com>.

142 Combe, pp. 217–218.

143 At least two Member States.

144 The second, entitled "European Battery Innovation", involves 12 Member States that will provide up to €2.9 billion in funding over the next few years, with the aim of mobilising a further €9 billion in private investment. It will cover the entire battery value chain, include 46 projects and lead to the launch of more than 300 partnerships (*EDB* 12664 of 27 January 2021, pp. 15–16).

145 F. Dèbes et D. Perrotte, "L'Europe à la relance pour les puces électroniques", *Les Echos*, 22–23 January 2021, p. 26.

If aid is envisaged, it may be preferable to give it a sectoral scope so as not to favour one or more specific companies[146] (while factoring into the overall assessment a higher cost for public finances and the risk of distortion with other sectors/industries).

European industrial policy is a key area for reflection on the relationship between respect for a market economy and the place and forms that public initiatives can take. It can help to overcome the opposition between those in favour of private initiative and those in favour of public interventionism, and move pragmatically towards coordination and synergies that combine the best of both worlds. In particular, if a public initiative makes it possible to achieve important objectives for the European economy and/or society that are unattainable by current market forces alone, with a minimum of resources and restrictions on competition, why deprive ourselves? However, we must be careful not to undermine too much the principles of state aid, whose contribution both to the health of public finances and to economic vigour has been tried and tested.

Dynamic, Yes, but With Discernment

In this respect, the Swiss experience gives us cause for reflection. There has been no deindustrialisation in Switzerland. Not only has the proportion of the workforce employed in industry remained stable for a quarter of a century, but this economic sector has also gained in added value. "However", Switzerland has no industrial policy in the sense of promoting certain sectors. It favours horizontal measures without seeking to favour a given sector.[147] Once again, the watchword is the quest for high *productivity*, which results in companies specialising in promising sectors.

---

146 In a similar vein, *see* Aghion et al., p. 96.

147 D. Farman, J. Cosandey and S. Rutz, "Continuing Swiss Industry's Success Story: Embracing structural change rather than fighting it", Avenir Suisse, 8 October 2021; *see* E. Garessus, "Non, la Suisse n'est pas victime d'une désindustrialisation", *Le Temps*, 8 October 2021.

In any case, we must be wary of rehashing the "old tricks" of industrial policy from the 1970s. That policy contributed to stagflation and growing public debt. Let us avoid a disastrous repeat.

Nor is market failure (e.g. a lack of European industry in a key sector) sufficient to justify any public initiative. But it must be effective and capable of catching up and closing the gap with competitors from third countries. Otherwise, public money and energy go down the drain. The project needs to be carefully thought through, focusing on strategic products and services. Sometimes it is better to "cut your losses" and concentrate your efforts on another technology or a new innovation.[148]

Re-industrialising Europe will also require support from the financial system. The financial system will have to take its share of risks in the business world, as well as in other areas of modernisation of the European economy and society. It will therefore have to perform well. As we shall see, the reforms undertaken since the 2008 crisis in this area have not improved its record in this respect. European financial services policy needs to be rethought.

3. A Safer, More Efficient and More Complete European Financial System

Part One: The Benefits of a Strong Financial System for Europe

The single market makes it possible to produce more wealth, which in turn grows and can be invested. This wealth and the growing needs of businesses call for an integrated financial area and system. Major financial centres can develop and attract capital from all over the

148 Combe, p. 44.

world. The more efficient the European financial system becomes, the more financial resources can be made available to the EU economy at lower cost.

(i) Finance: A Second Engine for the Real Economy

The financial sector can boost and sustain over time the prosperity generated by the production of goods and services in Europe. With the huge amount of money it brings in, the European economy can finance projects that facilitate tomorrow's growth.

So finance is very important. Contrary to a ninth common misconception, it does not replace the "real" economy, nor does it swallow it up, but rather it complements and enhances it.[149] In the event of a slowdown in the real economy, it can also soften the blow and temporarily take over.[150] It then acts like the electric motor in a hybrid car that has run out of petrol.

These points are at times misunderstood. All too often, finance conjures up images of dubious combinations, excessive risks, honest people's savings going up in smoke and the impunity of financiers. Finance does not kill the real economy if it is properly managed. On the contrary, it preserves its benefits, perpetuates them and even increases them.

Finance also provides a large number of direct well-paid jobs (depending on the Member State, the financial sector can employ more than 10% of the working population).[151] What's more, the abundance of capital means that employees are generally well paid, through a transfer effect, given the reduced costs of financing businesses.

---

149 Think of Tesla's stock market valuation, which is ten times greater than that of the two biggest car manufacturers, Toyota and VW.

150 For example, after the economic boom of the 16th century, the financial system of the Netherlands helped to overcome a bad period in the 17th century and to finance their commercial expansion around the world.

151 Unlike many service sector jobs, labour productivity in the financial sector is generally high.

This is important if we want to maintain our social democratic model. Insofar as this system involves paying workers well, having an abundance of financial resources at low cost facilitates its viability. *The vitality and efficiency of the financial system are all the more crucial at a time when other non-economic objectives must be pursued at the same time (making the economy greener, strengthening European military defence).* Finance can be an ally of labour, contrary to a tenth prejudice.

(ii) The Financial System: The Equivalent of an Export Sector

The European financial system can also attract capital from the rest of the world. There is also an external dimension: the interest that the EU represents for customers from third countries.

Europe is a stable region, founded on the rule of law. People who have become wealthy in emerging countries fear a change of regime or direction. As soon as they can, they seek to shelter their money. Why is Miami so rich? Because it is the gateway to the United States for people from South and Central America. They open an account there or, better still, buy a property there for reasons of security. Europe can be another refuge for the wealth of the rising classes in emerging countries.

Similarly, the European Investment Bank (EIB) is raising a growing proportion of capital in third countries. As the world's largest multilateral development bank with a triple-A rating, the EIB raises €55–60 billion each year on the financial markets. Today, a third of this sum comes from non-EU countries.

The European financial sector is therefore comparable to an exporting sector in the sense that it can attract money from the rest of the world, which it will then make available to the real European economy. It can also invest in the rest of the world to generate future income.

This is why we need to move beyond the eleventh cliché, which is that finance must not be too large in relation to the real economy. It is not a question of the proportion between the two spheres that counts (what country would want to reduce the size of a sector that exports heavily on the grounds that it is disproportionate to the rest of the economy?) but rather the solid foundation of the European financial system and the sound management of its risks. Provided these conditions are met, it is in our interest to develop a financial system that is attractive to the rest of the world. We will see that we have not done enough since the 2008 crisis.

A powerful European financial system is essential for Europe's recovery. It can be a lever facilitating private and public initiatives, whether in a separate or combined manner, as we have outlined and will examine in more detail.

(iii) The Euro: A Potential Additional Driving Force

The single currency, the euro, can constitute a third engine, alongside that of the real economy and the financial economy. It can represent additional added value for the European Union.

Firstly, the euro has eliminated exchange risks and costs in a substantial part of the EU. Secondly, it has facilitated the merger of national financial systems into a European financial system. This has increased the financing opportunities for European companies. For example, they have been able to issue bonds in euros that can be subscribed to by many more investors. The European bond market has also enabled Europe to become one of the three largest markets in the world, alongside the United States and Japan (known as a liquidity pool). Think of the sums of money that, in one way or another, enter the European financial system as a result. If the European currency is in demand, Europe can obtain financial resources at a lower cost. It can therefore finance more projects.

Issuing the currency in which some international transactions are conducted also brings considerable advantages.[152] The sovereign privilege of minting the world's benchmark currency adds a few percentage points to GDP (via the right of seigniorage[153]). Not to mention the ascendancy it brings in a number of international forums. In addition, the international influence of a currency gives rise to a whole series of transactions that will benefit its economy. For example, more bonds will be issued in this currency and will probably be subject to the law of one of the Member States of the eurozone. Once again, a legal-financial industry is developing, generating jobs that are highly skilled to boot. Financial innovation in the EU also brings benefits. Finally, the idea is not far removed from that of standards, already mentioned,[154] or even from that of Marshallian districts. If the euro becomes an international benchmark, European society as a whole will benefit.

If Europe manages to develop a predictable monetary policy, based on sound fundamentals, and avoids changes of course dictated solely by its short-term interests, the euro can gradually become an alternative to the dollar. The international dimension is showing its face again.

However, such objectives require certain conditions to be met, as well as sustained rigour and exemplarity if we are to win and retain the confidence of the rest of the world in the soundness of our economy, our financial system and our currency. Current circumstances show that we are still a long way from achieving this.[155] The euro has lost a great deal of value and capital outflows from the eurozone are at record levels. What's more, the overall performance of the eurozone is unimpressive compared with that of Member States that are not

152 In this respect, issuing bonds as part of the European Recovery Plan will make the EU a major player on the financial markets. It should strengthen the international role of the euro (*see EDB* 12639 of 20 January 2021).

153 In other words, income from the issue of money.

154 *See* above, Title I, Ch. 1, "Introduction", 2.

155 On the ECB's cyclical temptations, *see* below, Title I, Ch. 2, C.

part of it.[156] This sub-optimality is striking. Sweden, which boasts a remarkable school of economics, was very wise, as things stand, to refuse to join the eurozone.

So we have a multi-layered structure, based on the internal market, with an integrated, high-performance financial system and a single currency with an international dimension.

(iv) Finance, the Technological Revolution and Other Challenges of Our Time

With the new industrial and technological revolution, it is all the more vital to have an efficient European financial system. We need colossal sums of money to ensure the well-being of future generations. We need to invest heavily to create a European Apple, Google or Tesla, to conquer space, to embrace digital technology, 5G, a greener economy and European defence. We need to devote more money to R&D&I than we have in the last 20 years if we do not want to fall behind permanently, if not irretrievably. Just for an increasingly green economy, we are talking about €260 billion a year, or 1.7% of European GDP, which is more than 1.5 years of the European budget. In the light of statements by the former Vice-President of the European Commission, Mr Timmermans, the needs could even be higher.

(v) Finance: A Relatively Clean Sector

The financial sector consumes little energy,[157] pollutes the environment less than other sectors and does not require a lot of space. These are considerable advantages in today's and tomorrow's world, and even more so in a microcontinent like Europe.[158] Space is at a premium.

---

156 *See* below, Title I, Ch. 2, D.

157 Subject to the energy required by IT and remote communication technologies to run servers, PCs, technological infrastructure, payment systems, clearing and settlement, etc.

158 *See* above, Title I, Ch. 1, "Introduction".

There are virtually no more areas available for storing sea containers within a hundred kilometres from the coast. We are in danger of bottlenecking.

Part Two: Weaknesses in the Policy Pursued Since the Financial Crisis

(i) A Cancer That Has Not Been Eradicated: Bad Bank Debt

Despite the European Central Bank's (ECB) low interest rate policy, a significant amount of bad debt continues to be owed by banks, fifteen years after the start of the banking crisis. There was talk of €600 billion before the pandemic, starting from a peak of €1,200–1,400 billion in 2013–2014. It has fallen to €350–360 billion (2.6%) by the end of 2020. A resurgence is feared, with the rate of underperforming loans starting to climb again during 2022, as figure 15 shows.

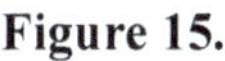

Figure 15.

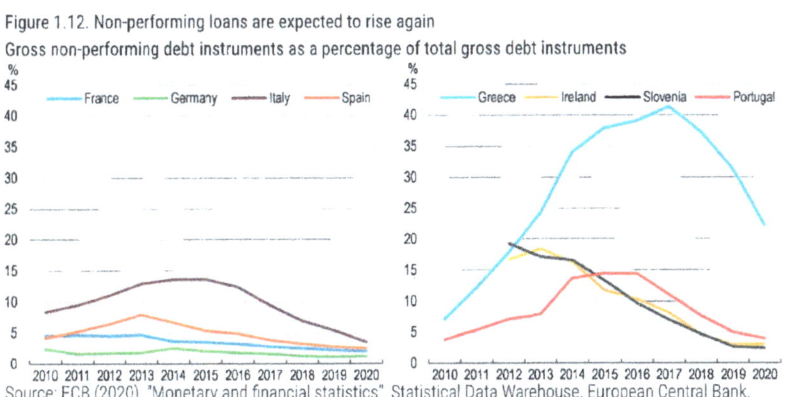

Figure 1.12. Non-performing loans are expected to rise again
Gross non-performing debt instruments as a percentage of total gross debt instruments

Source: ECB (2020), "Monetary and financial statistics", Statistical Data Warehouse, European Central Bank.

Bad debts reduce the capacity of the banks affected to finance the economy and strengthen their solvency. They also act as a deterrent to bank mergers, especially cross-border ones. They make European banks less competitive than American banks, which have half the bad debt ratio. They also lead to excessive costs (reserve requirements) for healthy banks. They also represent a risk to the stability of the European financial system. Finally, they provide an argument for the US to continue imposing new constraints on European banks.

The health of European banks is worrying. Increased capital requirements, other regulatory constraints and the ECB's long-sacrificial rates have reduced their profitability to an insignificant 1–2% on equity. They are also facing growing competition from technology companies (often non-European). This is a serious situation for the European economy, which the banks continue to finance to the tune of 70%.

We do not always realise the extent to which the 2008 crisis, which originated in the US, had a far greater impact in Europe, particularly given the difference in the relative importance of banks in the European and US economies.

(ii) Increasingly Burdensome, Destructive and Ineffective Regulation in Its Place

Instead of focusing on bad bank debt, European co-legislators have adopted thousands of pages of regulation and set up European Supervisory Authorities whose main activity is to draw up thousands more pages of implementing regulation.

Is this the result of the regulatory and prudential tsunami? The fact remains that the European financial sector is losing momentum. There is only one European bank in the world's top ten, in ninth or tenth place. There are now only two European asset managers in the top ten, compared with five before the 2008 crisis. Once again, Europe has fallen back in the rankings of the world's leading companies.[159] What's more, with London, we have lost what was until recently the world's leading financial centre.

159 *See* the Foreword above.

For example, the control and compliance functions have taken on too much indiscriminate importance in recent years. The European financial system is like a human being whose immune system works too hard: it becomes anaemic and sclerotic.[160] Banking, financial and insurance operators spend too much time and resources ensuring that they do not violate this or that requirement in terms of form, reporting, etc. The culture is changing. From being a partner to entrepreneurs and households, the financial system is turning into a bureaucratic, procedural and cumbersome machine which no longer finances the real economy. How many businesses have come up against a shortage of banking and financial services?

Once again, the level playing field heralded by the European Commission is proving to be a level dying field.[161] In flagrant violation of the principle of an open economy with free competition, the EU is restricting production and outlets for banking and financial services, strangling the European economy.[162] It oversizes the national and European authorities, which, having to justify their existence, sink into regulatory, cautionary and even repressive zeal.

In addition, heavy regulation kills off small operators, increases concentration in the sector and reinforces systemic risk with a market reduced to a few large players. Finally, the obsession with protecting investors and savers is preventing them from financing the European economy… and becoming wealthier.

Once again, Europeans have shot themselves in the foot.[163] They lacked the clarity to identify the problems and the political intelligence to define and defend clearly understood European interests.

---

160 Multiple sclerosis is caused by a dysfunction of the immune system.

161 On this question, *see* above, Title I, Ch. 1, A, 3.

162 For just one example, *see* S. Ruche, "La directive MiFID II bouleverse la recherche financière", *Le Temps*, 23 October 2023.

163 The two world wars, which were entirely due to the stupidity of Europeans, cost them world supremacy.

Part Three: Some suggestions

(i) For a More Targeted Approach

Let us opt more for a risk-based approach. Legislators and supervisory authorities should focus on the players and practices that pose the greatest threat to financial stability, starting with non-performing loans and the institutions that hold them. These must be subject to greater vigilance.

Interventions must also be more targeted and determined. Intrusive and authoritarian measures are recommended to clean up the financial system on a long-term basis. Otherwise, the system will not be able to fully finance the economy. If necessary, exemplary sanctions must be taken, including against individuals. This is a question of accountability and social justice.

On the other hand, let the other banking and financial operators breathe a sigh of relief and make money available to economic operators and households. Let us drastically reduce the volume of regulation. The financial sector must once again be able to assume its primary role: finance the economy.

(ii) Let Us Rehabilitate Financial Innovation and Invest in Financial Education

More room must be given to financial innovation in order to improve the sector's performance. Technological developments (digitisation, artificial intelligence, etc.) open up considerable prospects for progress.

Let us give investors more proportionate protection by facilitating access to investments that may be risky, but may be promising and essential to the dynamism of the European economy. In this respect, part of the population no longer needs paternalistic protection. Financial education would be more rewarding, more promising and more effective. European society can only benefit from citizens who are more aware of financial realities. What is more, such an approach would democratise financial knowledge. It is also a component of a more open and inclusive society, which effectively enables citizens to develop, grow and become more prosperous.

(iii) For a Structural/Modern Supply-Side Policy

We therefore need to clean up Europe's financial system, recalibrate regulations and controls in line with the risk that operators and operations pose to the system, simplify and breathe new life into the engine. We also need to complete the single financial area, as national barriers still exist in this sector,[164] and enable more citizens to become dynamic and informed users of the financial system.

In a nutshell, it is once again an appropriate structural/supply-side policy that needs to be pursued at European level. At the moment, we are a long, long way from achieving this. The EU has behaved like a tourist reading a city map upside down: it is gradually and methodically moving away from the objectives to be achieved, with new regulation after new regulation. To err is human; to persist in error is diabolical.

(iv) Towards More Market Finance? An Ill-Considered Debate – Towards a Multipolar European Financial Sector

The Capital Markets Union (CMU), one of the Commission's major objectives to move towards more market-based finance, has been a flop.[165] It is all the more worrying in that, with Brexit, the EU has lost its leading financial position, as already mentioned.

---

164 In the same vein, *see* the aforementioned *EIB Investment Report 2019/2020*, pp. 21–22.

165 One might even wonder whether, rather than moving forward, the CMU is moving backwards. More and more companies are delisting. One of the reasons for this is a change in European regulations which means that fewer and fewer listed companies are subject to independent analysis, further widening the asymmetry of information between the issuer and the circles that gravitate around it, on the one hand, and public savings on the other. Another is that European companies prefer to list in the United States, as we have already seen with Spotify.

If the CMU is to be relaunched, it must also be rethought. This must not be achieved at the expense of the banking sector. The driving force of the capital markets should be added to that of banking, not replace it. Why deprive ourselves of an asset? So, yes to more market finance, but with a strong or even strengthened banking sector. You cannot win a match by working only on your weak points. You have to continue to maintain and even improve your strengths. A balance between the banking sector and market finance is a laudable but secondary objective. The priority is to have a sufficiently large and efficient financial sector, particularly given the growing and more diversified needs of the European economy.

Moreover, the current average size of EU companies and their consequent inability to benefit from the single market makes it doubtful that they will have access to financial markets solely as a result of the Union of capital markets. Nor can the (cultural) financing habits of economic operators be changed by legislative reform, especially in the face of such structural problems.[166]

In this respect, the improvement in the functioning of the single market advocated above should help. In particular, the recommended common foundation[167] should reduce the asymmetry of information between companies and potential investors. The deepening of the internal market should also lead to more medium-sized companies with greater cash flow and therefore self-financing capacity, as mentioned above.[168] This must be promoted alongside the European banking sector and the CMU.

Self-financing is a third source of financing. It is invaluable, as stock market listing does not only offer advantages. In particular, it can

166 This is exacerbated by a number of European regulatory reforms, which mean that fewer listed securities are subject to independent analysis, and by the fierce competition from US financial centres, which a growing number of European issuers are joining.

167 *See* above, Title I, Ch. 1, A, 1.

168 Larosière, pp. 153–160.

lead to a tendency towards short-termism. For example, family-run businesses tend to invest more and to question winning formulas more than those whose shareholders are widely dispersed and/or made up of investment funds. This would explain BMW's lead over other brands in electric motors.

The Union of capital markets must not blind us to the potential of a fourth component of the investment fund industry, i.e. collective investment vehicles managed by professionals, whose assets are entrusted to the supervision of a separate custodian and which, depending on their investment policy, are more or less open to the general public.

To date, European initiatives in this area have been far more successful than those relating to financial markets in the strict sense. Why? Like banks, and unlike financial markets, investment funds represent a more pronounced form of financial intermediation. Investors do not invest directly in financial instruments issued by companies (shares, bonds). Instead, they buy units in funds that select and diversify their "targets". In a way, the fund fills the gap between investors and companies whose value is difficult for them to judge. Its units are distributed by… banks, which can offer them to their customers more easily than shares in a particular company, given the advantage of the greater risk diversification inherent in a collective vehicle. The fund plays the role of the financial markets to a greater or lesser extent, since it is obliged to repurchase or redeem the shares of any investor wishing to leave the fund at their net asset value.

The insurance sector, and even that of pension funds, must also be the subject of particular attention. These operators can make long-term investments that are extremely useful and beneficial to the European economy. Instead of exploiting this potential, the European legislator has restricted the investment possibilities of insurance companies since 2008.[169,170] The pension fund sector could be reactivated, especially in Member States where the statutory pension pillar is in deficit.[171] The more diversified the European financial system, the better off the European economy will be.

A sixth dimension is Europe's ability to attract capital from all over the world, as mentioned above, as an area where the rule of law and legal certainty prevail. This is another source of funding that should not be overlooked.

Finally, in addition to a multipolar structure, the European financial system needs to develop the expertise required to support change, particularly technological change. The financing of innovative activities, whatever the vehicles and techniques used, requires specific know-how (analysis of the market, the reliability and potential of the operator, risk-taking and management, vision, etc.).

From an economy with 70–80% bank financing, Europe could therefore, while maintaining or even strengthening its banking industry, evolve towards a financial system with several pillars: banking, market finance, fund finance, insurance, pension funds and corporate self-financing. It could also seek to attract more capital from the rest of the world.

(v) For a More Aware Europe That Looks After Its Own Interests

If the European financial sector is to assert itself, Europe must also be clearly aware of its interests and free itself from American tutelage in this area, particularly in the intellectual sphere. For a long time, finance was an Anglo-Saxon affair, with London and then New York

169 On this issue, *see* B. Spitz, *Merci l'Europe ! Riposte aux sept mensonges populistes*, Paris, Grasset, 2019, pp. 114–115 and 130.

170 It was not until September 2021 that the EU began a U-turn on this issue.

171 Larosière, pp. 151–160.

(from... the end of the First World War[172]). The architecture was built by the United States after the Second World War. They continue to dominate it.

Europe is too complacent and naive. Here are a few examples.

First, after 11 September 2001, the Americans succeeded in obtaining information on their residents who had accounts in Europe (FATCA[173] system). The reverse has not been true. What's more, FATCA is such a complicated mess that a number of operators in Europe prefer not to deal with American residents. The European financial system has lost this clientele.

Secondly, the banking crisis originated in the United States. Who dictated the measures to be taken to avoid another crisis? The United States. Which sector did they focus on? The banking sector. Yet this accounts for only 30% of the financing of their economy, compared with 70% in Europe.[174]

4. Worker Mobility and the Development of Human Capital

Mobility

(i) An Asset Against Unemployment – The Prospect of a Better Life

The single market is another chance for people to get a (better) job. You just have to cross not the street, but the border.[175]

172 This was Europe's first act of suicide.

173 For Foreign Account Tax Compliance Act.

174 What's more, they were careful not to transpose all the solutions identified to the international level!

175 To paraphrase a famous and controversial statement by French President Emmanuel Macron.

Many Italians found work in the coal and steel industries in France and Belgium in the 1960s. After the 2008 crisis, young Spaniards fled mass unemployment in their own country and went to work in Germany or Luxembourg, for example. The single market does not just exist for capital. It opens up opportunities for people who lack them in their Member State of origin.

The European Union multiplies by 27 the territory in which a national of a Member State can work, live and travel.

One of the best associates I have ever worked with – I launched a European law practice in Luxembourg (where I myself had emigrated) 20 years ago – came from Montpellier. I took him on for an indefinite period when he was 23. Much to the astonishment of his friends. In his region – and even in Paris – young graduates only had access to insecure, generally unpaid, work placements. In some cases, they were not even reimbursed for their expenses. That was in 2006. Since then, he has lived in London, married an Irish woman, started a family… and continues to maintain close links with Montpellier.

Unemployment is a waste on every level: human, cultural and economic. It is a part of life that is not lived to the full, a potential that is not exploited. Unemployment among young people is a scourge because it delays their take-off and compromises a series of essential stages in adult life, including the building of a couple and a family. Job vacancies are also missed opportunities for businesses.[176]

176 Greater worker mobility would also enable the eurozone, as a monetary zone, to function better in response to asymmetric shocks, i.e. shocks that affect only certain Member States of the zone (*see* in particular P. Krugman, M. Obstfeld and M. Melitz, *Économie internationale*, Montreuil, Pearson, 10th ed., 2015, p. 693).

(ii) Mobility: A Freedom That Is Insufficiently Used

Worker mobility in Europe is ten times lower than in the United States.[177] Only 3.9% of workers are mobile. Member States have more third-country nationals on their territory than nationals of other Member States, as shown in figure 16 below![178] It is true that for the former, Europe is a paradise, in comparative terms. Being able to live here justifies efforts that a national of another Member State is less inclined to make.[179]

Figure 16.

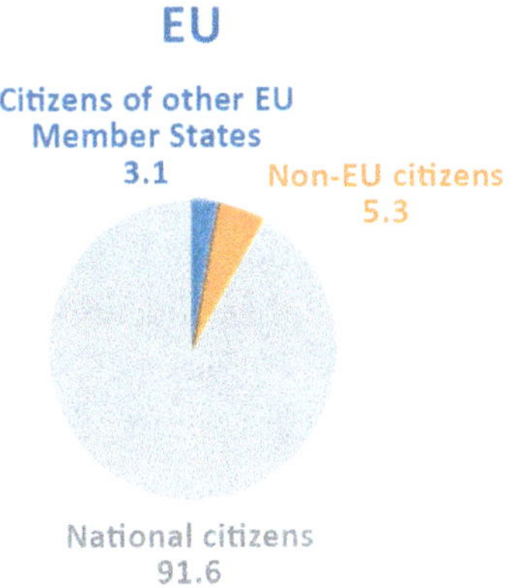

On the positive side, the number of intra-Community expats has doubled over the last ten years. This development is comparable to that of the proportion of SMEs involved in intra-Community trade.[180] European integration is becoming a tangible and sensitive reality for a growing number of people and businesses, even if it remains marginal due to the incomplete nature of the internal market.

177 Verhofstadt, p. 237.

178 "Citizenship of the population", *Key figures on Europe*, 2022 and 2023, p. 13.

179 As in many areas, however, the reality is not monolithic. On the one hand, the younger generation is probably better equipped today to move around Europe. On the other hand, talent can be as nomadic as money (on this last point, *see* Attali, p. 13).

180 *See* above, A, 1.

(iii) Mechanisms to Promote Personal Mobility

Various mechanisms are already in place to improve worker mobility. However, they need to be better known by the public (there is still a lack of education and public awareness of the potential of the internal market). They could also be improved and supplemented.

Erasmus, which enables higher education students to study for six months in another Member State, is a major success of the EU.[181] Thanks to this programme, which was launched some forty years ago and had a budget of €3.3 billion in 2022 (i.e. 2% of the European budget), tens of thousands of students have had the opportunity to discover or perfect their knowledge of another university education and another language.

Even though Erasmus has been open to them since 1995, apprentices make far less use of it than higher education students. Greater use of this mechanism would also enable socio-professional categories who may feel excluded to access some of the tangible benefits of European integration.

A funding programme organised by the EIB-FEI Group[182] cuts the cost of an Erasmus student's stay abroad in half. Like EURES, it is not well known.

EURES (European Employment Services) is both a European network and a European job mobility portal. Launched in 1994 to combat unemployment and the economic crisis, its aim is to facilitate mobility on a European scale by disseminating job offers and applications. It is managed in cooperation with national labour placement and job search organisations. Every year, 1.5 million people find a job in another

181 And it's proving to be an undeniable success (*see EDB* 12413 of 29 January 2020, p. 17).

182 European Investment Bank-European Investment Fund. On these two European banking and financial bodies created by the European treaties, *see* below, Title II, Ch. 1.

Member State through this channel. There are currently 4.6 million job offers published on EURES. Unfortunately, too many people (including European civil servants) are unaware of its existence.

The coordination of national employment agencies could be further improved. Information technologies make it possible to list job applications and vacancies on a European basis. Google launched an application in this area in 2017, Search Jobs (Google Careers). Market mechanisms are not just for finance. Constant advances in network technologies should make it easier to match job offers and demands at European level. Once again, the "technical progress" dimension could be strengthened in Europe.

Recently, a European Labour Authority was set up to facilitate the regular cross-border mobility of workers. For example, it must facilitate access by employees, employers and national administrations to information on rights and obligations in the event of cross-border mobility.

The European professional card[183] is reportedly a relative success: 1,750 had been issued by the end of November 2017.[184]

(iv) Suggestions for Other Mobility Incentives

We could also think about using incentives: one from the Member State of origin, which would save on unemployment benefits, the other from the host Member State, for moving house, etc. Perhaps we should think about the practical obstacles to the free movement of people and how to overcome them (learning a foreign language, immersion programmes, preparatory courses, specific costs generated by the exercise of freedom of movement, etc.)? Once again, there is a need for work along the entire chain, in terms of awareness, preparation and education.

183 Electronic procedure for obtaining simple, fast and transparent recognition of a professional qualification in another EU Member State.

184 *EDB* 11999 of 12 April 2018.

Is it conceivable that the obligation for an unemployed person to respond positively to a suitable job offer should be extended to an offer from another Member State? Shocking? What if the move was reasonable (neighbouring region…)?

Active labour market policies[185] that take greater account of the European dimension can therefore be put in place. This brings us back to a structural/modern supply-side policy,[186] to the need for the affirmation of a European workers' area.

(v) Freedom of Movement and Solidarity

Facilitating the intra-Community mobility of EU Member State nationals is also a question of European solidarity. As soon as a Member State encounters unemployment problems, structural solutions should be envisaged with the EU or even with the other Member States, for example within the framework of the European Semester.[187] The nationals of such a Member State come before those of third countries. The justification given by certain Member States for accepting migrants from third countries, based on the jobs to be filled, is questionable in view of the unemployment rate in certain other Member States, especially the unemployment rate of young people, the most mobile population but also the one most affected by unemployment.[188] This in no way detracts from our international obligations or our moral duty towards migrants. However, we must not level the whole playing field or confuse the issues.

185 For example, in its communication of 30 September 2020 on a new ERA for research and innovation, the Commission is seeking to increase the mobility of researchers in industry and academia.

186 *See* below, C.

187 *See* below, Title I, Ch. 2.

188 Subject to the observation that third-country nationals seem to be prepared to make more of an effort to gain access to an EU country than nationals of another Member State!

Human Development

(i) EU responsibilities in Employment, Education and Training

The EU must contribute to achieving a high level of employment in all its policies and actions. This transversal and therefore important objective of European integration[189] is, for example, one of the priorities of the European Semester. The sustained efforts made within this framework have probably contributed to the spectacular fall in unemployment in the EU between 2013 and 2019 (down 45%, from 12 to 6.2%),[190] as shown in figure 17 below[191].

Figure 17.

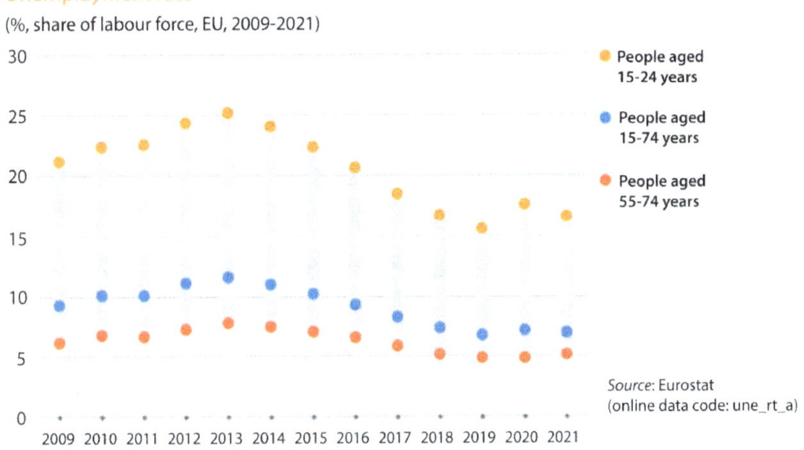

189 *See* Arts. 9 and 147 of the Treaty on the Functioning of the European Union (TFEU).

190 *See* below, Title II, Ch. 1; in December 2022, despite the pandemic and the war in Ukraine, this rate had fallen to 6%.

191 *Key figures on Europe*, 2022, p. 24.

A target for 2030 is for at least 78% of the population aged between 20 and 64 to have a job.[192]

The development of human resources has been identified in the construction of Europe as a means of achieving a high and sustainable level of employment.[193] Beyond the purely economic dimension, Europe has a role to play in human capital, in developing people's skills. Today, this is a major challenge if we are to enable people to (re)find a job that is properly or even well paid.[194] Given the technological revolution on the horizon, this is essential. With regard to professional qualifications linked to the digitalisation of the economy, "the Commission has estimated that 800,000 jobs could go unfilled by 2020 if training programmes are not adapted to this new demand on the labour market".[195]

A second target for 2030 is for at least 60% of adults to participate in training courses each year. The EU is falling behind the USA, which has a higher percentage of graduates.[196] This has an impact on a key indicator that we have already seen, namely productivity. In particular, productivity does not depend solely on scientific and technological research; know-how and excellence[197] in all areas are essential.

Beyond that, this policy has the potential to help Europe's population grow.

---

192 In 2022, this rate is 74.6% (*Key figures on Europe*, 2023, p. 22).

193 *See* Art. 151 TFEU.

194 For example, underqualified adults account for 23% of the working population in France compared with 20% in Germany (Larosière, p. 123).

195 Defraigne and Nouveau, 2nd ed., p. 312 (in French). The forecast has been confirmed. In 2020–2021, there will be one million vacancies for digital technology experts. Seventy per cent of companies are postponing investments due to a lack of skilled personnel.

196 The United States devotes more resources to higher education than European countries: "In 2007, while the United States spent 2.9% of its GDP on higher education, EU countries spent only 1.4% of their GDP, and France only 1.3%. Looked at in another way, the United States spent more than twice as much per student as Europe and more than three times as much as France" (P. Aghion et A. Roulet, *Repenser l'État : pour une social-démocratie de l'innovation*, Paris, Seuil, 2011, p. 19, footnote 3 (in French)).

197 *See* in particular Combe, pp. 15, 17–18.

More can and is being done to make people more employable.[198] In 2020, for example, the European Commission adopted an action plan on digital education to adapt education and training systems to the digital age, as well as a communication on the European Education Area as a driver for job creation and growth.

There is also a link between the quality of continuing education and the reindustrialisation of Europe.[199]

Finally, education, together with research and innovation, was one of the sectors on which the Juncker Plan[200] focused.

The European dimension of employment and technological developments[201] should be more fully integrated into national employment policies. Without the relevant skills, the chances of (re)finding a job are reduced.[202]

(ii) Towards Better Support for Workers Wanting to Start a Family?

The employment rate of the European population (73.1%) remains below the target (80%). At the same time, Europe's demography is in decline, with an average of 1.5 children per woman, whereas a fertility rate of 2.1 is needed to maintain the population. All too often, one of the members of a couple, often the woman, has to put her professional ambitions on hold when children come along. Even today, it is a challenge for both of them to continue working full-time with children.

---

198 *See* the Skills Agenda (*EDB* 12386 of 10 December 2019).

199 On this subject, *see* in particular F. Chombar, CEO of Melexis, a Belgian company in the chip sector, Interview in *L'Echo*, 6 February 2021, pp. 26–27.

200 *See* above, B, 1 (iv).

201 *See* in particular M. de Lathouwer, "L'algorithmique, l'informatique et la relance économique", column in *L'Echo*, 6 February 2021, p. 19; L. Berny, "EDTECH : l'heure de la reconnaissance", *Les Echos Week-End*, March 2021, pp. 22 *et seq*.

202 *See* Larosière, pp. 121–123 and 127.

Why not allow those who wish to do so to both work full-time and have two or three children, or even more? It would be a win-win situation for our society.

This requires the creation of an appropriate framework: sufficient crèches and after-school childcare facilities, and a legal and fiscal framework that does not penalise or even encourages the hiring of in-house staff. There is a wealth of personal development opportunities for parents, jobs and new practices in terms of supervision, monitoring, occupation and education of children to be explored and exploited. At the end of the day, this could create a considerable economic, demographic and human development dynamic.

(iii) Music, Images and Languages

Promoting music education would also be a good thing. Studies have shown the contribution that learning music makes to brain development. It increases IQ and EQ. A country like Switzerland has enshrined this in its Constitution, convinced of the positive aspects of this education for emotional control, precision, particularly manual precision, discipline and concentration.

Learning music also makes it easier to learn foreign languages. In a multilingual Union, it is important to encourage practices – positive ones at that – that enable people to communicate despite the diversity of languages.

This last consideration should also lead to the promotion of graphic and (tele)visual arts and imaging technologies.

Quite apart from translation applications, there is the politically more sensitive issue of foreign language teaching in schools. The Member States remain primarily responsible for teaching programmes. However, some harmonisation has been achieved at European level to promote the recognition of diplomas and the free movement of people. Would it not therefore be possible to require each Member State to teach a second language, which would necessarily be that of a Member State or a language of international importance?

Once again, it is the impact that must be taken into account in identifying the measures to be prioritised, and their added value, particularly for the well-being of the population and European prosperity.

Underlying all this is the same approach, inspired by a structural/modern supply-side policy: creating the basic conditions to generate more activity, jobs, creativity, productivity and innovation.

(iv) Towards a Reorganisation of Education Systems?

One proposal that may provoke strong reactions, precisely in view of the competences of the Member States, would be to open up the field of education more to the diversity of players. Why, after all, should education be confined to state schools and to a single ministry? Especially in these times of intense technological change and disruption? Would it not be good for European society to be able to rely more on agile, flexible, innovative players in education? The lesson in a number of areas is that an "incumbent operator", especially when it has a monopoly, tends to rest on their laurels and slow down or even discourage improvements and innovations.

Would it not be conceivable for states to separate the organising authority, which sets the curricula and monitors the quality of the teaching provided, from the teaching itself, and for there to be independent private or public institutes alongside the latter, which would be accredited and monitored? All would be financed on the basis of objective criteria, in particular according to the number of students and the achievement of a series of qualitative objectives (including the degree of efficiency of the teaching, i.e. the success rate at a constant or even increased level of demand).

As in other areas, we can no longer afford to waste potential, not to mention the "human waste" of certain education systems. A dissociation between the organising authority and the service providers exists in a series of so-called network activities, such as telecommunications, energy and transport.

The remuneration formula could result in both a reduction in operating costs and an improvement in the services provided. In particular, as long as minimum targets are met, service providers could be rewarded for innovations, better service, etc.[203]

With the advent of new technologies, the development of soft skills, advances in teaching methods and a better understanding of the brain, the range of educational possibilities is expanding. The evolution of education should not necessarily be regulated by the pace of certain national ministries.

As we have seen in relation to the internal market and financial education, it would also be a good idea to integrate into national education systems a greater awareness of, and preparation for, the use of all that European integration is likely to bring to people, particularly in their daily lives.

203 We will come back to these points in relation to services of general economic interest (SGEI). *See* below Title I, Ch. 2, D.

5. Transport

Transport Networks and Prosperity

If people, goods and certain services are to move around Europe smoothly, we need to have the right transport infrastructure in place.

Everyone can probably think of an example of a region that has been decompartmentalised thanks to a transport infrastructure or, on the contrary, that continues to lack one. The northern and southern shores of Lake Geneva are a case in point. In the 1970s, the Swiss built a motorway, impressive in places, from Geneva to Valais. Savoie, on the other hand, has kept a tiny road. It crosses the towns on the south bank, in particular Evian, nicknamed, and one can guess why, the Sleeping Beauty. The difference in economic development between the two banks is clear to see.

I remember a conference given by a former European Commissioner for Transport, Jacques Barrot, who explained how prosperity had returned to a Savoyard valley following an improvement in communications. Another example, concerning Belgium. Why did Flanders attract a lot of American investment in the 1960s? Not least because it was much more accessible than the southern part of the country from the national airport where American investors landed. The quality of transport is essential. In particular, it influences the location of companies and their productivity.

European Deficiencies

In this respect, Europe lags significantly behind the USA. With 60% less surface area, half as many goods are transported from one state to another. Rail operating costs are 40% higher than in the USA.

Air regulations are unnecessarily fussy in Europe, preventing the development of this mode of transport, particularly in poorly connected regions.

What is more, the networks continue to be configured in national terms. Try to reach the various institutional capitals of the EU by train (Brussels, Luxembourg, Strasbourg, Frankfurt). The Brussels-Luxembourg link is slower than it was 20 years ago, when it was considered a priority that had to be improved!

Protectionism and obstructionist policies are marked in this area. We continue to reason excessively on the basis of national areas. This is an area where the EU's competences (particularly in terms of impetus) could be strengthened, for example by taking inspiration from the American model.

Investments to Be Planned and Carried Out

We have the advantage of living in a microcontinent with short distances between centres of activity, which are incomparable with those in the United States and even more so in Asia.[204] We need to exploit this and capitalise on it.

The trans-European transport network (TEN-T),[205] depicted in figure 18 below, must therefore continue to be developed to link up the Member States, decompartmentalise certain regions, ensure the interoperability of the various land, river and air networks and integrate the new Member States.

204 *See* above, Title I, Ch. 1, "Introduction", 2.

205 Programme for the development of infrastructure in the European Union. Its aim is to facilitate connections between the road, rail and inland waterway networks, as well as the ports and airports of the Member States (*Touteleurope.eu*).

Figure 18. The nine TEN-T core network corridors

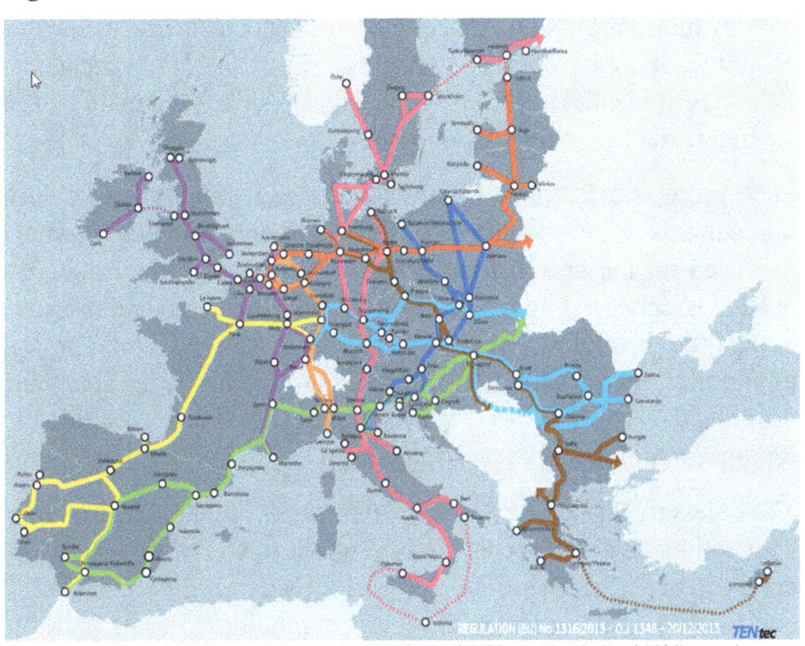

Atlantique, Baltique-Adriatique, Méditerranée, Mer du Nord-Baltique, Mer du Nord-Méditerranée, Orient-Méditerranée orientale, Rhin-Alpes, Rhin-Danube, Scandinavie-Méditerranée

(Source: European Commission)

The roadmap for a single European transport area lists 29 projects to be completed by 2030 in order to reduce bottlenecks, which cost the EU27 0.5 GDP percentage points, in other words €72 billion. The priority TEN-T projects include the 18 kilometres Fehmarn Belt undersea rail and road tunnel, which will link Denmark to Germany, and the future Warsaw-Helsinki rail link. The former, which will almost halve the journey time between Copenhagen and Hamburg, will only be financed by Europe to the tune of 5%. The rest will be financed by the concession holder, a subsidiary of the Danish state, which will repay its loan from toll revenues over a period of around 30 years.[206] There

206 M. Chauvot, "Vinci va construire un tunnel géant entre l'Allemagne et le Danemark", *Les Echos*, 7 January 2021.

is also the Lyon-Turin rail tunnel, 40% of which is financed by the EU, 34% by Italy and 26% by France, and which should have considerable economic and environmental benefits. Since 2022, the spectacular Pelješac Bridge, 85% funded by the EU, has linked the main part of Croatia to the Dubrovnik region.

Such projects are a priority. The impact and added value of such investments are significant for Europe's economic development and even for the preservation of the environment. Once again, we need to adopt a rigorous method for quantifying the overall positive impact (the breakdown of which can vary greatly from one project to another), the construction and maintenance costs, the financing formula, the eco-responsibility of the project, and its contribution to regional planning and even management.

The necessary financial resources will have to be found. The Commission estimates that the cost of investment to complete the central core of the TEN-T is €500 billion between 2020 and 2030,[207] equivalent to three years of the European budget. For its part, the EIB has signed financing agreements for €15 billion for transport in 2021–2022.

The question may also be raised as to whether the TEN-T needs to become even more ambitious.

Environmental Dimension

Integrating the environmental dimension is a benefit at every level: health, preservation of the environment, competitive advantage for Europe, lower energy bills.

Paradoxically, the current lag in transport infrastructure could be an asset in terms of sustainable development and environmental

207 *EDB* 12154 of 7 December 2018, p. 12.

protection.[208] Europe could make a quantum leap in investment by choosing the most innovative formulas appropriate to the new environmental, energy and land-use challenges.

Integrating the environmental dimension into transport policy is all the more crucial given that transport is responsible for around 20% of carbon dioxide emissions. It is also the only sector where pollution is increasing in absolute terms, as figure 19 shows.[209]

Figure 19.

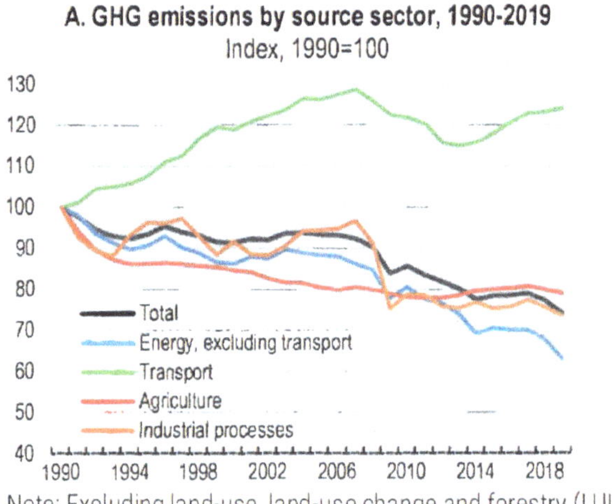

One of the four pillars of the InvestEU programme[210] is sustainable infrastructure. Priority is given to clean modes of transport, multi-modal transport, and the renewal and maintenance of rail and road infrastructure. Once again, this means more favourable treatment

208 Transport accounts for a quarter of the EU's greenhouse gas emissions. This share is constantly increasing. To achieve climate neutrality, emissions from the transport sector should be reduced by 90% by 2050 (Communication from the Commission, "The European Green Deal", COM(2019) 640 final, 11 December 2019 (hereinafter the "European Green Deal"), section 2.1.5. "Accelerating the shift to sustainable and smart mobility").

209 *OECD Economic Surveys: European Union 2021*, p. 14.

210 *See* above, B, 1 (iv).

for clean technologies. For example, in June 2022, the European Commission selected 135 transport infrastructure projects to which it allocated €5.4 billion, including the Fehmarn Belt project mentioned above. The EIB finances projects that are green, innovative and efficient, safe and secure, inclusive and accessible.

More Balanced and Complementary Modes of Transport

Given the current state of the art (I will come back to this question later), the preferred modes of transport include inland waterways and rail.[211] These can substantially reduce carbon dioxide emissions.[212]

(i) Inland Waterway Transport

Inland waterway transport emits three to four times less carbon dioxide than road transport, relieves congestion on the roads and causes fewer accidents. Technological innovations have made it possible to navigate small-gauge rivers in an environmentally friendly way: barges with a capacity of up to 1,500 tonnes (the equivalent of 50 lorries) are propelled by small pusher craft (tugs).[213] If necessary, the digging of canals, diversions, etc. would make it possible to prevent floods, the number of which is set to increase with climate change. Killing two birds with one stone. A variant on the multiplier effect of an initiative.

The Seine-Nord-Escaut Canal will link Rouen to the Canal du Nord and, more widely, to the very dense network of waterways in north-west Europe, and should be open to navigation in 2027. The EU has made a substantial contribution to its funding. Another project,

---

211 Fourteen times less carbon dioxide emissions than aircraft (*EDB* 12407 of 21 January 2020, p. 23):

212 The European Green Deal refers to shifting a substantial proportion of the 75% of domestic freight currently carried by road to rail and inland waterways (section 2.1.5 "Accelerating the shift to sustainable and smart mobility").

213 The ERDF (European Regional Development Fund) contributed 50% to a project in this field.

blocked in its day by the ecologist minister, Dominique Voynet, is the Rhine-Rhône Canal, or more precisely the Rhine-Saône Canal. Its profitability is perhaps problematic in a strictly French context. As part of the European navigable waterway network, it would make more sense.[214]

We need to look at the extent to which the Iberian peninsula, with its many waterways, might not be able to reactivate them.

(ii) Rail Motorways and Combined Transport

Rail freight has a carbon footprint four times better than road haulage. More generally, rail takes up less space than road transport, a significant advantage in a densely populated microcontinent like Europe. The lifespan of railway equipment is also particularly long.

An interesting concept is that of rail motorways. Containers, used in maritime and river trade (as well as road), or even semi-trailers or road units, are transported on railways from rail terminals. In France, rail accounts for 4% of long-distance traffic. It is faster than road transport.

Complementarity and intermodality between inland waterway and rail transport should be further exploited. The EU has set up the European Interconnection Mechanism (EIM) programme for the transport, energy and digital services sectors. Twenty-four billion euros were available for the development of transport networks between 2014 and 2020, and €25.81 billion for the following seven-year period,[215] i.e. around €3.5 billion per year. A significant proportion has been allocated to combined transport.

---

214 Similarly, in the rail sector, there is talk of bringing back into service the sumptuous Canfranc station, which used to link Pau to Saragossa (*see* F. Delétraz, "Canfranc, la renaissance d'une gare fantôme au cœur des Pyrénées", *Le Figaro*, 3 April 2020).

215 Duration of EU budget planning.

(iii) What About Road and Air Transport?

That said, let us not be prejudiced about road transport, which, it should be pointed out, has grown considerably because the rail sector has been unable to innovate and transcend national boundaries. We cannot rule out the possibility that technical progress will reduce the harmful effects of road transport, particularly in terms of emissions (with hydrogen, electricity and new fuels). It is both good policy and fair to give it a chance (*the principle of technical or technological neutrality*). For the same reasons, let us not exclude air transport a priori, where major technological advances are likely to be made over the next few years.[216]

The solution will not necessarily be rail and/or inland waterway transport, but a combination of the various modes of transport.

Complementary and Alternative Measures

Transport markets should also continue to open up in order to improve mobility in Europe. Further steps to liberalise maritime, river, rail, air and even road transport are still needed. The potential gains from liberalising ports and port activity should not be underestimated, particularly given the favourable carbon footprint of sea and river transport.

Improving transport within the EU should not, of course, obviate the need to reduce transport requirements, thanks to technological progress (remote technologies such as teleconferencing, digitisation), improved coordination of flows (smart cities, 5G, etc.), or even the promotion of short distribution channels (for food, for example).

216 Paraffin could be replaced by non-polluting fuels in the years to come (biofuels, synthetic paraffin). On this point, *see* Piccard, p. 123. Airbus is working on a new, more fuel-efficient wing shape. A French firm has just announced a 19-seater aircraft powered by electric motors, ideal for routes of around 500 kilometres in terms of both air pollution and noise (*Les Echos*, 26 May 2023).

6. Energy

Issues

Today's European energy policy is all about securing the EU's supply at an affordable cost for households and competitive for businesses, while polluting and wasting as little as possible (two efficiency requirements).[217]

Therefore, European energy policy must ensure that the EU becomes increasingly self-sufficient in energy, diversifies its sources of supply, promotes the production and consumption of green energy, provides energy at the lowest possible cost, and is ever more efficient in capturing, storing, distributing, using and even reusing energy.

We do not sufficiently appreciate the extent to which these parameters determine the prosperity of our populations, the health of our ecosystem and regional planning.[218]

Energy Self-Sufficiency

Europe's energy autonomy is a cause for concern. The rate of energy dependence, i.e. the percentage of imported energy in relation to that consumed, is almost 60%.[219] What's more, current tensions with Russia make the risk of over-dependence on a single third country very real.

This rate falls to 44% in Denmark, due to its offshore wind programme. Sweden's rate is even better, at 33.5%, probably due to a very proactive programme in which the "prosumer" plays a key role, the best score being that of Estonia (10.5%).[220] France, with its nuclear facilities,

217 In this respect, *see* the European Green Deal, section 2.1.2 "Supplying clean, affordable and secure energy".

218 *See* J.-M. Jancovici and C. Blain, *Le monde sans fin*, Paris, Dargaud, 2021, esp. p. 45.

219 *Key figures on Europe*, 2021, p. 59; 55.5% in 2023 (*Key figures on Europe*, 2023, p. 67).

220 *Key figures on Europe*, 2022, p. 64.

achieved a fine performance of 44%. This is a sobering comparison with Germany's average performance in this area (63.5%), despite all the efforts – technical and financial – that Germany has made.

Efforts must be made to avoid the EU becoming too dependent on certain external producers or certain transport routes.

Seventy-six per cent of the gas consumed in the EU is produced outside the EU. It is mainly supplied by Russia and Algeria, and since the war in Ukraine, increasingly by Norway. This dependence is all the more problematic given that, in the fight against global warming, gas has advantages over oil, at least for use in large infrastructures (e.g. factories). Hence the agreement between Greece, Cyprus and Israel on the construction of a gas pipeline.

Diversification of Supply

Today, there is a wide variety of energy sources. In addition to hydrocarbons. In addition to gas, in its various forms, these include biofuels, especially second-generation biofuels, biomass, hydroelectric power, hydrogen, nuclear power, solar power, coal, wind power (including offshore wind power), cogeneration, pumped hydroelectric storage, tidal power, fuel cells, osmotic energy, etc.[221]

The EU is seeking to exploit maritime energy resources in the broadest sense and to make the most of the diversity of the seas surrounding it.

As part of a policy to diversify energy sources, small energy-producing units should be promoted: wood-based collective heating in forested areas, small hydroelectric power stations, small wind turbines, water and wind mills, hydropower and its variants, net energy-producing houses, biomass, etc.

221 Energy produced by the meeting of two waters of different salinity.

The Place and Role of Nuclear Power?

There is also the sensitive and passionate issue of nuclear power. Despite its risks (waste treatment, accidents), nuclear power offers many advantages: energy autonomy, absence of carbon pollution, continuity of production (it is not intermittent, unlike solar and wind power), dual nature and a small footprint. Moreover, nuclear fission can lead to nuclear fusion. For this reason, more and more people, including some environmentalists, are calling for its temporary retention.[222]

It is also an area in which Europeans have (had?) a technological lead, but which they are in the process of losing. Why give it up? For example, waste treatment can be improved.[223] More generally, technical progress is possible. A Geneva-based company, Transmutex, is planning to create a safe power plant that would run on thorium, a metal that is much more widespread than uranium, and that would release almost no radioactive waste.[224] There is also talk of small power plants.

Nuclear energy also appears to be important in an energy transition process whose duration and outcome are unknown. We might as well keep a reliable source of energy for as long as it takes. In this respect, it is risky to set exit dates. Every effort must be made to do without nuclear fission as quickly as possible in its current state of development, but the speed of the transition to other energy sources will depend on the pace of technological progress (including in the nuclear field). It cannot be predetermined.

It is also preferable to keep the specialists who have been trained here in Europe rather than have them working for powers that are no great friends of democracy and human rights.

---

222 In this regard, *see* the explorer Jean-Louis Etienne, *Les Echos*, 31 December 2019, p. 5.

223 *See L'Echo* of 9 January 2021 on the major advances made by Myrrha in Belgium, pp. 18–19. They would enable radioactive waste to be reused to produce energy and would divide its toxicity by 1,000.

224 *Le Temps* of 23 December 2021.

As part of the future strategy for decarbonising the economy by 2050, the Commission has put forward scenarios envisaging a larger share of nuclear energy.[225] The Intergovernmental Panel on Climate Change (IPCC) accepts that a small share of nuclear power could help to combat global warming in a transitional phase. In the draft taxonomy of investments,[226] some Member States have managed to have nuclear energy included as a green investment.

If Germany had not turned its back on nuclear power so abruptly after the Fukushima disaster, would it have been forced to increase its dependence on Russian gas and exposing itself to the American sanctions threatening the Nord Stream 2 project? What's more, isn't it paradoxical to close nuclear power stations for environmental reasons and reactivate hyper-polluting (but highly profitable) coal-fired power stations, as Germany has done and as France is now being forced to do following the closure of Fessenheim? Once again, this European tendency to cut off the branch on which we are sitting, to fall from Charybdis into Scylla, to play the fool by pretending to be angels.

Maintaining and developing nuclear power[227] is a way of increasing our energy autonomy vis-à-vis both Russia and the USA (without opening ourselves up to American criticism), as well as improving the carbon footprint.

And let's be realistic. The risk of a nuclear disaster threatens Europe, whether or not it has nuclear power stations. All we have to do is list the nuclear power stations on the fringes of its territory, which were built and operate to safety standards that fall short of European requirements.

---

225 *EDB* 12163 of 20 December 2018, p. 9.

226 European classification of economic activities that contribute to environmental objectives.

227 With technological advances such as small modular reactors.

Nuclear power is an asset for Europeans. We might as well keep it, maintain it and even develop it as long as it does not appear to be clearly useless, especially in such uncertain times when Europe is facing challenges of a different nature.

However, the nuclear industry must not be given a free pass or a blank cheque. It must be subject to independent and strict controls on its safety[228] as well as its construction, production and maintenance costs. Neither damned nor sanctified, but admitted and administered under strict conditions.

In any case, it is important to conduct a rational and calm debate on this subject. Switzerland, which decided to abandon nuclear power by a slim majority (the cantons with nuclear power plants voted to keep it), recently succeeded in doing so.

In this debate, we must also consider the consequences of our choices and take responsibility for them. In this respect, nuclear power is a bit like Brexit. Many people want to get out without paying the price. Then they regret their decision.

Security of Supply and Whether or Not Energy Sources Can Be Controlled

Security of supply includes the ability to control an energy source. Solar and wind power do not guarantee a given quantity of energy at all times, unlike other sources where the quantity available can be modulated.

For a Principle of Neutrality

As in the case of transport, a principle of neutrality must prevail. An energy source must not be irretrievably condemned, for example on the basis of its current environmental record. With technical progress, an energy source can improve its environmental performance.

228 On this question, *see* in particular H. Murakami, *Novelist as a Vocation* (transl. P. Gabriel and T. Goossen), New York, Knopf, 2022.

A prime example is coal, the most widespread energy source in the world and present in the European Union. The prospect of *clean coal* is no pipe dream. For example, the Bluegas process developed by US company Great Point Energy turns coal into gas. The Swedish company Alfa Laval is developing a technique for separating the sulphur from the carbon in coal.[229]

Cost of Energy

The cost of energy is higher for European companies than for their American counterparts. There is talk of a 60% surplus for electricity. Energy is only more expensive in Japan. Given the importance of energy in the costs of businesses, governments and individuals, this is a major issue. Half of imports from third countries consisted of oil and gas bills, even before the war in Ukraine.

Energy sources also differ in terms of cost. Depending on technical progress in particular, they will be more or less competitive.

European Achievements in Renewable Energy and Energy Efficiency

Europe is not inactive in this area. The 20-20-20 programme aimed to achieve the following by 2020:

- to increase the share of renewable energy in the EU's energy consumption to 20% by 2019;[230]
- improve energy efficiency by the same proportion.[231]

There is now a 30-30-30 programme for 2030, aiming for at least a 32% and 32.5% improvement respectively.[232] The 30-30-30 framework

229 R. Etwareea, "Et s'il fallait dédiaboliser le charbon", *Le Temps*, 19 January 2023.

230 *Key figures on Europe*, 2021, p. 60.

231 In addition to reducing greenhouse gas emissions by 20% compared to 1990 levels.

232 Forty per cent for reductions in greenhouse gas emissions.

adds a 15% electricity interconnection target, i.e. the possibility of transporting 15% of all energy produced in the EU to other EU countries,[233] in the interests of efficient resource allocation. A European energy area is emerging, a trend that is to be welcomed.

As we have already seen, we are not thinking "European" enough in a number of strategic areas (research, transport, employment, education, regional planning, economic, social and territorial cohesion, etc.), which is confirmed by figure 20.[234]

Figure 20.

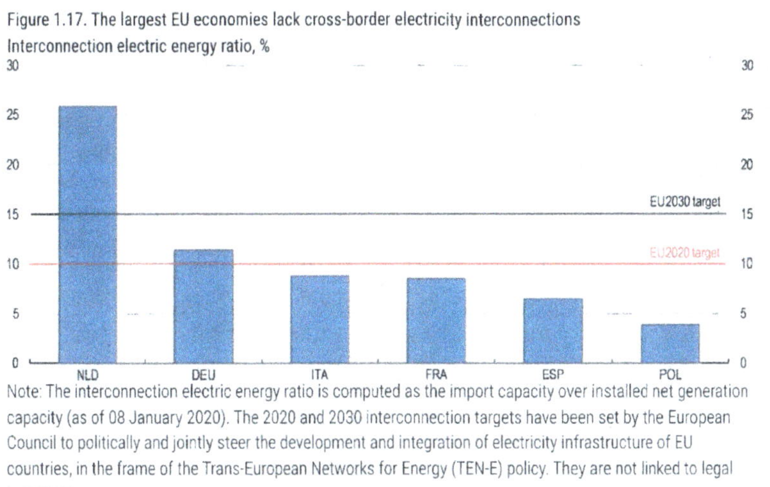

Note: The interconnection electric energy ratio is computed as the import capacity over installed net generation capacity (as of 08 January 2020). The 2020 and 2030 interconnection targets have been set by the European Council to politically and jointly steer the development and integration of electricity infrastructure of EU countries, in the frame of the Trans-European Networks for Energy (TEN-E) policy. They are not linked to legal sanctions.

Source: ENTSOE-E Winter Outlook (2019-2020), https://www.entsoe.eu.

Member States have been dragging their feet in implementing the target set by the 2014 European Council of 10% electricity interconnection by 2020. However, the war in Ukraine seems to have shaken some

233 *See*, for example, the Belgian-Danish agreement of February 2021 to import electricity from Danish wind farms into Belgium via a high-voltage undersea link (*L'Echo*, 6 February 2021, p. 6).

234 *OECD Economic Surveys: European Union 2021*, p. 35.

national circles out of their narrow calculations to protect their markets. As a result, the project by RTE (France) and REE (Spain) to build a 370 kilometres direct current interconnector, mainly underwater, between the Bordeaux and Bilbao areas, has been accepted as a European Project of Common Interest (PCIs).[235] It will considerably increase electricity exchange capacity between the two countries.

By the end of 2018, the Member States were to submit their draft integrated national energy and climate plans, and by 1 January 2020 their long-term national energy and climate strategies. Consistency must be ensured between these plans and strategies.

Some Member States are aiming to do even better. For example, Germany's proactive policy since the Fukushima disaster in 2011[236] is beginning to bear fruit. Today, Germany produces more electricity from renewable energies (solar, wind, biomass and hydro) than from coal and lignite. In 2019, it has adopted an ecological transition plan worth €100 billion (thanks to the room for manoeuvre afforded by its sound management of public finances[237]). Denmark is aiming to reduce its CO_2 emissions by 70% by 2030. It is banking heavily on offshore wind power. On certain days, wind generation covers 130% of Denmark's electricity demand.[238] Coal mines were closing in most Member States before the war in Ukraine.

Decarbonisation, energy efficiency and the transition to renewable energy are transversal objectives, integrated into a series of European policies. For example, they are taken into account in the allocation of funding from the Structural Funds. The European Investment Bank focuses on financing projects aimed at improving energy efficiency[239] or the production of green energy.

235 On this concept, *see* above, B, 1 (iv).

236 However, there are questions about its nuclear phase-out in view of the carbon dioxide emissions generated by the resumption of coal and lignite-fired power stations.

237 On this point, *see* below, Title I, Ch. 2.

238 *Les Echos*, 9 October 2019, p. 7.

239 This must become a priority, as the production and consumption of energy by all economic sectors account for more than 75% of the EU's greenhouse gas emissions (European Green Deal, section 2.1.2.).

R&D&I and Energy

There is a case for specific R&D investment in this sector in order to improve Europe's energy autonomy and competitiveness, as well as the carbon footprint of all energy sources. The European battery industry (particularly lithium batteries) is the subject of proactive projects, for example by Germany and France, acting jointly.[240] Hydrogen, in particular generated from renewable energies, is also seen as a solution for the future, particularly for sectors where electric batteries will be insufficient (heavy and chemical industries, lorries, ships, etc.). As part of the European Recovery Plan,[241] Germany and France are planning to invest heavily in the green hydrogen sector. The prospect of European energy autonomy based on the hydrogen-electricity combination no longer seems utopian.

Dozens of projects of common interest (PCI) in the field of "energy infrastructure", totalling around €90 billion, are also planned.[242] Progress in these infrastructures is essential for the proper distribution of energy across Europe.[243]

We can also think of more open markets and liberalisation.

Another Key Index: The Energy Intensity Rate

When it comes to optimising the use of resources, one indicator is increasingly important: the quantity and cost of primary energy required to generate wealth (energy productivity, energy intensity). At a time when resources are increasingly scarce and expensive, this parameter is becoming ever more important.

240 *See* above, 2, Industrial Policy.

241 *See* below, Title I, Ch. 2, D.

242 *EDB* 12294 of 12 July 2019, p. 12.

243 *See* the European Green Deal, section 2.1.2.

In this respect, the Nordic countries, with their more fragile ecosystems, are at the forefront. Our neighbour Switzerland, whose alpine environment also requires a great deal of care, is not to be underestimated. This competitive parameter is becoming increasingly essential. The performance of the Member States in terms of energy intensity is mixed, and further efforts need to be made.

Once again, Europe's spatial concentration is an advantage. It needs less energy than the USA and Asian countries to produce the same amount of wealth. We can though still significantly improve our performance. Encouraging the financial sector to give priority to financing eco-responsible projects, within the broader framework of responsible finance (ESG[244]), could have a significant indirect effect in this respect.

Certain remote communication technologies (videoconferencing) make it possible to hold meetings at a distance and avoid the need to travel. Admittedly, they are not as effective or instructive as a physical meeting. The latter remains irreplaceable for delicate discussions. The rationalisation of community infrastructures, especially in cities, through technology (smart cities), also holds out the promise of energy savings.

We have the sensitivity and the technological resources (or we can acquire them through research). We also have major energy operators, which is an asset in the energy transition. For example, the EU is home to one of the world's 10 largest companies, Total, which is active in the energy sector.

Energy Intensity and Efficiency: A Shared Responsibility

Improving performance in terms of energy intensity and efficiency is everybody's concern: individuals, households, municipalities, intermediate levels of government, states and businesses, to the best

244 For Environment, Social and Governance.

of its ability. Progress in this area can be facilitated by awareness of the climate challenge and social, media and reputational pressure, but also by technological leaps and measurement tools. It is now possible to reduce domestic energy consumption substantially without reducing comfort, using moderately priced applications (there is no comparison with home control systems).

Alongside technical progress, greater moderation will therefore be required in order to achieve decarbonisation and improve the environmental balance sheet. Once again, this points to the need for awareness-raising, involvement and appropriate education of the various players in European society.

C. Preferred Method: A Structural or Modern Supply-Side Policy and a Systematic Search for Added Value

1. Working on the So-Called Missing Factors: A Structural or Modern Supply-Side Policy

To perform better, an athlete has the choice between working hard or doping.

The first aims to remedy his weaknesses, one by one, and to work on their strengths. For example, to compete with Nadal and Djokovic, Roger Federer has favoured the topspin backhand over the sliced backhand, considerably increasing his speed on the return of serve. To better counter spinning balls, he has opted for a larger racquet head and taken the ball more by the scruff of the neck. He continued to work on his extraordinary reactivity. Djokovic follows a strict gluten-free diet. Before them, Andrés Gómez, a highly gifted but nonchalant left-hander from Ecuador, finally won the French Open after undergoing drastic physical preparation. In particular, it enabled this tall player to bend his legs better on low balls and reduce errors. In football, Belgian striker Romelu Lukaku has greatly improved his back-to-goal game at Inter Milan thanks to coach Conte.

This fundamental work requires effort, but the results are long-lasting. Quite the opposite of doping, which is effective and painless at first but generally harmful to performance and health in the long term.

In economics, both options are on the table.

The easy solution is to stimulate the economic fabric by injecting money (often made from nothing). We do not work on the engine and its intrinsic qualities of power, torque and moderate consumption. Instead, we introduce more fuel, create a temporary euphoria, clog up the engine and… add to the public debt, to the misfortune of future generations. In short, we are more like a petrol station attendant than an engineer or tuner.[245]

A *structural or modern supply policy means working on the conditions for economic activity*. The aim is not only to free up economic activity, but also to create an optimal environment for it to flourish. The aim is to improve the efficiency of the goods, services and capital markets, through structural measures rather than cyclical stimuli. To draw a comparison with a car, the focus is on the design quality of the engine, chassis and brakes, so as to make it intrinsically and sustainably more efficient and safer.

In this approach, particular attention is paid to the *missing factors*, i.e. the links that are missing or insufficient in the chain of

245 Having said that, the comparison is not the same. Cyclical stimulus, as long as it remains limited in time and exceptional, can have a positive effect on the economy by helping to get the economy moving again. But it is all a question of dosage… and withdrawal.

prosperity: a truly integrated market, physical, technological and communications infrastructures,[246] protection of property, innovations and the innovation process, incentives for innovation and technical progress, the level of training of workers, the quality of information, matching supply and demand, improvements in the operation of institutions (a better ratio between the effectiveness and weight of regulations, the *fitness* principle – more and better with less – digitalisation of the administration, speeding up the course of justice, reducing its cost, etc.), education of consumers, savers and investors, and the general public. By acting on them, we ultimately increase the potential for prosperity and growth.

This approach involves working by *intermediate objectives*. Public authorities do not take the place of operators. Once they are in a favourable position, it is up to them to play their part and assume their responsibilities,[247] in accordance with the European principle of a market economy.[248] Confusion between the two must be avoided.

A modern supply-side policy can also help with transitions (digital, agricultural, energy, etc.) by developing an enabling framework and providing assistance in the initial phases, while once again leaving the final responsibility to businesses and the public. The aim is also to help them grow by enabling them to adapt their freedom of enterprise and consumption to a new context.

In a nutshell, the aim is to improve the pitch and playing conditions, and to train players by working on the ground; not to boost them through

246 The latter are set to play an increasingly important role. Information is essential in a market economy because it brings supply and demand closer together, whether they already exist or are simply in the pipeline. Today's technology enables information to be disseminated more widely and at lower cost than in the past. Portals and platforms are one example of an increasingly common way of doing this. For example, to support start-ups in the EU, the European Commission has launched an online platform to encourage the development of start-up activities throughout Europe (*EDB* 12418 of 5 February 2020).

247 Another key point of this essay. The principle of the responsibility of economic operators, states and the European Union, including a separate European body such as the EIB, is one of the foundations of European integration.

248 On this principle, *see* below, C, 5 and Ch. 2, F.

economic measures of indefinite duration, to distort competition through subsidies, or to relieve companies of their responsibilities, particularly financial responsibilities.

Structural or Modern Supply Policy: Avoiding Confusion

This work on the fundamentals is quite distinct from what is sometimes referred to as supply-side policy, i.e. reducing the tax burden on companies and individuals, who are often the most affluent. This is not one of my recommendations.

In addition, the proposed land approach can improve demand and purchasing power in a sustainable way and without cyclical stimuli. Structural policies include measures such as a ban on roaming, so that mobile phone users can effectively enjoy a seamless space in Europe, price moderation through a combination of a monetary policy geared to price stability and a vigorous competition policy, a high-quality energy policy that lowers energy costs not only for businesses but also for households, and so on.

The EU's Ability to Pursue a Structural/Modern Supply-Side Policy

The EU is well placed to pursue a structural/modern supply-side policy.

Firstly, the creation and smooth operation of the single market presuppose the removal of barriers to trade and the promotion of trade (for example, by proclaiming the mutual recognition of goods and services). The European project calls for work on market structure.

Secondly, as it is not responsible for day-to-day economic policy[249] or local public services, the EU can concentrate more on long-term

249 And so escapes its "pernicious rattling", to paraphrase the novelist Colette (*La maison de Claudine*).

structural reforms and developments. It is also less exposed to instability and turmoil than national governments. However, a modern supply-side policy requires in-depth work and a certain amount of time to unfold its effects, since it operates indirectly, through the economic players.[250]

It can also be reconciled with the division of competences between the Union and the Member States: the development of the general framework at European level, aimed at optimising the potential and advantages of a large market, the definition by the Member States of their public service offering, their social, societal and economic policies, and even economic stimulus measures. It can also be reconciled with the division of roles between public authorities and economic players, whether private or public (principle of neutrality of ownership). The former must respect the principle of an open social market economy with free competition.

European integration is also focused on the long term. It aims to strengthen and perpetuate national democracies, protecting them from their inner demons, and seeks sustainable growth through a highly competitive social market economy and sustainable public finances.

In these respects, the EU offers valuable complementarities with the Member States. It would be a shame not to exploit them to the full. *The EU is not a superstate and must therefore carry out its tasks in a different way.*

In any case, the EU has neither the budget nor the power to raise taxes to pursue a classic policy of stimulating demand by distributing money. So – without giving gifts to certain economic operators and therefore without creating burdens for taxpayers – it must make life easier for businesses and citizens through general measures, enabling them to make an effective and healthy contribution to growth.

250 On the success of the supply-side policy pursued in France from 2015 to 2019, *see* E. Le Boucher, "En revenir vite à la politique de l'offre", *Les Echos*, 18–19 December 2020, p. 12.

Conversely, it is important that the EU does not become a duplicate of the Member States. Otherwise, criticism of the "Brussels" bureaucracy becomes justified. Europe must increase potential (as we shall see), act as a lever and not impose a second straitjacket, as it increasingly tends to do.

Many of the suggestions outlined above and in the rest of the essay relate to a structural/modern supply-side policy. This is not a dogmatic prejudice on my part. A number of the proposals made, inspired by my various professional experiences (assistant judge at the European Court of Justice, lawyer, university lecturer), were drawn up before I realised that, in theoretical terms, they were measures falling within the scope of such a structural policy. The EU must help Europeans, their businesses and the Member States to grow, in a way that is sustainable rather than cyclical. Given the current state of European integration and economic theories, a structural/modern supply-side policy is an appropriate instrument for this purpose.

2. Any European Initiative Must Deliver Significant Added Value

The Union's DNA is to increase the room for manoeuvre of its Member States, the quality of life of its people and the health of European businesses. This is the purpose of economic integration, which is first and foremost what the EU is all about: making the people of Europe stronger and more prosperous so as to contribute to their well-being.

Its main objective is to enable *sustainable growth* (which now includes an environmental dimension) and the *well-being of its people* through a "*highly competitive social market economy*".

The EU must therefore be a lever for the Member States, their populations and their businesses, an enhancer. It must help them to grow.

By the same token, it is in the EU's logic that any European regulation should provide an undeniable plus. It must be synonymous with *added value* and have a *significant positive impact.*

In particular, the EU must facilitate economic development. Consequently, a European regulation or directive should only be adopted if it improves the framework for economic activity.[251] The European Parliament and the Commission sometimes tend to forget this, dreaming that they have an unlimited mandate. They need to refocus their initiatives.

Particularly in view of Europe's decline, which has been exacerbated by the pandemic, the war in Ukraine and the Palestinian-Israeli conflict, systematic priority must be given to prosperity, competitiveness and, as we have already seen, innovation, technical progress and education. The pursuit of other objectives is possible (provided that the EU is competent). Provided it is not at the cost of a HIGHLY competitive social market economy and sustainable growth, which are the preconditions for all other progress.

Towards More Stringent Monitoring of Compliance With the Principle of Subsidiarity

The principle of subsidiarity only allows the EU[252] to deal with a problem if it cannot be resolved effectively at national level.

In my opinion, this condition for European intervention should not simply be negative (inadequacy of national action). A poorly calibrated European measure can be just as unsatisfactory. An intrinsic *qualitative* added value of European action should be required in addition to the effect of mass or size. The European measure should have its own clear merits in terms of *added value*.

251 Members of the European Parliament should be more aware of this priority. They should curb their tendency to behave like national parliamentarians. The EU is not a state with full powers and sovereignty. Its purpose is more specific. It must ensure the economic prosperity of today and tomorrow, a highly competitive social market economy. The European Parliament should focus first and foremost on these tasks.

252 In the areas it shares with the Member States.

This intrinsic added value should be rigorously assessed. In particular, the positive economic impact of European measures should be systematically evaluated. Between two measures that are equally effective in pursuing secondary objectives, the one that is most effective for the economy should be favoured. The search for the most efficient measure (i.e. the one that best achieves the objectives pursued at the lowest cost in the broadest sense) should also be promoted.

This impact should not be measured solely in terms of costs for public authorities, taxpayers and economic operators. The return on investment, both direct and indirect, should also be included in any calculations. The net contribution of a measure to the European economy should be determined, its multiplier coefficient: what additional prosperity, what positive spin-offs is it likely to generate?

Perhaps we should even require the European institutions to respect a certain level of multiplier, or at least force them to calculate the multiplier for the planned measure. The EU needs to grow too. Its *raison d'être* obliges it to do better; its privileged position (sheltered from the vicissitudes of day-to-day management)[253] allows it to do so, and current circumstances oblige it to do so.

The CJEU's monitoring of compliance with the principle of subsidiarity and of a real contribution to improving the European economy should therefore be substantially strengthened. In particular, it is striking that the CJEU has never censured a European text for violating the principle of subsidiarity.

In our view, a more dynamic approach, more demanding of the European institutions because it requires the demonstration of significant positive added value, would also be likely to reduce the obsession of Member States with a fair return on their budgetary contribution. They already benefit from a dividend in kind, namely the positive

253 *See* above, C, 1.

spin-offs of EU membership, which we have seen is already a multiple of their contribution.[254] If the value of their participation in European integration were to increase as a result of more development-oriented initiatives, they would be less concerned about the immediate recovery of their budgetary contribution.

A more dynamic and economically demanding approach could also reduce the reluctance of the so-called frugal Member States (the Netherlands, Germany, Austria, the Nordic countries) to any increase in the EU budget.

It would therefore be useful to be able to determine not only the general positive effects of European integration, but also the contribution of each new European project, its return on investment.

3. The Principle of an Open Market Economy With Free Competition

In sport, a good referee is one who does not stand out, while ensuring that the rules are respected and that the players are safe, by intervening proportionately and wisely.

In a similar way, greater weight could be given to a European principle: that the action of the Union (but also those of the Member States; we will come back to this in Chapter 2) respects the principle of an open market economy where competition is free, where factors of production circulate freely and can seek an efficient allocation.

The principle of non-interference by public authorities in the market economy and the prohibition of undue disruption of the interplay of supply and demand are, in the final analysis, just as fundamental as

254 *See* above, Introduction.

the freedoms of movement. They are inextricably linked to each other and condition their effectiveness, as does an undistorted system of competition.

A large market is useless if it is over-regulated. It loses interest and even becomes less attractive than a more liberalised local market. What is the point of moving around in a vast environment if it's oxygen-poor?

The economy should be as free as possible, and public intervention should only be permitted where it is necessary and proportionate to the pursuit of a general interest objective.[255] The potential for creativity, initiative and production must not be unnecessarily undermined.

Consequently, the EU should establish a market failure before taking any initiatives. It would have to prove that the situation is unsatisfactory and that, without intervention on its part, it will remain so.

This principle is closely linked to the responsibility of economic operators. Let them try things, develop technologies and projects. They are in a better position than politicians and public authorities to determine what is economically and technologically feasible.

In this respect, the Commission's initial proposal to ban combustion engines by 2035 was a mistake. It is wiser to set targets and leave it to economic operators to develop the means of achieving them. How can the EU say today that the internal combustion engine is a dead end in more than 10 years' time? Would that not be a rather light-hearted and counterproductive statement, given that about 15 years ago both VW and GM developed prototypes that consumed just one litre per 100 kilometres; that second-generation biofuels are very promising, particularly in terms of CO_2 emissions; and that synthetic fuels are currently being developed? It is not the

255 On this question, *see* below, Title I, Ch. 2, F, on budgetary, monetary, and economic policies.

combustion engine that pollutes, but the energy used up until now![256] It is to be welcomed that the proposal has been corrected – *at the last minute* – on this point.

In Favour of a More Binding Principle of Respect for an Open Market Economy

In a controversial decision, the CJEU considered that the principle of respect for an open market economy with free competition was not binding.[257]

European and national regulations would gain in quality and economic efficiency if legislators had to justify their interventions that infringe economic freedom by establishing that they are necessary and proportionate to pursue objectives of legitimate interest.

Yes to a Level Playing Field, No to a European Level Dying Field

Priority must be given to a legal framework that is conducive to business development, simple, secure, stable and ingenious.

One of the reasons for America's success is that it does not over-regulate. They allow economic players freedom. Donald Trump has been much criticised. However, he took a "very simple" step at the start of his term of office: for every new regulation, three had to be repealed. Such a constraint forces legislators to cut to the chase and design frameworks that offer the best balance of benefits and burdens for businesses, the public and even the public sector. Closer to home, Switzerland has once again been recognised as the European country that most respects economic freedom. Its success is well established. So, no to the regulatory rage, the gasworks, the strangulation. Yes to

256 In this sense too, *see* Piccard, p. 114.

257 CJEC, 3 October 2000, *Echirolles*, case C-9/99, ECLI:EU:C:2000:532, para 25.

promising and fruitful frameworks, on which a modern supply-side policy must be based. In “level playing field”, there is “playing”, which evokes play, movement and pleasure, not “dying”,[258] not asphyxiation.

The Juncker Commission has been careful to reduce the number of proposals and focus on strategic issues. This course must be maintained and the effort amplified. The European institutions must be prevented from taking the easy way out. They too must grow.

The option of proposing a new regulatory measure only if another is abolished (the so-called *one-in, one-out* rule[259]), put forward by the von der Leyen Commission, is therefore a first step in the right direction. We probably need to be more radical, in particular to encourage a more substantial overhaul of European regulations than a simple arithmetic game of zero sums. The effort should therefore be stepped up: two to five existing regulations should be repealed for the adoption of a new one.

In this period of great technological progress, it is not out of the question for legislators to be able to do away with some of the red tape. Ultimately, the political world faces a challenge comparable to that of industry: we need to get rid of processes that pollute unnecessarily in order to achieve greater efficiency, i.e. efficiency that is accompanied by less collateral damage than in the past.

Regulatory cutbacks should be all the more marked since, as we have seen,[260] as things stand at present, the overwhelming majority of European businesses are SMEs or even micro-enterprises.[261]

---

258 On the causes of the EU’s tendency to over-regulate, *see* S. Schepers, “Comment sauver l’innovation industrielle en Europe”, *Le Journal de l’école de Paris du management*, 2016/5 (no 121), pp. 23–28.

259 Each legislative proposal that generates a new burden must relieve citizens and businesses of an equivalent burden at EU level in the same policy area (Eur. Comm., press release IP/19/6657 of 4 December 2019, “The Working Methods of the von der Leyen Commission: Striving for more at home and in the world”). On the subject, *see also* *EDB* 12423 of 12 February 2020 and 12430 of 21 February 2020, pp. 5 and 7 respectively.

260 *See* above, A, 1.

261 And European law is severely over-regulated.

Consequently, it is with them in mind that European legislation must be drafted today. I do not rule out the possibility that, if the average size of companies in Europe increases, as a result, for example, of the measures recommended in this essay, the needle on the compass may move in the right direction. But, heaven forbid, in the meantime, a little sense of proportion and "*Bodenhaftigkeit*" (awareness of the reality on the ground).

4. Towards a Virtuous Triangle of the Eco-Responsible Social Market Economy

A Twelfth Duck Whose Neck Needs Wringing: "The Race to the Bottom"

When Europe harmonises, it often does so from above. It aligns itself with the best standards or even creates new requirements (e.g. REACH for chemical substances). Rarely has it aligned itself with the average or the lowest bidder. Here too, it is raising the bar.

Each country or group of countries brings its own treasures, which have become established as the "best product" and the "best practice". France has brought its administrative tradition and value-added tax (VAT), Germany its fundamental rights, an independent central bank and ordoliberalism,[262] and the Nordic countries their transparency.

What is more, and this is a point ignored by many, the pooling of diverse expertise and approaches does not necessarily lead to laborious compromises or muddled solutions. It can lead to qualitative leaps,

262 Developed in reaction to Nazism in the 1930s by German intellectuals in exile, ordoliberalism is a doctrine that assigns the state the role of guaranteeing free and undistorted competition and setting the general framework for activities, while refraining from further dirigisme or ad hoc interventionism. It also implies a central bank independent of the government, working to ensure financial stability and low inflation, as well as a balanced fiscal policy.

to new, better, more ingenious approaches. Just think of the UCITS that are the envy of the United States, the GDPR,[263] the financing techniques developed by the EIB and the EIF, and Airbus.

These points are not anecdotal. They reflect both the richness and diversity of Europe and one of the advantages of a large market. The margins generated by a large market for companies (or at least for some of them[264]) make this extra quality possible, in areas as diverse as product composition, consumer and personal data protection, fundamental rights, financial vehicles, etc.

The more effective the single market becomes, the higher our social, environmental and societal standards will be.[265] *The liberalisation of energies generates a surplus of wealth that makes it possible to finance more generous and ambitious policies.*

The priority given to the single market is therefore far from incompatible with ambitious social and environmental policies, contrary to a twelfth common misconception.

The aim must be to generate a positive spiral, an upward dynamic between the economic, social and environmental poles. This means getting the order of the sequence and the proportions between the components right. As recounted by the journalist Rouletabille, the character created by Gaston Leroux, we have to tackle it from the right angle.

In this respect, the environmental challenge, on top of social expectations, is also forcing the Member States and the EU to be more effective and efficient in the pursuit of qualitative policies, of which there are now many. If we add to this the growing international competition

263 General Data Protection Regulation.

264 On the fact that, even today, the benefits of the single market are essentially reserved for large companies, *see* above, A, 1.

265 This is contrary to the fixed idea of certain political movements that the market is synonymous with the jungle and the lowest bidder (and state interventionism with paradise). No. If a large market makes it possible to free up more financial margins, it opens up more space for non-economic policies of general interest.

and the European military defence project, we are going to have to redouble our ingenuity and excellence. In particular, we can no longer afford to be indulgent towards Europe.

For a Clever, Well-Tempered Approach

As long as it does not compromise the competitiveness of the European economy, the inclusion of qualitative ambitions is to be welcomed.

In this respect, the challenge that new, more demanding regulations represent for companies may, paradoxically, ultimately give them a comparative advantage. In a way, this is the idea of the fruitful constraint dear to the theorist of history, Toynbee: faced with a reasonable obstacle, human societies surpass themselves. But the reform must have been well conceived and the effort required to adapt must be bearable.

The subject goes beyond the limits of this essay: how can we distinguish between new restrictive regulations that are excessively damaging to the economy and those that are bearable or even beneficial in the long term? Which constraints have development potential? For example, I have suggested the idea of a minimum organisational base for businesses, which could increase their productivity and facilitate their growth.[266]

Can a well thought-out "quality label" that meets a market need and offers a good cost-benefit ratio for economic operators, support and facilitation measures (once again the idea of modern supply-side policy), a realistic timetable, etc. help to distinguish between good and bad "constraints"?

The inventiveness and care with which politicians and administrators draw up this framework are essential, as is the phasing-in of its implementation.

---

266 *See* above, General Part, A, 1.

Towards a Fair Share of the Fruits of New Regulation

We can also think of a balanced distribution of the products of a reform between the economic, social and environmental spheres. The benefits of a new framework should not be monopolised by one section of society. The idea is likely to preserve or even increase social cohesion. However, the EU should ensure that its initiative is likely to generate additional prosperity, without which the pursuit of non-economic objectives is illusory.[267] In addition, the weighting between the different poles must depend on the priorities of the moment.

5. A Major Asset for European Society: Standards

The dynamic between the activity of economic operators and public action can give rise to recognised products and standards, comparable to designations of origin in the agricultural and food sectors.

Far from preventing private economic activity or even innovation, public action adds a distinctive quality compared with other products and services, giving them an extra halo of quality. Recognition by the market, possibly aided by judicious promotion (branding), can make them must-haves, likely to conquer external markets.

Progress in the single market can therefore lead to more European products being exported. We shall see in the next section to what extent the common commercial policy is the external extension of the single market.[268]

Europe can become the world reference, given the size of its market. The EU's neighbours closely follow European regulations. Switzerland

267 In this respect, the vagueness in the European Green Deal about the direction in which the "potential trade-offs between economic, environmental and social objectives" will be regulated is worrying (*see* section 2.1.).

268 *See* below, D, 1.

ensures that its products are euro-compatible, or even *euro-compliant*. It is a safe bet that, despite the rhetoric of its former Prime Minister Boris Johnson, the UK will do the same.

Well-designed standards[269] can also be seen as part of a modern supply-side policy, because of the advantage they give European companies.

Some Examples of European Standards

Europe has been able to create certain standards or benchmark products. For example, its mass-market investment funds, UCITS, are a global success that is the envy of the United States. They are marketed particularly in Asia. They have enabled Europe to become one of the world's leading financial centres in this field. The fund industry (the expression is revealing) has generated tens if not hundreds of thousands of jobs in Europe. It also attracts thousands of billions of euros from all over the world. This money benefits the European economy. The asset management sector makes it possible to finance a range of projects in Europe on advantageous terms.[270] In 2011, Europe extended this framework to managers of so-called alternative investment funds, which invest in companies whose shares are not (yet) listed on the stock exchange.

REACH is an integrated system for the registration, evaluation, authorisation and restriction of chemicals. Initially, this demanding certification system subjected European companies to stricter rules than their competitors in third countries. Today, it has become a quality label. Companies that do not meet the requirements are excluded

269 Unfortunately, the European Commission's main concern seems to be to establish global standards by taking advantage of the single market (*see* "A New Industrial Strategy for Europe"). Rather than thinking in terms of power and the balance of power, it should be working to develop a supportive legal framework that is a prestigious brand and a lever for European production, and that has more to do with soft power.

270 On the contribution of an efficient European financial sector to prosperity, *see* above, B, 3.

from a series of markets.[271] Since 2015, South Korea has instituted a chemical product control system openly inspired by the European model: K-REACH.[272]

Another example of a European standard being exported is value-added tax. As taxes are not the preferred mechanism of citizens, the painless side of VAT has charmed the Gulf countries. European law and audit firms are training civil servants in the United Arab Emirates. The result: jobs, business and tax revenues for Europe.

The GPDR is becoming the most demanding standard in the world in terms of data protection and privacy.

Standards: Implications for European Legislators

The international dimension must be integrated into European legislative activity. In today's globalised world, the EU naturally has an interest in taking account of the rest of the planet. If the compromise acceptable to 27 Member States can also be a model for third countries, that is an additional added value for Europe.

The issue is becoming crucial with the emergence of China. There are now three blocs and potentially three competing systems. Companies around the world will adopt one or even two nomenclatures, not three. As a result, Europe needs to be able to come up with a standard as quickly as possible, one that is likely to win the support of as many different non-EU countries as possible. There is also a premium on speed when it comes to standards, as illustrated by the competition in the past between the VHS, Betamax and VCR systems for video recorders: it was not the best technique that won the day.

---

271 Defraigne and Nouveau, 3rd ed., p. 370.

272 Ibid., p. 262.

6. Towards Self-Limitation and More Evaluation

A Concise Legal Framework

A rule of self-limitation would be welcome. A master is only as good as his constraints. Why not limit the number of regulations and directives, the number of pages, and focus on the essentials? Concision takes work. A constraint in this area would be a spur to greater design quality.

Another advantage of such a proposal is that it would strengthen the debate and therefore transparency and democratic legitimacy. Who today can take an intelligent position on a proposal by the European Commission? The mass kills democratic debate. It prevents the exchange of views and the improvement of proposals. It removes the real issues from adversarial scrutiny, in violation of the European principle of openness, which aims to involve the public as much as possible in decision-making.

It excludes small operators from the discussion (this is a Europe that is not very accessible to SMEs) and, in any case, increases the cost of participation for large operators. It therefore imposes excessive burdens on businesses and citizens, in violation of the principle of proportionality, right from the stage of drafting proposals for directives and regulations.

Towards Independent Impact Assessments

In setting European objectives and the measures envisaged, the EU should be able to rely on high-quality independent economic research centres. However, impact studies are often weak and serve to endorse prior political choices.

Independent economic institutes are important in Germany. They are a key element in the overall doctrine and system that has formed the matrix of German economic and monetary policy for more than half a century, with the success that we all know. For example, it was the president of one of Germany's economic centres who sounded the alarm under Chancellor Schröder.[273]

These centres take part in the public debate in Germany. In part, they act as a counterweight to the demagogic temptations of.[274]

At European level, there is nothing comparable. This is a sign of the absence of a European political society in the broad sense.[275]

In addition, there is no systematic examination of the effectiveness and efficiency of the measures adopted in the past.[276] It is as if the EU felt that critical reports would damage its credibility. For example, critical reports are sorely lacking in the area of the Common Agricultural Policy.[277] Any regulation that proves ineffective or inefficient should be withdrawn after a few years.

7. Conclusion: Towards a Structural/Modern Supply Policy for the Internal Market

The pandemic and the Russian invasion of Ukraine only serve to reinforce the urgent need to deepen and improve the single market, so as to generate additional growth, provided it is eco-responsible and socially equitable. Awareness of this seems to be growing.[278]

---

273 H.-W. Sinn, *Ist Deutschland noch zu retten?* [Can Germany Be Saved?], Munich, Econ, 2004.

274 In particular, they are involved in verifying the realistic nature of budget revenue forecasts within the "Commission des évaluations fiscales" (Larosière, p. 64).

275 On this subject, *see* below, Title IV, Ch. 2.

276 Such a posteriori controls do exist (Fit for Future, Refit) but they are not practised systematically.

277 *See* below, Title III, Ch. 2.

278 *See* the conclusions of the Council of the European Union of 11 September 2020, "A Deepened Single Market for a Strong Recovery and a Competitive, Sustainable Europe"; *see also* the priorities of the Swedish Presidency for the first half of 2023.

In my opinion, a modern structural/supply-side policy is an effective approach for the EU to deploy, given its limited powers and means of action.

What Gains in GDP Can Be Expected From the Above Proposals?

Such an assessment is difficult. However, on the basis of recent studies and in view of the fact that measures not otherwise envisaged are proposed above, we can reckon on at least 5% of GDP just for defragmentation and completion of the single market and 2% for its lasting improvement, i.e. almost *€1,120 billion.*

For example, the removal of barriers to intra-Community services should increase the GDP of the EU27 by €575 billion, and barriers to trade in goods from €228 billion to €372 billion.[279] A 2015 study by the European Parliament came up with comparable figures: €1,030 billion, including €615 billion for the single market for consumers and citizens and €415 billion for the digital single market.[280] The same study, updated in 2019, puts the figure at nearly €900 billion.[281]

The considerable investment needed (i) in R&D (between €320 billion and €500 billion per year), (ii) for the ecological transition (we are talking about at least €260 billion per year, which corresponds to almost 2% of European GDP in 2020[282]) and (iii) the digital revolution, (iv) in transport infrastructure (€50 billion a year, or more than 0.3%

279 E. Prouzet, "The cost of non-Europe: Impact on the internal market", *Open Access Government*, 1 December 2022.

280 European Parliament, *Mapping the Cost of Non-Europe, 2014-19*, Brussels, European Parliament, March 2014; based on the 2019–2024 version of the European Parliament's study, the Commission puts forward, in March 2020, a figure limited to goods and services of €480 billion to €560 billion, or 3 to 4% of GDP.

281 European Parliament, *Europe's two trillion euro dividend: Mapping the Cost of Non-Europe, 2019-24*, Brussels, European Parliament, April 2019.

282 *See* the European Green Deal, section 2.2.1, "Pursuing green finance and investment and ensuring a just transition".

of GDP), (v) for our common defence (former President Trump spoke of a 2% contribution to NATO), and (vi) for a more inclusive society argue for decisive action in favour of greater prosperity.[283]

In this respect, we also need more determination than that shown today against protectionism of all kinds. In general, the EU is too soft. Europe is weak. One might even wonder whether its insidious and methodical unravelling was not launched some twenty years ago. We need to wake it up and reverse the trend.

To return to the myth of Europa, let us take our inspiration from the statue in Athens: a powerful, conquering bull, well-poised, led with a light, confident hand by an accomplished Amazon Europa.

D. Afterword: Two Pillars to Maintain, the Common Commercial and Competition Policies

Let us say a few words about two policies closely linked to the single market. The first, the common commercial policy, is its extension towards third countries. The second, competition policy, is its cornerstone. Their essential contributions are not always well understood or perceived by the public.

By way of a common introduction, it seems that international trade and a vigorous competition regime encourage innovation, productivity and growth. An emblematic example is South Korea. After 1998, South Korea accepted foreign direct investment and introduced more competition into its economy. Whereas in the early 1990s, South Korea filed eight times fewer patent applications than Germany with

283 *See also EIB Investment Report 2019/2020*, p. 7.

the US Patent Office, 20 years later it filed 30% more patents than Germany. Considering that it has 50% less population, the growth is spectacular (12.5 to 130%).[284]

1. Common Commercial Policy

An extension of the single market is the EU's common commercial policy, i.e. its relations with the rest of the world in terms of trade in goods and services. The aim is both to ensure outlets for European products and to regulate imports from third countries into the EU.

In recent years, under the impetus of the European Commission and especially its former Swedish Commissioner, Mrs Malmström, the EU has pursued a judicious policy of free trade agreements. This has focused on trade relations with third countries that are "socio-compatible", i.e. where the standard of living of the population and the standards of social protection (but also the values) are relatively comparable to our own.

As a result, the economic benefits of these agreements have been less outweighed, or even overshadowed, by social disruption (for example, French car manufacturers have made very good exports to South Korea, against the expectations of a number of French business circles). Once again, European policy has had a positive impact, creating added value.

2. The Contribution of European Competition Law

On Saturdays, I buy a foreign newspaper and its weekly supplement. Half the time, I do not receive the supplement. But I'm always billed for it. The fault lies with the distributor, who has a virtual monopoly

284 Aghion et al., p. 185.

and therefore could not care less about the quality of the service. During a property development, a friend was shocked by the prices quoted by electricians. Shortly afterwards, the French Competition Authority opened an investigation into a cartel in this area. On three occasions, the European Commission rejected Ryanair's acquisition of Aer Lingus because the merger would create a monopoly on 46 air routes. Recently, the *collectivité territoriale* (territorial collectivity) of Corsica was ordered to pay more than €80 million in damages. It had granted favourable treatment and subsidies to SNCM, whereas a private operator, Corsica Ferries, could provide the same service without subsidies.

An essential component of the internal market is free and undistorted competition. It is important that, for the benefit of other businesses and consumers, companies and governments do not restrict or distort competition. Competition law has several components. The first are aimed primarily at companies (merger control, antitrust law). State aid control and a subset of this, the discipline of services of general economic interest (SGEIs), place obligations primarily on the Member States. We will deal with these in Chapter 2, on the EU's current and possible contribution to better public management.

The Role and Added Value of Antitrust Law and Merger Control

Businesses are free to compete with each other, for their own good, the good of consumers, innovation and growth. The economic freedom of companies is protected against certain illegal actions by other companies (cartels, abuse of dominant position). In addition, control of mergers before they take place aims to preserve a certain amount of competition on the markets and a healthy market structure.

Competition law aims to protect the principle of an open economy, based on private initiative and entrepreneurial freedom, against abuses and excesses by companies. It is a corollary of the single market.

What is the point of opening up borders if companies, acting alone or together, can maintain or restore obstacles to intra-Community trade as formidable as state protectionism, thus preventing new entrants?

Competition law exerts downward pressure on prices, encourages a more diversified supply and encourages greater innovation. A number of goods and services are comparatively cheaper today (i.e. taking inflation into account) than in the past. A good Côte du Rhône cost €5 in 1994. Today, the same bottle costs €6.5: barely a 30% increase in 25 years. Champagne was only drunk on very special occasions, and people were content with the generic product. In 50 years, despite two oil crises and the hyperinflation of the 1970s, this product has only doubled or tripled in price and has become more democratic. What's more, today's range is much more diversified: special cuvées, blanc de blancs, extrabrut, growers' champagnes, rosé champagnes, etc.

Look at the innovations that we have witnessed in cars: aerodynamic progress with the first mass-produced family car with an air penetration coefficient of 0.30, the Opel Omega in the early 1980s, widespread use of four-wheel drive, airbags, longer service intervals, hybrid and electric cars, driver assistance instruments, considerable reductions in fuel consumption (in the 1970s and 1980s, a litre of petrol was needed per 100 kilograms; today we do much better[285]). The Commission has also put the brakes on a cartel between German manufacturers who were trying to slow down the pace of innovation in catalytic converters.

More generally, the Commission is keen to ensure that companies do not rest on their laurels or abuse their privileged positions. For example, the EU initially welcomed payment and credit card systems as a new facility for merchants and consumers. Then it became more vigilant, eventually outlawing certain commissions. Such an approach maintains downward pressure on prices and encourages innovation.

285 Even if the weight of the cars has increased too much.

Furthermore, it is not companies that dictate the rules to the EU. The framework is defined by the European authorities, who are more sheltered from pressure from business circles than national or regional officials. This applies to both large American companies (Microsoft, Google, Apple) and European companies (Alcatel Alsthom and Siemens).

Proximity to citizens and businesses is not always an advantage for the smooth running of public activities. One example is the successful liberalisation of Poland, carried out under the supervision of the European Commission. This contrasts with the corruption that has characterised privatisation in Ukraine and the unsatisfactory competitive situation there.[286] As a result, Poland's level of prosperity has grown much faster than Ukraine's over the last twenty years.

Corporate power can also be turned against the population and political power and, in the long term, threaten democracy and, more generally, our pluralist society. Historically, antitrust law has curbed the excessive power of certain companies (Rockefeller in the United States, IG Farben, the great German chemical conglomerate). Because of their technology and financial resources, certain companies are likely to pose a threat to our free society and to the conduct of democratic elections.[287] Competition law can be a guarantor of democracy.

A Policy Worth Reviewing?

Eventually, competition policy will have to undergo certain changes, particularly in the light of the new global situation. Consider the kind of competition coming from China, with companies that are supported or even encouraged by the public authorities. The European Commission's rejection of the Siemens-Alstom merger opens up a fundamental debate in this respect.

286 *See* J. Tirole, *Economics for the Common Good*, Princeton University Press, 2017.

287 On this point, *see* in particular "Tim Wu, l'avertissement de Biden aux géants du net", *Les Echos Week-End*, March 2021, pp. 32–33.

However, it remains to be seen whether the response should take the form of an adaptation of the competition rules or be based on trade relations with the third countries concerned (WTO, etc.). These are therefore delicate issues that require careful consideration.

In this respect, knee-jerk reactions from politicians (such as those following the European Commission's decision to oppose the Siemens-Alstom merger project) cannot be solutions, just incentives for in-depth work. The Alcatel story confirms this. The Commission has authorised a merger between Alstom and the Canadian company Bombardier, subject to commitments that Alcatel had initially refused as part of the project with Siemens. In the end, much ado about nothing?

It might be in the EU's interest to have more companies with the requisite size to become global players (rather than European champions). This consideration could lead to a change in the criteria for assessing mergers and acquisitions, which are perhaps too focused on affecting the structure of the European market or even national markets.[288] Without being the only option in such a change in merger control, another solution, as we have seen, would be to improve the functioning of the internal market so as to increase the size of SMEs, the number of medium-sized companies and operators making use of the freedom of movement and to accelerate the emergence of new giants. In this case, the geographical dimension of the markets could widen. It may not be necessary to change the assessment criteria.[289] Once again, the question of the appropriate remedy arises.

At a time of great technological change, when Europe is lagging behind, it is even more essential to encourage and preserve the innovative

288 The delimitation of markets regularly on a national basis confirms the predominance of SMEs in the European economic fabric and the confinement of their activities to the national territory.

289 The speed with which the European Commission can abandon national definitions of product and service markets will be a very good indicator of the success of the completion and deepening of the internal market advocated in this essay.

process.[290] To put it plainly, the European Commission must do more than just look after the immediate welfare of consumers. It must resolutely combat the acquisition of promising new technologies by the major players in order to neutralise them (predatory acquisitions) and any manoeuvre designed to slow down the pace of innovation. As a first step in this direction, the Commission has invited national competition authorities to refer to it for review mergers without a Community dimension involving advanced technologies or sensitive areas. The initiative was taken in connection with the acquisition by a Californian company of another Californian company, which had developed a revolutionary technique for detecting certain cancers (*Illumina/GRAIL* case).[291]

The current rules of competition law are not obsolete. They can, however, be improved or adapted to changing circumstances. They are, tried and tested and represent progress in relation to the economic regime that preceded them.[292] Let us beware of regression; of a form of nostalgia and intellectual laziness. Yes to constructive criticism of competition law and to its improvement; no to the temptation of (false good) ideas that have failed. In public economic law, there are counterparts to those nostalgic for the monarchy!

290 In this respect, *see also* Aghion et al., in particular pp. 25 and 80.

291 This resulted in the European Commission prohibiting Illumina's already completed acquisition of GRAIL on 6 September 2022, imposing a fine of €432 million on the acquirer for failing to comply with the obligation to notify the European Commission in advance, and requiring Illumina to divest GRAIL as soon as possible on 12 October 2023.

292 For example, the injection of a dose of competition into the German healthcare system partly explains its better performance in dealing with the pandemic than the French healthcare system, which has the same budget in terms of percentage of GDP.

Chapter 2

Prosperity and the Public Sector

At the beginning of Title I, reference was made to two horns of plenty on which Europe was leaning in a 16th century representation.

Today, the internal market is the first. We showed that it can bear even more fruit in the first chapter.

The second horn that needs to be addressed today is the public sector.

Until now, the EU has sown the seeds of progress in this field. Since the banking crisis of 2008, the EU, with the help of the Member States, has been sowing the seeds. Over the *past 15 years, it has probably been more concerned with improving public management than the internal market*. It could still do much better. Public leverage could become another powerful lever for development.

Indeed, given that around half of the European economy is publicly controlled, improving the performance of the public sector in Europe will have substantial consequences. Secondly, unemployment is falling, so Member States no longer have to maintain fictitious jobs.

Finally, given the scale of the economic, social, environmental and military challenges, it is essential that the public sector becomes more of a driving force in Europe's economy and society.

Let us take a look at the instruments available to the EU to boost the public sector: the health of public finances, fiscal governance, economic policies, monetary policy, the recovery of the European economy after the pandemic, the control of state aid and SGEIs, and respect for the principle of an open market economy with free competition. Given their specific characteristics, we will discuss public investments in the following section.

A. Sound Public Finances and Budgetary Responsibility

Pillars of European Integration

The sustainability of public finances is a cornerstone of the EU.

On the one hand, the EU cannot run a deficit and accumulate public debt, which is the norm for an international organisation. The most tangible advantage is its triple-A rating, which few Member States have, and which enables it to borrow on better terms.

On the other hand, Economic and Monetary Union (EMU) has introduced rules of budgetary discipline, with ceilings of 60% public debt and 3% public deficit.

The budgetary responsibility of public authorities, both European and national, is in line with the responsibility of each component of European society, particularly that of economic operators. Everyone must look after their own financial viability and cannot rely on the help of others as a matter of principle. This is also a characteristic of a market economy, itself another foundation of European integration.

Limits on Member States' indebtedness also protect the 27 Member States from demagoguery, from jeopardising the opportunities of future generations and from short-termism. It is a condition for the sustainability of our democracies and the well-being of our populations, two of Europe's fundamental missions. The budgetary discipline imposed by the EU is an additional added value of the EU.

A Discipline That Respects National Diversity

Member States remain largely free to define their economic, social, societal and even environmental policies, subject to compliance with the main European principles, including the sustainability of their public finances. It is therefore up to them to set tax levels accordingly. Tax levels can vary considerably from one Member State to another (by as much as double, from 22.7% in Ireland to 47.4% in France in 2019). Once again, European requirements are respectful of specific national characteristics.

These differences are misunderstood by some, who equate them with freebooting, tax dumping, a thirteenth common misconception. In fact, these differences in tax levels – which can be found within many states at local or even regional level – are the consequence of the autonomy of Member States (and the differing expectations of their populations) in a range of policies, but also of their greater or lesser quality of management. Why force a Member State to levy 50% tax if it covers its operating costs with 35%? Furthermore, because of their geographical location or their lesser attractiveness, some Member States cannot apply the same level of tax as countries that more naturally appear to be havens on earth.

Perception of Budgetary Discipline in the Member States

The Germanic, Nordic, Baltic and Slavic states consider these to be rules of good management. For example, social democratic states such as Sweden and Denmark have public debt levels well below 60% (30.7% and 30.2% in the second quarter of 2023), even though their level of public taxation is comparable to that of France. They plan to further reduce their debt to better face the challenges of today and tomorrow.[293] Germany, whose public debt had fallen from 80% after reunification (an immense effort) to 58% before the pandemic, wanted to reduce public debt to 40% by 2040.[294] In 2023, it will have to deal with a debt of 64%. The Netherlands was at 52.4% and is now down to 46.9%. Despite the 2008 banking crisis that hit it hard, Ireland was at 64.8% and will be at 43.1% in 2023. Luxembourg was at 22% and has "risen" to 28.2%.

There has also been a moderation in the public deficit and public debt in the new Member States in general. Some Western countries are quick to lecture them on a range of subjects, but should take a look at their own figures.[295]

Latin countries are generally more closed to the benefits of moderate indebtedness. Before the pandemic, Greece was at 181.1%, Italy at 132.2%, Portugal at 121.5%, Cyprus at 102.5%, Belgium at 102%, France at 98.4% and Spain at 97.1% of GDP as figure 21 below shows.[296] In the second quarter of 2023, Greece – which is making considerable progress – is at 166.5%, Italy, France and Spain – which are following the opposite trajectory – are at 142.4%, 111.9% and 111.2% respectively, Portugal is down to 110.1% and Belgium is at 106%. Cyprus has also made significant progress, reaching 85.3%.

293 At 42% in 2016, Sweden was aiming for 35%. By the end of 2018, it had reduced its debt to 38.8%. Denmark was at 34.1% and Finland at 58.9% at the end of 2018.

294 Larosière, p. 65.

295 Hungary is at 70.8%, Slovenia at 70.1%, Poland and Slovakia at 48.9%, Romania at 35%, the Czech Republic at 32.7%, Latvia at 32.4%, Lithuania at 32.4%, Bulgaria at 22.6% and Estonia's at… 8.4%. The low level of public debt in the Member States of Central and Eastern Europe is probably due to the more limited financial development of their economies.

296 *Key figures on Europe*, 2022, p. 41.

Note the spectacular progress made by Greece where, in 12 months, public debt has fallen from 195 to 171%, is at its lowest level since 2012 and will be accompanied by a primary budget surplus (i.e. excluding debt charges) of 0.1% by 2022.[297]

Figure 21.

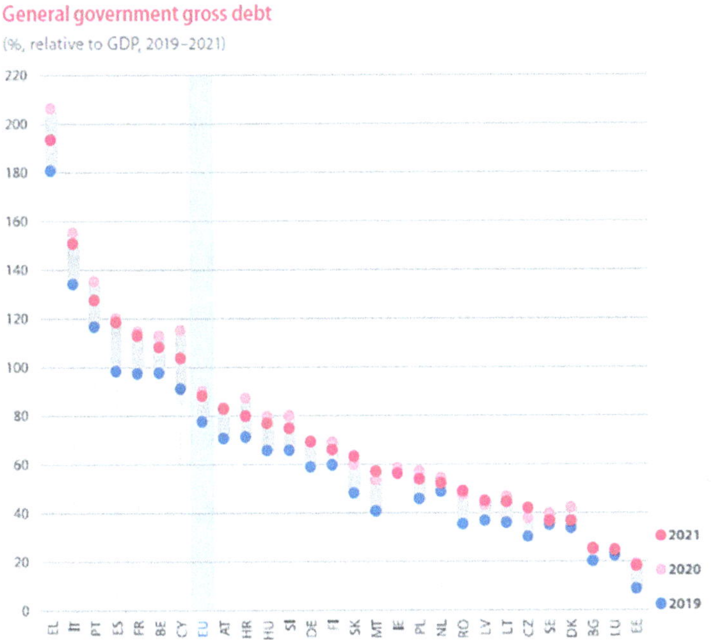

Be that as it may, the Latin countries must realise that they are largely outnumbered in the EU of 28, or even more so in the EU of 27, representing only a quarter of the Member States. Indeed, with the exit of the United Kingdom, whose public debt was then above the European average of 80%, the average level would have fallen below this threshold, to around 78%, in the absence of the pandemic.

297 *Les Echos*, 19–20 May 2023, p. 6.

Healthy Public Finances: An Asset or a Weakness for Europe?

Whatever the opinions on the subject, it is generally considered that a level of public debt in excess of 70–90% is counterproductive.[298] Of course, I am comparing apples with pears, a stock (debt) with a flow (national product). However, generally speaking, countries with a large public debt do not have the most dynamic economies, especially those with a large public sector. Their need for money absorbs savings and reduces private sector investment, which is potentially more productive. Most of their public spending is not (often) investment.[299] Furthermore, what is the profitability of public investment?

A high level of debt can also have a deterrent effect on economic operators, who will fear future tax increases.[300] Interest payments on the debt are the second or third largest item in the French budget, about the same as national education. So much money that is not being allocated to policies of general interest. This is a growing concern as interest rates rise. For example, public debt servicing represented 1.5% of GDP in France, compared with 0.5% in Germany… and 3% in Italy before the rise in interest rates. The quality of the borrower certainly qualifies the argument. The fact remains, however, that a one percentage point difference in the deficit of GDP at the level of the 27 represents €160 billion.

If its GDP is growing strongly, a country can afford a higher level of debt. This puts into perspective the public deficit and debt of the United States, which, thanks in particular to[301] its policy of investment

298 J. de Larosière, *Les lames de fond se rapprochent*, Paris, Odile Jacob, 2017.

299 In France, "operating expenditure, social benefits and debt servicing account for more than 90% of the total" (Larosière, *40 ans d'égarements économiques*, p. 55 (in French)).

300 On this issue, *see* Ibid., p. 54.

301 Private consumption is also a driver of US growth.

in research and development (not to mention its sovereign privilege and military leadership, as well as its population's propensity to consume), is enjoying higher growth.

But few, if any, of the Member States, especially among the Latin countries, are in the same position as the United States.

The moderation of public debt is accompanied by reduced public deficits or even surpluses. It provides room for manoeuvre in the event of unforeseen difficulties and for pursuing policies in the general interest.

Germany, for example, has released billions of euros in public bonuses in 2019 and said it was ready for a fiscal stimulus to counter the threat of recession. It has launched a €100 billion programme to make its economy greener. In 2022, after Russia invaded Ukraine, it announced a similar effort to strengthen its defence policy. Recently, it demonstrated its ability to protect its businesses against the rising cost of energy. Its budgetary rigour in normal times and during phases of prosperity enables it to pursue a counter-cyclical economic policy during crises, especially when they are severe.

Not surprisingly, the Nordic countries are particularly well placed to pursue counter-cyclical policies, unlike Greece and Italy, as figure 22[302] below shows.

302 Aghion et al, op. cit. p. 355.

Figure 22.

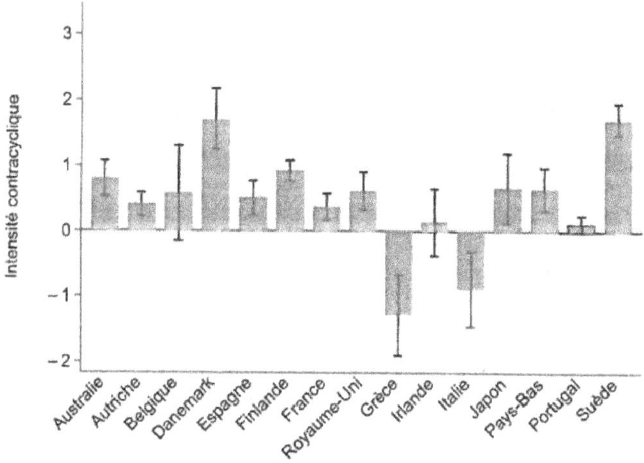

Figure 14.3. Mesure de l'intensité contracyclique de la politique budgétaire, 1980-2005.
Note : un signe positif reflète une politique budgétaire contracyclique, alors qu'un signe négatif montre une procyclicité de la politique budgétaire.
Source : Aghion, Hémous, Kharroubi (2014).

There is also a trend towards better public management in Member States with good budgetary positions, as revealed by the pandemic crisis. While Germany and France devote the same percentage of GDP to health spending, Germany's performance has been far superior. Germany has three times fewer managerial posts in the health sector than France. It has also accepted a degree of competition in the field.

In addition, Member States with low levels of public debt invest more. R&D&I investment rates are generally higher. There is also a higher level of growth, greater productivity gains, lower unemployment and a better employment rate, as figure 23 below[303] shows.

303 J. de Larosière, *Putting an end to the reign of financial illusion: For real growth*, Paris, Odile Jacob, 2022, p. 60.

Figure 23.

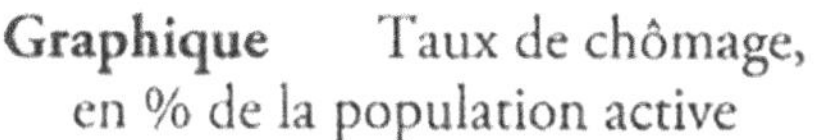

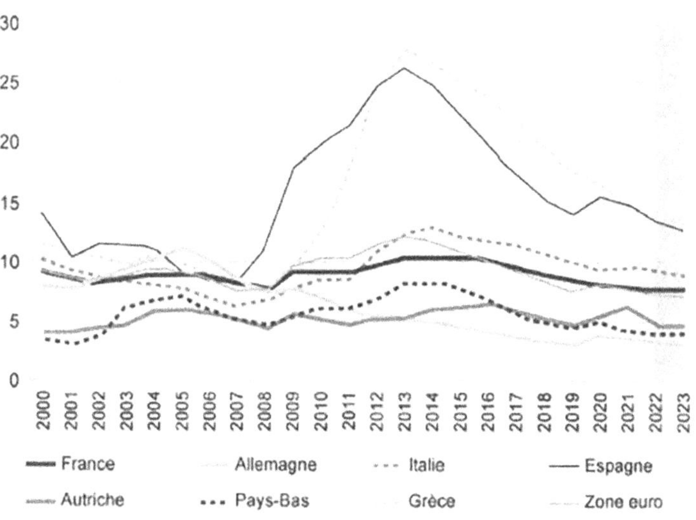

Sources : Commission européenne, Eurofi Macroeconomic Scoreboard, septembre 2022.

Budgetary discipline also makes it possible to be… more generous towards the rest of the world. The Member States have signed up to the target of devoting 0.7% of their GDP to development aid. The average today is only 0.48%.[304] Which countries exceed the target? Sweden (1.14%), Luxembourg (1.02%), Denmark and Germany (0.73%), four of the best performing Member States in terms of budgetary health.

So, as long as the Member States do not achieve higher growth, it is advisable to force them to respect a certain budgetary orthodoxy if they want to retain the room for manoeuvre to pursue ambitious

304 *See* above, Introduction.

policies and face up to the challenges of today and tomorrow (digitalisation, artificial intelligence, making the economy greener, defence policy, etc.).

Sound public finances are vital to any political system. The Roman Empire died of financial mismanagement. It is essential to maintain a certain proportion between public revenue and expenditure, and also to have room for manoeuvre, a cushion against unexpected events such as pandemics, natural disasters, changes and, as the events in Ukraine have reminded us, international conflicts. "To govern is to plan ahead." This well-known saying has a double meaning; in addition to the ability to look to the future and to have a vision, it means showing foresight in the face of hardship, in short, having reserves.

The Maastricht Criteria: Not All That Ineffective

Thanks to the Stability Pact and the European Semester,[305] Member States' debt has fallen by 10 percentage points between 2013 and 2019, from 90 to 80%. This trend is likely to continue until we produce more detailed assessments of the sustainability of public deficits and debts.

What is more, for the first time since the introduction of the euro as a physical currency (2002), none of the eurozone Member States was in excessive deficit before the pandemic. The 3% rule is therefore not as ineffective as some claim. Yet a fourteenth lie! Figure 24 below shows that, of the EU Member States, only Romania, which is not part of the eurozone, had a budget deficit of more than 3% in 2019.[306] Furthermore, just before the pandemic, 13 Member States had budget surpluses, i.e. almost half.[307]

---

305 *See* below, B, 1.

306 *Key figures on Europe*, 2022, p. 40.

307 This was written before the pandemic.

Figure 24.

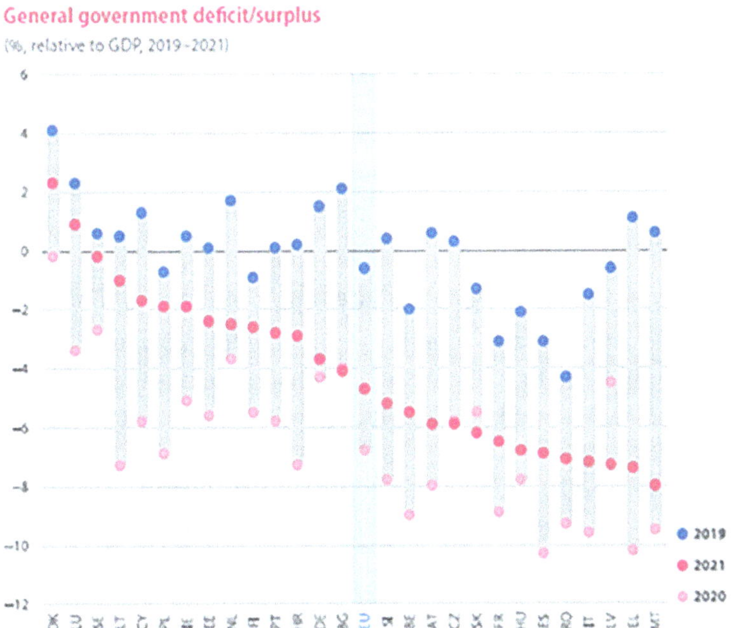

These margins for manoeuvre were useful in cushioning the shock of Covid-19 in 2020.

Towards a Change in European Budgetary Rules?

If there is a way of achieving a finer adjustment in this area, one that generates greater wealth for the states and peoples of the EU in a sustainable way, so much the better. Rates of 3 and 60% are not absolute fetishes or monolithic parameters. However, it is better to have clear, poorly tailored benchmarks than more benchmarks or opaque methodologies!

It is often suggested that certain public spending should not be subject to these criteria, such as spending to combat global warming. The road to hell is paved with good intentions. It is not enough to describe an item of expenditure as an investment for it to bear fruit. The approach must be serious.[308, 309]

On the other hand, if we start making exemptions to the budgetary rule in the name of some emergency, it will be stripped of its substance. A penny is a penny, and certain balances are fundamental. Projects and dreams are unlimited, but means are not. That is why economics is a gloomy science.

To conclude, just as there is room for improvement in the rules on competition, there is also room for improvement in the rules on public debt and public deficit. However, the changes envisaged should not be regressive, inspired by ideas that have failed.

European Integration, Fiscal Responsibility and Solidarity Mechanisms

As indicated, each Member State is responsible for its own finances. In this respect, it remains a sovereign state, a subject of international law with the resulting financial obligations. Conversely, the other Member States are not liable for its debts. One reason for this is that a politician is elected by a population, represents it and is committed to it. It is not up to the population of another Member State to bear the consequences of this more or less fortunate choice.

The risks of imbalance, instability and difficulties in one or more Member States nevertheless raise the question of the appropriateness of certain mechanisms to accompany the larger integrated market. The disappearance of internal borders, the impossibility of re-establishing

308 On this concept, *see EDB* 12412 of 28 January 2020.

309 In this respect, the considerations developed by the European Commission in its communication "The European Green Deal" of 11 December 2019 on green public investment and green budgeting are reassuring. Both the concern to improve the EU's budgetary governance and the concern to safeguard guarantees against risks to debt sustainability are mentioned (section 2.2.2. "Greening national budgets and sending the right price signals").

them, the common destinies, and solidarity lead us to think about collective intervention in the event of serious disruption in a Member State. For example, recent years have highlighted the financing difficulties of certain states, with the soaring interest rates they were asked to pay (spread).

Given the gains that the single market represents for all, temporary and conditional solidarity mechanisms may be considered.[310] They must not, however, release either party from its commitments. This brings us back to the principle of responsibility, which is fundamental to the construction of Europe and applies equally to the European Union, the Member States, companies and the general public. In addition, assistance must not undermine the whole structure. There is a proportionality to be respected: solidarity does not mean everyone being dragged down together.

Europe is an added value, a complement to the national level: it does not replace it or release it from its commitments. On the other hand, it can help to a certain extent and under certain conditions. "Europe helps you, but help yourself too."[311] It also means acting as a lever.

Let us take the case of a Member State's deficit and/or debt slipping. In order to discipline Member States, there is a "no bail-out" rule: neither the Union nor the other Member States can be held responsible for a Member State's commitments or take them over. This does not, however, preclude conditional financial assistance. This reconciles the individual responsibility of states, temporary assistance and the concern for added value and sustainable progress

310 Of course, they do not rule out other solutions, which may take precedence. For example, under Mario Draghi, the ECB was able to resolve the problem of spreads by implementing a differentiated policy of buying the bonds of the Member States most exposed to them, in the name of the need to maintain the unity of monetary policy and therefore its effectiveness.

311 A softer version of the German "*fördern und fordern*" (help and demand).

(difficulties must remain exceptional and not recur, and the Member State receiving assistance must take structural measures to improve its management).

It was on the basis of these principles that the European Stability Mechanism (ESM) was set up, a treaty between the Member States of the eurozone.

This logic leads to a preference for alternatives to Eurobonds that do not commit Member States to the debt of other countries.[312]

We could, for example, imagine that, as progress is made in the management of its public finances (measurable in terms of the primary budget balance[313]), a fraction of the debt accumulated by a Member State could benefit from favourable refinancing conditions via a mechanism involving all the Member States (or members of the eurozone) or even the EU, as long as these improvements persist.[314] However, the debt would continue to be serviced by the Member State concerned alone. In a way, the mechanism would take over from the ESM on the road back to sustainable finances. After the rescue, it would contribute to the restructuring of a Member State's public finances.

It is not a question of substituting oneself, of taking on obligations or a role in someone else's place, but of helping them to fulfil them. Once again, the ideas of leverage, added value, facilitation and synergy. It would create a solidarity that does not take away responsibility and does not appease. Helping[315] those who have stumbled to get up again and helping them to grow in the long term.

---

312 This is a fundamental question of respect for democracy and public accountability. The voters of one country do not appoint the elected representatives of another Member State. Consequently, they cannot be held responsible for the mismanagement of the latter. It is up to the voters of the latter Member States to take responsibility.

313 Budgetary position before debt servicing. For example, Greece had a positive primary balance of 2% in 2023

314 In the event of a further deterioration, Member States would lose access to this mechanism for the future, as long as their primary balance is not positive.

315 Without placing them under guardianship, which would be the logical consequence of pooling debts.

B. Fiscal Governance and Macroeconomic Surveillance

1. The European Semester

The European Semester is an example of close coordination between the Member States, the European Commission and the Council. The Member States draw up their draft budgets, which are submitted to the European Commission for comment. The latter examines them in the light of a series of European objectives and priorities.

The European Semester was introduced in 2011 in response to the banking crisis of 2008 and the subsequent budget crisis. The exercise has a disciplining effect on Member States, as they have to reflect on a series of issues, formalise a project and present it in the face of contradiction. Gradually, a European budgetary culture is developing, with an exchange of best practices. Through this exercise, carried out within a specific framework and timetable, which is renewed each year, the Member States and the European institutions learn from each other ("learning by doing"). The approach is empirical.

The European Semester is another way in which the EU intervenes. The EU does not legislate but provides technical advice to Member States on their draft budgets. It cooperates with them to improve budgetary practices in Europe. Without prejudice to the economic and social policy options of the Member States, it conducts a dialogue to achieve greater efficiency.

On the economic and budgetary fronts, this involves improving resilience to external economic shocks, contributing to a prosperous economy in the long term (back to a modern supply-side policy, a structural policy), ensuring the sustainability of Member States' public finances and preventing excessive macroeconomic imbalances through competitiveness adjustments.

The European Semester also helps to ensure that certain issues that are important to all 27 Member States receive ongoing attention.

In addition to the budgetary criteria of 3 and 60% mentioned above, the Commission's objectives include improving the employment rate and combating unemployment, as already mentioned.[316]

Even if the level of follow-up to the Commission's recommendations by the Member States is uneven, after a few years, the points on which the EU is particularly vigilant have seen considerable progress. The fight against unemployment is one area where European recommendations are particularly well integrated into active labour market policies.[317] Unemployment fell by more than 45% between January 2013 and August 2019, from 12 to 6.2% in the EU, as figure 25 below shows.[318] An unprecedented performance. Remember how difficult it was to reduce unemployment after the two oil shocks of 1973 and 1979.

316 *See* above, Title I, Ch. 1, B, 4 (ii).

317 *See EDB* 12490 of 20 May 2020.

318 Eurostat, Euro indicators, 17/2024, 1 February 2024. In December 2023, the unemployment rate had fallen at 5.9%.

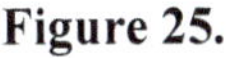

Figure 25.

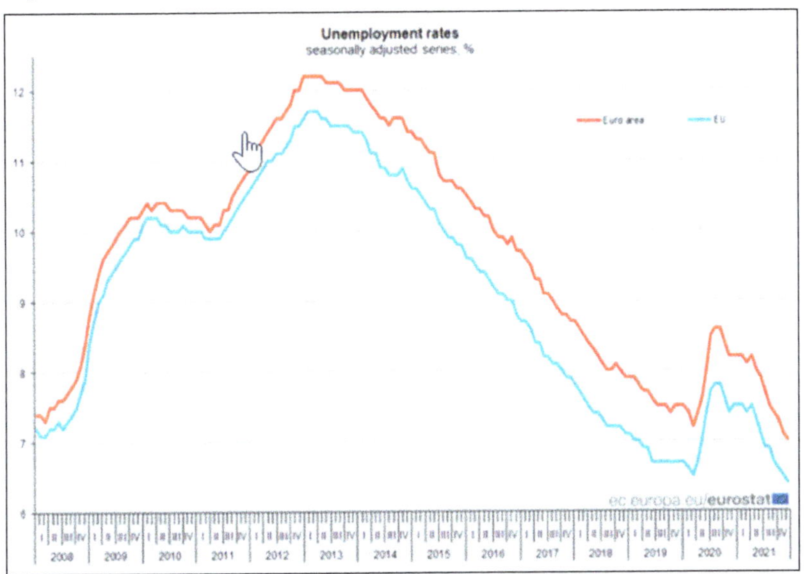

Other Topics Examined

There has also been a gradual integration of social and ecological issues.[319]

The European Social Charter of Rights is now taken into account. Proclaimed in 2017, it sets out 20 principles for a social Europe in terms of equal opportunities, access to the labour market, fair working conditions and social protection and inclusion.

Recently, the Semester has included the United Nations Sustainable Development Goals.

319 *See EDB* 12430 of 21 February and 12441 of 7 March 2020; the introduction to the Commission Communication "The European Green Deal".

There is also a focus on promoting economic growth, the digital transition, preventing excessive macroeconomic imbalances in the EU, and monitoring the implementation of national recovery plans in the wake of the pandemic.

The European Semester, a Potential Goldmine

Given that the European Semester focuses on national budgets, which currently represent 51% of the GDP of the 27 Member States, any improvement brought about by this collective exercise could have a substantial impact. The approach could therefore be much more ambitious than it is today, leading to a major project, *the Union of Public Sectors*. The aim would be to systematically seek to improve the quality of public management in the European Union – again, with a view to adding value.[320]

In the paragraphs that follow, we raise a number of issues that deserve attention and reflection.

(i) Budget Preparation Procedure

For example, the German budget is drawn up on the basis of revenue, which is estimated independently and reasonably, even conservatively. In France, by comparison, the starting point is the Ministry of Finance's determination of expenditure.[321] The first approach is more effective than the second in preventing any slippage in public finances. Should greater harmonisation in this area not be addressed as part of the European Semester?

---

320 A first step in this direction is the establishment of independent national supervisory institutions whose mission is to contribute, through their public assessments, to better governance of public finances. However, regardless of the lack of effective powers, these institutions operate in a purely national context.

321 Larosière, *40 ans d'égarements économiques*, p. 63.

(ii) Composition of Budgets

Consideration could be given to the way in which public spending is financed, depending on its characteristics (running costs of the state apparatus, percentage of managerial posts, budget for general public services, public investment), its size, the measurement of its effectiveness (leverage or multiplier effect; achievement of several objectives by a single measure, etc.), the productivity of the public sector and the gains it has made in this area.[322][323]

There are, for example, good arguments for prohibiting borrowing to finance the operation of public services and the pension scheme. On the other hand, borrowing is a legitimate means of financing medium- to long-term investment.

One might wonder about the rules that should be observed when creating civil servant posts. Such a decision is akin to taking on a virtually perpetual debt. On the one hand, the recruitment of a young civil servant commits the state for the duration of their career, i.e. 40–45 years. Secondly, it is unlikely that the post will be abolished once the incumbent has retired. Is it reasonable for a political majority, sometimes short-lived, often ephemeral, to be able to commit the national budget for so many years, without also having to meet certain objective conditions?

(iii) Managing Member States' Public Debt

Rather than envisaging the Copernican revolution of mutualisation, is it not more realistic and in line with the main thrust of European integration to develop cooperation and even coordination in order to

---

322 From the 1970s to the 1990s, the concern of some Member States was to contain the unemployment rate. The price was sometimes the creation of "convenience" jobs in the public sector. Today, both the structural fall in unemployment and the limited room for manoeuvre available to public authorities mean that this approach needs to be reviewed.

323 For a number of suggestions in this area, *see* section F below on the optimal allocation of public resources.

improve the management of Member States' debt, alongside the limited and conditional mechanism of mutualisation of their refinancing suggested above?[324]

(iv) Extending the Areas Covered

Given their importance for prosperity and the environment, energy issues should be integrated into the European Semester. A series of key indices in this area should be monitored: the percentage of energy dependence on third countries, energy productivity/intensity and efficiency rates, CO_2 and methane emission levels and trends, and progress towards energy sources and practices with a better energy balance.

2. Multilateral Surveillance

The surveillance of national economic policies tends to go beyond budgetary discipline. The EU is gradually monitoring the macro-economic balances of the Member States, in order to prevent any slippage in this area and to help them remedy it. In this way, the EU and the Member States have a scoreboard with which to measure the evolution of certain parameters that are essential to the health of the economy and of national societies.

The scoreboard includes detectors of internal imbalances (public and private debt, speculative bubbles on the financial and asset markets, changes in the flow of credit to the private sector and unemployment) and external imbalances (current account balance, Member States' net external positions, export market share, competitiveness, etc.) as well as specific alert thresholds.

324 *See* above, A.

Particular attention is paid to developments in the real economy: economic growth, employment and unemployment, productivity and its driving forces (research and development activities, foreign or domestic investment) as well as sectoral trends, particularly in the energy sector, which affect GDP and current account results.

For the reasons given above,[325] the increasing emphasis on productivity monitoring is to be welcomed. The September 2016 European Council adopted a recommendation calling on eurozone Member States to set up a national productivity council.

If the European Commission identifies imbalances, it may issue preventive recommendations, require a corrective action plan and impose financial penalties (for eurozone countries).

Are We Moving Towards an Extension of Surveillance to Include Major Economic, Soci(et)al and Environmental Balances?

The examination of macroeconomic balances should include a dimension of sustainable development and social cohesion. It should also identify the structural weaknesses and vulnerabilities of an economy (over and above cyclical developments), which the state in question would be invited to work on, where appropriate, with conditional support, particularly financial, from the Union.

Let me give you an example. A number of Central European countries have seen most of their "national champions" come under Western control. This makes them objectively more dependent on foreign direct investment. The relative weakness of transfers from Western countries has not been able to offset the negative effects of such a loss of control over the production apparatus. In order to develop (or, more prosaically, to provide bread and butter for

325 *See* above, Introduction, "A Balance Sheet in Jeopardy?"

their populations), they have specialised in sectors with low added value. Their populations have had to accept low wages and long working hours. These countries are lagging behind technologically. One of the challenges for them is to move up the added-value ladder, to develop domestic players so that they are less dependent on international trade. Poland, for example, no longer wants to be Europe's assembly plant,[326] an activity which, as we have seen, does not offer the greatest added value.[327]

Such a monitoring of the major balances would also enable the EU and the Member States, in their relations with each other, to take better account of the needs, vulnerabilities and sensitivities of each state. As the former president of the European Commission, Jean-Claude Juncker, has pointed out, the Member States know little about each other.

More generally, macroeconomic, social and environmental monitoring would help the EU in its overall strategy.[328]

It is essential in order to maintain and improve certain fundamental balances in a body like the EU. We need to be able to detect risk situations early on and constantly work to improve living conditions. When drawing up a policy or legislative reform, the EU must have a clear idea of the needs of the 27. It must also work on this issue.

For example, the Eurosceptic regions are not necessarily the poorest ones, but those facing conversion, whatever their original level of wealth. For the moment, these regions are "slipping through the cracks" and are not identified as priorities by European policies, particularly in terms of economic, social and territorial cohesion.

326 J. Iwaniuk, "La Pologne ne veut plus être 'l'atelier d'assemblage de l'Europe'", *Le Monde*, 19 October 2019.

327 *See* above, Introduction, "A Key Indicator: Labour Productivity".

328 On this, *see* below, Title II, Ch. 1.

C. ECB Monetary Policy

Underlying Principles

The ECB must first and foremost ensure price stability. Only in this way can it contribute to the Union's other policies.

The underlying mandate is that monetary policy should reduce the risk of inflation and establish conditions conducive to economic activity, savings, investment and hence sustainable growth. Economic operators' investment decisions require predictability. The ECB must also be immune to political pressure and not finance public authorities "by printing money" or acquiring public debt. Once again, preference is given to hard work over "doping", i.e. the artificial and temporary improvement of performance.[329] In a similar vein, it is expressly stated that ECB policy must respect the principle of an open economy with free competition. It probably follows that its interventions and its approach to monetary policy must not distort the markets, particularly the bond and financial markets, or the price formation mechanism.

This approach aims to preserve the expectations of citizens and businesses, their confidence in the currency as a purchasing power and a means of saving, and to discipline public authorities. Preserving the value of the currency is also likely to attract external capital and make the euro an international or even reserve currency.

Temperaments and Trends Since 2008

Since the banking crisis of 2008, the ECB has sought to favour short-term economic activity and Member States, some of which are major debtors. Hence its artificially low interest rates and massive purchases of government bonds on the secondary market.

329 On supply-side policy, already discussed in Title I, Ch. 1, C, 1.

In the end, the ECB opted for a policy that was more cyclical than structural, believing that it had to deal with the most pressing problems. The problem is that exceptional measures have become the norm and have become part of the long term.

Risks and Challenges

The result was abnormally low interest rates and a great deal of money creation.

Savers and pensioners are feeling the pinch (particularly in Germany, where the level of pensions in relation to final salaries is not high); with negative interest rates, savers are no longer being remunerated but taxed! Banks are suffering from lower margins.

The ECB's massive new interventions in the wake of the pandemic, particularly on the secondary market for Member States' debt, are also the subject of debate. While they are likely to guarantee a certain level of liquidity, necessary to maintain economic activity, their long-term effect on the economy if they persist could be counterproductive.[330] They have already fuelled inflation, despite the warnings of leading economists.[331]

There is also a risk of increasing Member States' debt and reducing the borrowing and investment capacity of European businesses.

Informed observers have also noted a depressive effect of this expansive policy on productive investment[332] of this expansive policy,

330 Their legality could pose a problem if the ECB undertook indefinitely to systematically renew its stock of bonds when they reached maturity, as this would be tantamount to cancelling the debts of the Member States (in this regard, Larosière, *40 ans d'égarements économiques*, pp. 80–81).

331 *See*, as early as 2020, P. de Grauwe, who saw a return to inflation of between 4 and 6% (S. Diessner et P. De Grauwe, "What price to pay for monetary financing of budget deficits in the euro area", *Vox EU*, quoted by Combe, p. 166); Larry Summers, February 2021 (on the subject, V. Le Billon, "Inflation : quand Larry Summers avait raison", *Les Echos*, 12 January 2022); Jim Rogers, co-founder of the Quantum fund with George Soros, March 2021 (YouTube); IMF, 14 October 2021.

332 Larosière, *40 ans d'égarements économiques*, p. 175.

due to the setting of an inflation target of 2% instead of 1 or 1.5,[333] the creation of asset bubbles, and a preference for liquidity,[334] the maintenance on the market of inefficient companies (so-called zombie companies), which undermines overall productivity[335] which, as we have seen, is problematic in Europe, the depreciation of the average quality of debt issued by non-financial companies,[336] and the widening of social inequalities.[337]

These artificial conditions on the interest rate market are also undermining the confidence of international investors in the euro. For months now, the eurozone has been recording significant capital outflows.

Today's monetary policy would produce economic decline and even tomorrow's crashes.[338]

Another point of concern and its long-term implications is the vertiginous expansion of the balance sheets of central banks,[339] including that of the ECB (which has risen from 12% of GDP at the end of 2000 to 39.1% at the end of 2020 and 73.8% on 13 May 2022[340]). If we put together public debt, the debt of non-financial companies, households, the financial sector (particularly non-performing loans), central bank debt, speculative bubbles linked to certain assets and the mass of liquidity held and compare them with the real level of economic activity, wealth creation and productive investment, we find fundamental imbalances that herald upheaval and even major disruption in the long term.

---

333 Ibid., pp. 173–174.

334 Ibid., p. 202.

335 J. de Larosière, *Putting an end to the reign of financial illusion*, pp. 71 and 98.

336 Ibid., p. 17.

337 Ibid., in particular p. 33 and pp. 48–51; in particular, the wealthiest were able to borrow via Lombard credit (i.e. by pledging their securities portfolio).

338 J. de Larosière, "Les banques centrales sont en train de fabriquer les crises de demain", *Les Echos*, 22–23 January 2021, p. 15.

339 Larosière, *40 ans d'égarements économiques*, pp. 171–172.

340 Larosière, *Putting an end to the reign of financial illusion*, p. 70.

The Transmission Protection Instrument (TPI), introduced in July 2022, is also the subject of much discussion. The instrument would allow the ECB to buy bonds from eurozone Member States that are experiencing "a deterioration in financing conditions not justified by the country's own fundamentals". The result would be that the ECB would gradually replace the bonds of healthy Member States on its balance sheet with those of less robust Member States. To what extent will this instrument, which is supposed to protect certain Member States against an excessive spread, not take away the pressure from them to carry out the necessary structural reforms and distort the market? Everything will depend on the discretionary power given to the ECB and the way in which it is exercised.

There is a great temptation to use and abuse the ECB. Indeed, it is one of the few concrete levers for action at European level, along with the European Commission via competition policy in the broad sense,[341] the European Investment Bank and the European Investment Fund in financial matters.[342] Mario Draghi had warned that he could help Member States temporarily, but that he was no magician and that they would have to carry out structural reforms. He was not listened to by a number of Member States. They found themselves at a loss when the pandemic broke out and war broke out in Ukraine.

In short, the ECB's tendency to take cyclical measures, announced as temporary and exceptional, is becoming the norm. Not only is the whole coherence of Europe's monetary construction at risk, but also its financial stability and current and future economic vigour (falling productivity, lack of responsibility, underinvestment).

---

341 This, too, is one of the characteristics of European integration. It can establish a quality framework. On the other hand, it has relatively few means of cyclical action.

342 *See* below, Title II, Ch. 1.

D. The European Recovery Plan

The European Recovery Plan is a set of measures adopted jointly by the EU and the Member States in response to the pandemic. The European and national levels combined their strengths, the EU's triple-A rating and the solvency of the Member States. The EU was thus able to make resources available to the Member States, particularly those most affected by the pandemic, on more favourable terms than could have been obtained by dispersed national initiatives. In addition, certain European intervention instruments have received more funding.

The European Commission has been, exceptionally, authorised to borrow up to €750 billion on the capital markets on behalf of the Union. This amount will be guaranteed by the Member States. It must be repaid by the end of 2058.

This plan is in addition to the €540 billion emergency support plan for jobs and workers, businesses and Member States presented by the Eurogroup in April 2020.[343] Seven hundred and fifty billion euros (Next Generation EU), i.e. almost 5% of the GDP of the 27, will be made available to the Member States, €390 billion in the form of grants and €360 billion in the form of loans through 7 programmes.

The largest of these amounts to €672.5 billion under the (i) Recovery and Resilience Facility, €312.5 billion in the form of grants and €360 billion in loans to Member States.

To qualify, Member States must draw up reform and investment programmes. These must respond to the challenges and priorities identified in the country-specific recommendations made in the context of the European Semester. They must also contribute to strengthening

343 The plan also includes a European guarantee fund (€24.4 billion) designed to facilitate the provision of liquidity through guarantees to fundamentally viable businesses facing cash flow problems as a result of the pandemic.

the growth potential, job creation and economic and social resilience of the Member States, as well as preparing them for the green and digital transitions: at least 37% of the plan's budget must support the ecological transition, and 20% the digital transformation. In addition, the measures must "not cause significant damage" to the environment. The greening of the economy is a priority for European action. These plans will be examined as part of the European Semester.

The six other programmes (€77.5 billion) are (ii) REACT-EU (€47.5 billion), (iii) the Just Transition Fund (€10 billion), (iv) Rural Development (€7.5 billion), (v) InvestEU (€5.6 billion additional to the flagship programme designed to succeed the Juncker Plan), already mentioned,[344] (vi) Horizon Europe: €5 billion, (vii) RescEU: €1.9 billion.

- REACT-EU, which stands for "Recovery assistance for cohesion and the territories of Europe", is made available to the *European Structural Funds*, including the European Regional Development Fund (ERDF), the European Social Fund (ESF) and the Fund for European Aid to the Most Deprived (FEAD).[345] In particular, this involves financing measures to maintain employment, including short-time working schemes and support for the self-employed. The funds can also be used to support job creation, particularly for young people, and healthcare systems, as well as to make working capital available to SMEs and provide them with investment assistance.
- The Just Transition Fund is designed to support and accompany territories that have further to go to achieve climate neutrality.

344 *See* above, Title I, Ch. 1, B, 1.

345 On the Structural Funds, *see* below, Title II, Ch. 1.

- The European Agricultural Fund for Rural Development (EAFRD) will receive €85.4 billion for the period 2021–2027, including €7.5 billion from the European Recovery Plan, in order to make agriculture greener, more efficient and more inclusive.
- Following on from the Juncker Plan, InvestEU[346] is the flagship investment programme proposed by the EU to relaunch the European economy and continue to make up lost ground in R&D&I. It will mobilise public and private investment through an EU budget guarantee of €75 billion[347] (to overcome risk aversion), which will support the investment projects of implementing partners such as the EIB and its specialised subsidiary, the EIF. Projects will be eligible in the areas of (i) sustainable infrastructure (€20 billion), (ii) research, innovation and digitisation (€10 billion), (iii) SMEs (€10 billion), (iv) social investment and skills (€3.6 billion), and (v) European strategic investment (€31 billion).
- The EU's main funding programme for research and innovation, Horizon Europe has a budget of €95.5 billion for the period 2021–2027, including €5.4 billion from the EU's recovery plan. It aims to strengthen the EU's scientific and technological excellence and the European Research Area, respond to strategic priorities, including ecological and digital transitions, and boost innovation capacity, competitiveness and employment.
- RescEU is the European Civil Protection Mechanism designed to protect citizens from disasters and manage new risks. It is fully funded by the EU.

346 Already discussed in Title I, Ch. 1, B, 1, on the importance of investment in R&D&I.

347 Thirty-one billion euros for European strategic investment has been added to the initial €38 billion, itself increased by €5.6 billion.

Assessment

The European Recovery Plan is an unprecedented synergy between the EU and the Member States. It is not only an economic instrument to combat the consequences of the pandemic, but also and above all a plan to modernise the economies of the Member States. Its aim is to help these economies grow in the long term.

The first regret is that 90% of the plan is a juxtaposition of national programmes; the opportunity has not been taken to make progress in integrating the European economy, for example through projects of common interest and cross-border projects. Reservations have also been expressed about the plan's contribution to inflation in Europe. Finally, while a public boost to the eco-responsibility of the economy may be justified, the shift towards digitalisation could be negotiated more easily and at a lower cost to the public authorities and taxpayers if the internal market in services were completed or if, at the very least, the opportunity presented by the pandemic had been seized to liberalise it. It should be remembered that the delay in Europe in terms of digitalisation is essentially due to the fragmentation, and possibly increasing fragmentation, of the internal market.[348]

"Now is not the time for grocers, but for architects", said Jean-Claude Juncker, the outgoing president of the European Commission, about the recovery plan.[349] But we need to work as architects, not as petrol pump attendants or even arsonists. This brings us back to the preference for working on the fundamentals rather than excessive recourse to cyclical stimulus, which mortgages the future without unmortgaging the past.

348 *See* above, Title I, Ch. 1, "Introduction", under 4 and A, 1.

349 Interview with C. Mathieu, "Jean-Claude Juncker : 'Il y a un défaut de construction en Europe'", *Le Quotidien*, 11 April 2020 (in French).

E. Control of State Aid and SGEIs: An Incentive to Better Design Public Initiatives

Alongside antitrust rules (cartels and abuses of dominant position) and merger control, European competition law[350] includes State aid control and, within this, a subcomponent relating to the discipline of services of general economic interest. In principle, Member States may not subsidise companies established on their territory.

Why is State Aid Banned in Principle?

Firstly, competition must not be distorted to the detriment of companies not receiving aid in the Member State in question and those in other Member States. The prohibition of State aid is designed to ensure that the opening up of the economy through the internal market is not thwarted by Member States. Subsidies are likely to kill off viable businesses that do not benefit from them and to dissuade businesses from competing with those that receive aid.

Secondly, State aid accustoms recipient companies to doping, takes away their sense of responsibility, reduces their dynamism and therefore their productivity. In short, they ultimately weaken them.

Lastly, aid is contagious, with companies that do not receive it claiming it back, particularly those in other Member States, by way of compensation. The end result? Considerable expenditure of public money in all the Member States, which cancel each other out. In short, a waste of public money.

In this respect, State aid law prevents Member States, whose budgets are substantial – much larger than that of the EU in relative terms

350 *See* above, Title I, Ch. 1, D, 2.

(between 30 and 60 times!) – from engaging in a costly and counter-productive battle amongst themselves. It saves a lot of public money. Controlling State aid has reduced public subsidies in the industrial sector by between 3 and 0.6% of the Union's GDP over 20 years,[351] representing a saving of around €380 billion a year.

As well as safeguarding competition and economic dynamism, state aid control therefore contributes to the health of national public finances. It saves money for other policies, such as social policies. It is also likely to reduce public levies and leave more resources available for financing private projects, which usually generate more economic growth than public intervention. A 10-point reduction in public spending leads, on average in the current state of affairs, to a 1.5% increase in GDP.[352]

The Discipline of State Aid Control

The ban on state aid is not absolute, but the granting of aid is regulated. In principle, Member States must notify any planned aid to the European Commission to receive prior authorisation. They must justify their plans, indicating the objective that has been set, why the aid is necessary and what harm it may do to competition.

The granting of aid presupposes a need that cannot be met by the market, i.e. by the interplay of supply and demand (in European jargon, this is referred to as a market failure). The cost to the state must be proportionate. The Commission is increasingly examining the effectiveness of aid. In particular, it has been looking at this question since 2014, as part of the a posteriori control of aid granted under the General Block Exemption Regulation.[353]

---

351 Defraigne and Nouveau, 3rd ed., p. 94.

352 For converging views, *see* F. Facchini, *Les dépenses publiques en France*, New Leuven, De Boeck, 2021, quoted by J.-P. Delsol, "Baissons les aides aux entreprises… et leurs impôts", *Les Echos*, 2–4 April 2021, p. 9.

353 In other words, without the need for prior notification to and authorisation by the Commission.

So there is a concern for *the concrete impact* of projects.

The specific interventions[354] by governments in the economy have become more disciplined as a result. They realise that they can no longer do whatever they want, however they want. Controlling aid helps governments to improve the quality of their interventions in the economy. Indirectly, it can encourage them, rather than subsidising certain operators, to develop general frameworks that are likely to benefit all companies established or simply active on national territory. Ultimately, it is an indirect stimulus to a preference for a structural policy, working on the fundamentals rather than putting plasters on wooden legs.

At the same time, European control of State aid does not prevent all public initiatives. On the one hand, Member States are free to make investments if they offer prospects of profitability, at least in the long term. On the other hand, if there is a good reason to proceed with unprofitable financing (promoting a new economic activity, decompartmentalising a region, protecting the environment, restructuring a viable business, etc.), national and subnational public authorities can act, but only on the basis of a serious project and dossier. There must be a business plan, reliable forecasts and a rigorous methodology.

In this way, State aid law is likely to contribute to improving the quality of Member States' intervention in the economy and to rationalising their action. It is another of Europe's contributions.

Towards an Improvement in State Aid Law?

The approach could be developed further. Originally, State aid is a transfer expense and is part of a redistribution logic. However, the

354 By definition, Sate aid is an advantage to one or more companies. However, Member States remain free to adopt general economic policy measures, subject to compliance with the main European principles (in particular freedom of movement).

aid must not be a zero-sum flow but generate a positive effect. The requirements in this respect could be increased. In particular, it should constitute an element in a development policy, presenting added value.

In this respect, we could consider – once again – requirements for a public investment multiplier.

Aid for a more eco-responsible economy is already subject to a more favourable regime. In order to accelerate the shift towards cleaner economic activities, this trend could be strengthened.

We might also ask whether the notion of SME in State aid law should not be reviewed. While this type of company can benefit from a more intense level of aid, its definition is both so complicated and strict that it is likely to reinforce the isolation of small companies in relation to groups of companies.[355]

Consideration could also be given to giving more of a counter-cyclical dimension to State aid. Admittedly, in a weak economic climate, there are more market failures that would justify the granting of aid. However, it is conceivable that the eligibility rate (the part of certain projects that can be financed by the public authorities) of certain types of aid, which are considered to be particularly beneficial, could be temporarily increased in the event of an economic contraction. For example, private funding for training and R&D&I runs a major risk of being cut back. In such a context, it is essential to equip workers[356] and to continue innovating.[357]

Finally, it would be useful to increase the number of staff dedicated to policing state aid by the European Commission, and even its powers of intervention.

---

355 A structural weakness of the French economy according to some observers (Larosière, *40 ans d'égarements économiques*, p. 103).

356 In a similar vein, *see* Aghion et al., p. 114.

357 Ibid., p. 353.

Services of General Economic Interest (SGEIs)

(i) Notion

Services of general economic interest (SGEIs) refer to economic services provided to all or part of the population, generally on a continuous basis and at advantageous rates for users, i.e. with no direct relation to the cost of the service. Service providers are obliged to serve everyone, or at least the entire population entitled to the service. They cannot choose their customers. These services include public transport, the basic postal service, energy supply, hospital care, social housing, access to a payment account, etc. The list is endless.

Users pay only part of the cost of the service, which is made quite high by the specifications imposed on the operator by the public authorities. The public authorities, and therefore ultimately the taxpayers, pay the difference, which can be considerable.

(ii) SGEI and Respect for National Diversity

European law has not called into question the possibility for Member States to create and finance SGEIs. On the contrary, it has expressly recognised it.

In passing, let us emphasise this often overlooked characteristic of European integration. Contrary to popular belief, it does not aim to achieve uniformity or level the playing field. The Member States remain masters of their own social, societal, economic and political organisation, for the most part. If the population of a Member State wants a lot of public services and a high level of social security, that is up to them.

As we shall see, the EU only requires compliance with the internal market (no unjustified barriers to trade and competition) and budgetary balances (a reduced deficit, contained public debt).[358] For the rest, the Member States remain free to set the level of taxes, levies and public spending, including the scope of public services. Europe respects national diversity.

At the same time, Member States remain solely responsible for balancing their public finances. They must assume the consequences of their political, economic and social choices and not pass on the budgetary burden to other Member States and/or the Union.[359]

(iii) The SGEI Matrix

European law has simply regulated and rationalised the creation and operation of SGEIs. The analytical framework safeguards the possibility for Member States to develop proactive or even progressive policies in a number of areas, but only where there is a plausible need. At the same time, it limits unjustified interference with competition and the costs to society.

Firstly, the public authorities must establish that the introduction of an SGEI is justified. This covers two aspects.

On the one hand, the existence of a general interest, a legitimate need of all or part of the population. In this respect, the Member States have considerable discretion. Take the silver economy: a Member State may feel that certain mechanisms need to be put in place to ensure that senior citizens do not fall behind in an increasingly technological society where, without an internet connection and so on, they lose access to a series of essential services such as a bank account.

Secondly, there must be a current and persistent market failure (two to three years). In other words, private operators would not be prepared to provide the service expected by the public

358 *See* above, Title I, Ch. 2, A.

359 *See* below, Title II, Ch. 1.

authorities, particularly in terms of quality, volume and price, without public funding, over a certain period of time. The aim of the SGEI discipline is to preserve existing and potential competition. For example, if technological developments mean that economic operators, whether public or private, are now or soon will be able to provide the desired service without public funding, it is important not to discourage them.

A similar trend exists in the medical field. Today's technologies are lighter and no longer need to be purchased by hospitals. Smaller care units are possible for a series of examinations or even treatments. This brings us back to the concern to preserve an open economy, entrepreneurial freedom and innovation.

Another example is Autolib' in Paris. It has been a financial drain. The service was used less than expected. Other means of transport competed with it. At the same time, the city of Lyon managed to set up a comparable system, but without public funding. In fact, there was no market failure. A final example, already mentioned, is the introduction and public funding of an additional maritime transport service between the Continent and Corsica for SNCM, while Corsica Ferries was offering the service without subsidy. The Marseille Administrative Court of Appeal ordered the Corsican regional authorities to pay Corsica Ferries €86 million in compensation.

The SGEI discipline developed by the European Commission makes it possible to avoid this type of misadventure. It also helps to progressively reduce the cost of these SGEIs without undermining their effectiveness, or even improving it.

Having been a legal clerk at the Court of Justice of the European Union (CJEU)[360] during the drafting of the founding judgment

360 In other words, a judge's assistant.

(*Altmark*) and, above all, having applied the SGEI disciplines in a series of cases as a lawyer thereafter, I can attest *that proper handling of these rules makes it possible to reduce the cost of SGEIs by at least 20%,*[361] *without reducing the quality of the service provided to the public.*

Given that general public services represented 6% of GDP in the EU in 2018 and health 7%, this suggests savings of 1.2 to 2.6% of GDP for the EU27, or €180 to €390 billion. These amounts are considerable, since they are comparable to the investment needed to green the economy!

In my opinion, some Member States could greatly improve the management of their public services. Again based on my experience, I am thinking in particular of France. The ratio between the level of public levies (around 60% of GDP), the cost of running the French state and other local authorities, and the generosity and quality of the services offered appears to be suboptimal.

(iv) Towards an Improvement in the SGEI Discipline?

Not only must the market be shown to be inadequate, but the added value of public action and the appropriateness of the resources chosen should also be proved. This brings us back to the *criterion of positive impact.*[362] Otherwise, public money is being misspent/invested. It would be a good idea to develop methods for measuring this impact (the multiplier). Efficient management of the SGEI and the absence of waste should also be required.[363]

361 In short, the same price reduction as the dismantling of a cartel (agreement between competitors).

362 However, in this case, it does not apply to a European initiative but to a national or subnational public authority (region, municipality, etc.).

363 *See*, in this respect, Title I, Ch. 2, F, the potential of the principle of an open market economy favouring an efficient allocation of resources.

Finally, as is the case generally in the field of State aid, the fight against non-compliance with European rules should be stepped up, and this will involve strengthening the teams and even the powers of intervention of the European Commission.

F. An Economic Policy That Respects an Open Market Economy With Free Competition

Presentation

In conjunction with a large market, a market economy and a system of free and undistorted competition, there is another principle.

In pursuit of European objectives (notably sustainable growth and a highly competitive social market economy), action by the Member States and the EU entails the establishment of an economic policy conducted in accordance with the principle of an open market economy with free competition,[364] favouring an efficient allocation of resources.[365] This also implies compliance with certain guiding principles: stable prices, sound public finances and monetary conditions, and a stable balance of payments.[366]

This principle is also applied to policies for monetary, industrial and trans-European networks. It must be taken into account by the ECB when pursuing monetary policy, without undermining the primary objective of maintaining price stability.[367] As already mentioned, action

364 Art. 119(1) TFEU.

365 Art. 120(1) TFEU.

366 Art. 119(3) TFEU.

367 Art. 119(2) TFEU.

by the EU and the Member States must ensure that the conditions necessary for the competitiveness of EU industry are guaranteed in accordance with a system of open and competitive markets.[368]

Potential of the Principle

This principle could lead the EU and the Member States to show greater respect for economic freedom. I say more because, until now, it has not been given enough consideration. In particular, the CJEU only recognises its general value as it merely lay down a programme and refuses to give it a binding effect, which is legally open to criticism.[369]

The implications of the guiding principle of an open economy could be substantial for the EU, but also for the Member States. They should be given more thought, particularly by economists.

It follows from this principle that freedom of competition must be preserved, that markets must remain open, particularly to new entrants, that a European initiative must have a proven positive economic impact, and that it must contain measured constraints for economic players. The need to keep markets open to competition implies particular attention to reducing barriers to entry. For example, it could justify a European initiative aimed at generalising the principle of mutual recognition of products and services legally produced in a Member State.[370] Furthermore, the functioning of markets must not be distorted.

368 Art. 173(1) TFEU.

369 In a judgment handed down by a single chamber of five judges, the CJEU ruled succinctly that this principle was merely programmatic and that no legal consequences flowed from it (*Echirolles* judgment, case C-9/99, para 25). In another judgment concerning the price fixing for books, it did not even bother to give reasons for rejecting the relevance of this provision. The Court was too hasty, even in *Echirolles*. The fact that a provision is programmatic and devoid of direct effect does not mean that it is devoid of legal value. It simply means that it does not have absolute value, since the principle of an open economy may give way to other requirements. The conditions for such a waiver must also be defined, met and monitored. It was up to the CJEU to develop a methodology, a test in this respect: under what conditions can the European or national legislator depart from this principle?

370 On this point, *see* above, Title I, Ch. 1, A, 1.

Respect for the principle of an open market economy is all the more important now that public spending, debt and deficits are increasing.

So What Are the Best Interventions?

Firstly, those designed to achieve an open economy with free competition. Measures aimed at deepening the internal market and removing barriers to trade and distortions of competition are therefore permitted. Liberalisation and even deregulation programmes do not raise any objections. The same applies to measures aimed at improving the functioning of markets and increasing the effectiveness of competition. The *same applies* to measures to ensure the continuity of the single market for consumers, such as the ban on roaming.

Then, assuming that this large market has been completed, if the results remain insufficient, there is room for public intervention. This will aim either to remedy the failures or deficiencies, or to ensure that the economy performs better. However, this public initiative must be effective and proportionate. Public authorities must refrain from making the situation worse or spending money unnecessarily. In particular, the allocation of resources must be efficient, as required by the Treaty. Market failure must not be compounded by government failure. *The first is not a blank cheque for the public authorities to adopt any measure they like.*

Open Economy and Public Economic Action

This principle raises the question of the effectiveness of public action. The legitimacy of the principle of public intervention is not in question. As has been said, it is up to the public authorities to set the general framework applicable to economic activities. However, it is important to ensure that this action provides real added value (supportive framework, optimal allocation of resources, support for retraining and transition, etc.).

In our view, this principle should permeate every EU action. The EU's primary mission is to contribute to sustainable growth and a social market economy that is highly competitive and, in the current circumstances, innovative. Consequently, the principle must influence and permeate every one of its interventions. The same cannot be asked of the Member States, or at least is less categorical, because some of their actions are unrelated to the pursuit of European objectives.

For example, the principle of an open economy could lead the EU to better adjust the corset of the financial system by lightening a whole series of formalistic obligations while tackling the problem of bad bank debts more head-on.[371] To regulate yes, to strangle no, as the Germans so aptly put it.

The principle of respect for an open economy should also encourage the Union and the Member States to make markets as open as possible to new operators and innovation. It must be regularly verified whether and to what extent continued public intervention is justified.

Space policy is a good example. Ariane has fallen asleep on its laurels. Europe is losing ground to the United States, which has successfully opened up the market to economic operators after a period of monopoly by NASA.

Foresight: The Link Between the Principle of an Open Market Economy and Public Economic Action

More thought needs to be given to the appropriateness, forms and dimensions of public initiative in the economic sphere, and to the ways in which it should be implemented.

Too often, things are approached in a binary way, between the advocates of private initiative and those of state interventionism. This

371 *See* above, Title I, Ch. 1, B, 3.

opposition is a long-standing one. Moreover, it raises the question of whether public and private initiatives should be placed on the same level and whether they are antagonistic.

Similarly, there is a tendency towards conservatism in the forms of state action. The simplest (the most media-friendly?) for the public authorities are often favoured, but so are the most brutal and potentially the most damaging for the economy: subsidies, nationalisations, taxes, penal repression.

I do not pretend to offer definitive solutions, just to start the process of reflection.

On the basis of the principle of private initiative and the subsidiarity of public intervention, the question arises as to under what circumstances public intervention is justified, and the nature and scale of that intervention.

(i) Public Initiative, Enhancing Economic Market Activity

If public initiative makes it possible to improve market performance without distorting competition between economic operators, why deprive ourselves of it? Let us assume that governments are able to borrow on better terms than the private sector. They would buy up loan portfolios from the banks to enable economic operators to be financed at lower cost. This would increase the volume of profitable investment, without favouring some companies over others. In addition, the governments would give the banks more leeway to lend again, which would also increase the number of bankable projects.

In this case, there is no market failure in the strict sense, but rather a situation that can be improved and that market forces alone will not improve. Public intervention would be justified provided it is effective and does not distort competition.

(ii) No Premature or Excessive Public Intervention

Where there is a suspicion of market failure, it may be wise to ensure that it could be long-lasting before considering remedying it by public intervention, which could be premature and unfairly counteract market forces.

Assuming that a market failure has been established, the public authorities should give priority to tackling its causes. If the causes are structural, they should identify the missing factors (for example, a lack of connection between labour supply and demand, scientific research likely to give rise to economically exploitable innovation) and try to remedy them first. They would only take the place of economic operators or consider continuing an activity within a restrictive framework as a last resort and, temporarily, if possible. They would leave as much room as possible for a dose of competition. They would also ensure the efficient allocation of public funds.[372] In the event of a monopoly, it would be subject to performance obligations, with incentives for constant improvement and regular review of its necessity and size.

Other hypotheses are conceivable. It is important for economic efficiency to think rigorously about this and to be able to test models.

The treatment of Member States with an interest rate spread lends itself to such questioning. Is it more appropriate to design a new interventionist monetary policy instrument or to encourage the state in difficulty to work on its fundamentals so that it is less penalised by the financial markets?

At the risk of being criticised as a logical contradiction, there are situations where early public intervention can avoid a large-scale

372 If we combine the principle of an open economy where competition is free with the principle of subsidiarity, possibly reinforced, we would arrive at a situation where, assuming it were competent, the EU would have to demonstrate three things: market failure, the inadequacy of action by the Member States and the added value of its intervention. Fourthly, intervention should be proportionate and not go beyond what is necessary, either in terms of intensity or duration.

disruption and save public money. For example, during the pandemic, Switzerland activated a plan to provide liquidity to businesses in record time. Switzerland was one of the countries whose GDP suffered least from the Covid crisis. In my opinion, the two situations are different and require different solutions. Covid is an exceptional calamity that is likely to harm fundamentally sound and responsible operators. It calls for emergency, temporary measures – in short, a short-term policy. A Member State in the grip of a spread generally has structural weaknesses resulting from a persistent accumulation of economic policy errors and fiscal complacency.

(iii) Typology of Combinations Between Private and Public Initiatives

We also need to think about the combinations and complementarities between private and public action. For example, the interaction, the passing of the baton, the initiative of the private sector or the public sector being prolonged by the other. The public sphere can extend a private initiative. It can also play the role of pioneer or initiator.

Let us not forget that a Member State may invest freely as long as its behaviour is rational in a market economy, i.e. aims to obtain in the (long) term the return that a large private holding company would seek. State aid law does not prohibit all specific economic initiatives by Member States.

A catalyst effect, a spillover effect, a leverage effect, a multiplier effect of private investment can be added to a public initiative. The Juncker Plan is a good example of this.

Another example: for infrastructure investments, the EU provides the financial impetus needed to attract private capital (an impetus that often goes hand in hand with an analysis of the project and the reduction of asymmetric information).

Public authorities can favour actions where the private sector is involved or would be involved if there were a limited public sector contribution. In fact, the number of projects that can be unblocked is much greater with the same amount of public money, or even less.[373] In other words, the public sector has to provide leverage.

The nature of the financial support may vary. The EIB and the EIF regularly innovate in this respect.

However, the added value provided by the public sector must not be too costly for the public purse. There is a question of proportion. All the more so as other general interest objectives must be pursued. It is a question of opportunity cost and trade-offs.

This kind of analysis would make it possible to refine the configuration of public action: no or little distortion of competition, a minimum of public resources committed for a maximum of positive effects and room left for the freedom of private business. The idea is not to prevent public economic intervention, but to rationalise or even optimise it. Nor is it a question of curbing innovation in economic public action, quite the contrary.[374] An orderly approach is simply likely to avoid abuses and harmful initiatives and to improve the productivity of public investment and private-public synergy.

In this combination of private and public forces, the European financial system can play an essential role, through the leverage effect and the catalysis of financial resources that it can facilitate, notably via innovative formulas.

Another factor to bear in mind is complementarity. This is closely linked to the idea of market failure. For the public sector, it means developing expertise that the private sector does not offer and is

373 Not to mention the time saved between public intervention and a return on investment.

374 Research in this area should be promoted.

unlikely to offer any time soon. Not least because its development costs are too high to be profitable. For example, certain analysis and information services such as meteorology, especially in certain very specific segments, the evaluation of SMEs, etc.

(iv) The Principle of the Open Economy and Technological Change

Another example, already in the pipeline in European law, is the revisiting of Schumpeter's theory of creative destruction. According to the latter, capitalism advances, in particular by technological leaps, which lead to upheavals in the economy.[375] These can be brutal and costly in human and social terms.

The EU has a range of instruments to alleviate this suffering without holding back technical and economic progress. For example, one of the EIB's missions is to provide financial support for redeployment, restructuring and the adjustment of worker training. This is also one of the objectives of the Union's industrial policy. Lastly, State aid law is more flexible when it comes to conversion aid. These various instruments are designed to limit social break-up and preserve and develop human capital (an area in which the EU also has responsibilities),[376] without standing in the way of technical and economic progress. The aim is to move forward in the most efficient way, reducing "collateral damage" as much as possible. Once again, a Europe that helps people grow and widens the circle of possibilities.

In a modern conception of structural/supply policy, it is up to the public authorities to support transitions and reconversions with the aim of facilitating them and cushioning the social and human cost. Such

375 Fortunately, this analysis is not always true. Some technological revolutions do not necessarily lead to the disappearance of old products, but add to them. As is generally said, the invention of the bicycle did not destroy anything.

376 *See* above, Title I, Ch. 1, B, 4.

intervention would also be justified, for example, in any development in agriculture that is more respectful of the environment and the health of consumers[377] and in the energy transition.

In my opinion, we can no longer be satisfied with Schumpeter's theory. Today, the social and human cost of this theory is no longer acceptable. The economic and even environmental costs will continue to rise. Given both the increasing scarcity of resources and growing competition from the rest of the world, we cannot afford to waste the assets represented by certain industries that are either in decline or doomed economically or politically. To give an example, it might be more in the common interest to organise an orderly energy transition so that the assets of European hydrocarbon companies do not fall to zero, but so that they can make their technical, intellectual and financial resources available to this development.

That said, we must avoid the mistakes made by certain Member States in their industrial policy in the 1970s, the supposedly Keynesian stimulus policies that result in a temporary boost to the economy at the high cost of public deficits, distortions of competition and support for lame ducks that put the brakes on economic change. I come from the southern part of Belgium, from Liège to be precise. The policy of blind subsidisation of the status quo has been disastrous and contrasts so much with the success of the Dutch, German and Luxembourg approaches, just a few kilometres away. Yet these three other countries were just as exposed, if not more so (in the case of Luxembourg), to the steel crisis.

Now, if it is possible to avoid this kind of misguided state interventionism, in favour of well-designed and reliable public authority strategies likely to generate added value, why not?[378]

377 *See* below, Title III, Ch. 2.

378 On a more active commitment by governments, *see* in particular M. Mazzucato, *Mission Economy: A Moonshot Guide to Changing Capitalism*, London, Allen Lane, 2021.

(v) The Potential for Promoting Efficient Resource Allocation

The principle of respecting an open market economy with free competition is based at least in part on the idea that this promotes the efficient allocation of resources.

At first sight, a measure that is detrimental to an open economy is more likely to be justified if it allows a better allocation of resources than a market economy. In particular, this may be the case in the event of market failure. However, it is important that there is no valid alternative that is less damaging to the market economy.

Conclusions and Costing of Gains From the Public Sector Union Project

The EU is already exerting an increasing influence on public management at Member State level.

It can, however, contribute to further improving the performance of public sectors in the EU through its various instruments (budgetary discipline, European semester, multilateral surveillance, monetary policy, European Recovery Plan, control of State aid and SGEIs, better respect for the principle of an open market economy with free competition).

Given that public authorities represent half of the GDP of the EU27, which is considerable, it is reasonable to expect a 10% improvement in their performance. At a constant level of services, this would mean almost €800 billion of additional room for manoeuvre, or 5% more of GDP27, or perhaps even more since it is generally accepted that such a reduction in public spending would generate

1.5% more GDP, or €12 billion, i.e. more than €810 billion. *If we adopt a conservative approach, we would only count on a 3.5% increase, or €540 billion.*

For the rest, the key words in terms of public economic intervention would be subsidiarity, multiplier effect, concern for impact and added value, complementarity, synergy and interaction with the private sector, proportionality, *fitness* (more and better with less), support for transitions, efficient allocation of resources, rigorous methodology, appropriateness, preservation of the competitive process, the search not only for effectiveness but also for efficiency.

We shall see that some of these features already underpin the EU's development and solidarity policy, especially the interventions of its two banking and financial operators, the EIB and the EIF.

TITLE II

DEVELOPMENT AND SOLIDARITY

European integration is not just economic,[379] thank God. A second axis is solidarity. Solidarity between Member States with a view to bringing the poorest up to the level of the others and contributing to global and harmonious development; solidarity within national societies, with a concern for justice and social inclusion.

However, these solidarity policies include a significant economic development dimension, which could be further strengthened. The European approach is not one of anaesthetising and disempowering solidarity, but one of dynamism and progress. Once again, the dual idea of providing temporary help and helping people to grow in the long term.

In this respect, European integration should make better use of two assets. Firstly, as a lean superstructure with low operating costs, it is able to allocate more of its budget to investment than a Member

379 Bearing in mind that this cluster has major soci(et)al implications, as we have seen: standard of living and quality of life, inclusiveness, etc.

State, in relative terms. Secondly and more importantly, some of its players, especially the European Investment Bank and its specialised subsidiary, the European Investment Fund, have developed financial techniques that have a far greater leverage effect than traditional subsidies (Chapter 1).

As far as social justice and cohesion are concerned (Chapter 2), while the construction of Europe mitigates international shocks, the scale of current challenges requires a substantial improvement in its performance in these areas. We will examine how this can be achieved without compromising the economic dynamism that we have seen also has to be perfected.

Chapter 1

Economic, Social and Territorial Cohesion Policy

Alongside its standard-setting activities, its dialogue with the Member States on budgetary and economic matters and its monetary policy, the EU has another course of financial action. Although this was only revealed by the Recovery Plan,[380] it existed long before it.

A. Cohesion Policy Through the Structural Funds

One of the priorities of European integration is to bring the poorest countries and regions up to the level of the richest.

380 Another way is to create European companies, such as Ariane, Airbus, Arte and EuroHPC (supercomputers).

Although the less prosperous original members received more in proportion to their population than the most recent members, this policy remains important. It is now the second-largest item in the European budget, after the Common Agricultural Policy (CAP), and accounts for 30% of the budget, averaging €50 billion annually over the period 2014–2020, as figure 26 below shows.

Cohesion policy is fundamental for a number of Member States. Before the 2008 banking crisis, it represented 4% of Greece's GDP. Today, it represents between 3.23 and 3.78% of the GDP of the countries of Central Europe.

Figure 26.

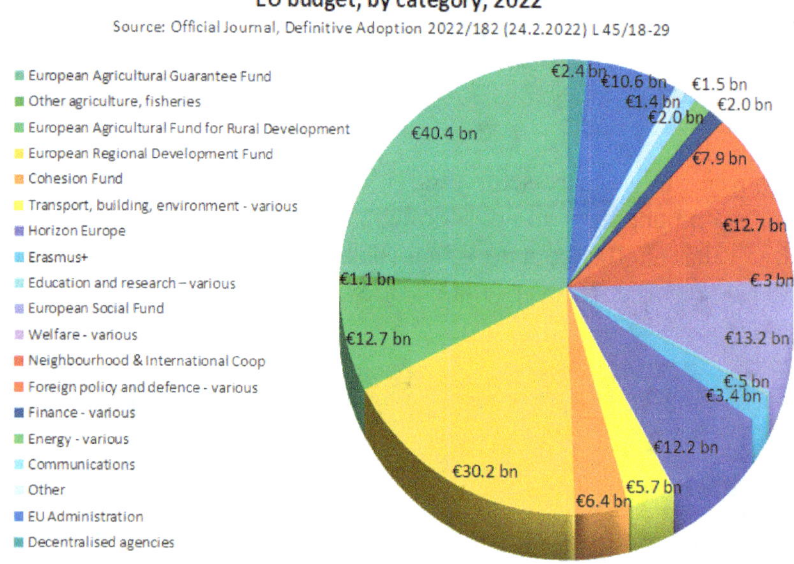

The Structural Funds

The latter, which we have already met,[381] are traditional instruments of public intervention, since they mainly provide grants. However, they can also provide repayable grants and, more recently, financial instruments. There are six of these: the European Social Fund (ESF), the European Agricultural Guidance and Guarantee Fund (EAGGF Guidance Section), the European Regional Development Fund (ERDF), the Cohesion Fund, the European Agricultural Fund for Rural Development (EAFRD) and the European Maritime Affairs and Fisheries Fund (EMAFF).

The Recovery Plan has not forgotten them: an additional €47.5 billion has been or will be made available to three of them, as has already been explained before.[382]

An Assessment of the Work of the Structural Funds

While the Structural Funds are useful, their record is mixed and could be improved.

(i) Positive Elements

On the plus side, in addition to the contribution to the assisted regions, the money injected has a secondary circulation (30% of the amounts distributed), via orders from the public authorities concerned. It therefore has a leverage or multiplier effect. This effect is reinforced by the obligation on beneficiaries of structural funding to use only suppliers established in the EU.[383]

381 *See* above, Title I, Ch. 2, D.

382 Ibid.

383 So, contrary to a fifteenth popular opinion, there is at least a partial counterpart to the Build America, Buy America Act.

Another, more recent, form of secondary circulation is the recovery by the Structural Funds of part of the sums paid out in the form of loans, guarantees or equity investments and their reinvestment, as already mentioned.

Since 2013, the emphasis has been on the contribution of eligible projects to combating unemployment and increasing the employment rate.

The Structural Funds also encourage cooperation between the European level and the national, regional or local levels. They make Europe a reality and encourage the exchange of best practice. In particular, some local or regional authorities are quick to call on the expertise of the European Investment Fund (EIF)[384] to implement certain programmes.[385] This is the case for the city of Montpellier.

(ii) Impairments

To be eligible, projects must pursue priority objectives. However, in practice, the positive impact is not sufficiently examined. The European contribution, which accounts for the lion's share, can have a disempowering effect on national or subnational public authorities.

Moreover, success varies greatly from one Member State to another. More than 60 years after the birth of the European Economic Community (EEC), the Mezzogiorno is still lagging behind. Why is this?

Too much emphasis is still placed on subsidies. As a result, money can only be distributed once.

384 The EIF is a specialised subsidiary of the European Investment Bank. Created in 1994 to combat the crisis and unemployment, it aims to facilitate the financing of small and medium-sized enterprises.

385 This is yet another way in which the EU can help Member States, or parts of them, to grow. The ingenious instruments and astuteness deployed at European level should not be underestimated.

There are also invasive and cautious controls. A portion of the budgets is never spent and is returned to the net contributor Member States. It is therefore a mass of financial resources that do not benefit the regions in need.

(iii) Suggestions

Greater emphasis could be placed on a development policy and concern for added value, the impact of European structural funding and therefore the real driving force behind the projects financed – in short, a culture of results. It would be useful for independent studies to be carried out and mechanisms put in place to assess the effectiveness of this method of intervention and to improve it (for example, via peer review, i.e. by the competent authorities of the other Member States, as is done in the area of financial supervision). One possibility would be to require a multiplier coefficient for approved measures and a country-by-country comparison of the results obtained.

If public authorities favour financial instruments (guarantees, loans, equity), they have a better chance of recovering part of their investment and being able to allocate it to new projects. This flexibility, which has been available since 2013, should be extended and used more widely (as should the policy of positive incentives for structural reforms).[386]

It is even questionable whether the subsidy instrument is compatible with the open and highly competitive social market economy that the EU aims to promote. At first glance, it is not aligned with the objectives of European integration.[387] In my opinion, it should only be used when absolutely necessary and as a last resort. *The place still given to subsidies in cohesion policy reveals too much conservatism, too much loyalty to the traditional mechanisms of intervention of certain*

386 Along these lines, *see EDB* 11191 of 24 November 2017.

387 *See* above, Title I, Ch. 2, F.

Member States. National interests see the EU as a windfall, which they finance only very marginally and are seeking to appropriate for themselves. The EU must move away from such failings. We can no longer afford to be so unambitious.

In a way, just as the pursuit of prosperity must not overshadow other dimensions, solidarity must incorporate certain elements of economic rationality.

The approach to determining the level of European support is also too arithmetical. As well as regions that are more or less poor, those that are in decline or in danger of being so should be treated more favourably. On the one hand, it is better to intervene quickly to halt such a spiral. On the other hand, empirical studies have shown that Euroscepticism thrives in such regions.[388]

An extreme solution would be to abolish the Structural Funds and transfer their powers and resources to the EIB, the EIF or even another specialised subsidiary of the EIB to be created, and to replace subsidies with financial techniques. In fact, as we shall see, their balance sheet is better while involving a lower cost for the community.

B. The Work of the European Investment Bank (EIB)

Financing metros, hospitals, eco-responsible social buildings, promising companies such as BioNTech and CureVac, etc., cohesion policy has been able to rely on one of the finest achievements of European integration: the EIB. In our opinion, the EIB has developed more effective means of action that consume less public money than the Structural Funds.

388 L. Dijkstra, H. Poelman and A. Rodriguez-Pose, "Géographie du mécontentement et du mal-être dans l'UE", *Telos*, 2 March 2020.

As the financial arm of the European Union, the EIB has a significant capacity to raise capital on the markets (over €60 billion a year). Its history should provide food for thought and inspiration. It was created in 1957 by the Member States in the form of a bank to limit their risk. The Member States were poor at the time. Unwilling to give the EIB a budget with the unlimited obligation to make up the deficit, they endowed it with capital. The EIB therefore had to borrow on the financial markets and then lend accordingly.

The rest we know, or unfortunately do not know well enough:[389] while financing public and private projects that make a tangible contribution to achieving European objectives, the EIB has been managed carefully to ensure financial responsibility, and has gradually become the world's largest economic development bank. It has the highest possible rating: AAA. It is to banking what Airbus is to aeronautics: a high-performance giant. When Europeans work together carefully on concrete projects, they need have no fear of anyone.

389 During an introductory course in European banking and finance law that I am giving at a prestigious Parisian university, I was struck by the fact that none of the students on the Master's course knew anything about the EIB.

Figure 27.[390]

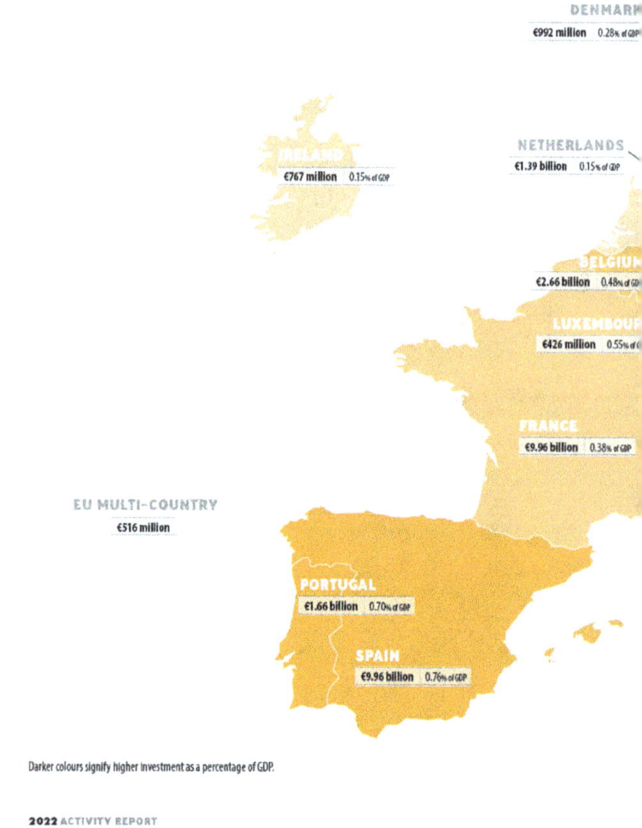

390 EIB, *Secure Europe: 2022 Activity Report*, Luxembourg, EIB, 2023, pp. 10–11.

FINLAND
€1.16 billion 0.43% of GDP
SWEDEN
€1.95 billion 0.35% of GDP
ESTONIA
€172 million 0.48% of GDP
LATVIA
€300 million 0.79% of GDP
LITHUANIA
€303 million 0.45% of GDP
POLAND
€5.45 billion 0.83% of GDP
GERMANY
€6.61 billion 0.17% of GDP
CZECH REPUBLIC
€1.85 billion 0.66% of GDP
SLOVAKIA
€54.5 million 0.05% of GDP
AUSTRIA
€1.62 billion 0.36% of GDP
HUNGARY
€804 million 0.50% of GDP
ROMANIA
€1.01 billion 0.36% of GDP
SLOVENIA
€42 million 0.07% of GDP
CROATIA
€218 million 0.33% of GDP
BULGARIA
€494 million 0.60% of GDP
ITALY
€10.09 billion 0.53% of GDP
GREECE
€2.19 billion 1.04% of GDP
€250 million 0.94% of GDP
CYPRUS
MALTA
€20 million 0.12% of GDP

The activity of the EIB and its subsidiary the EIF represents an average contribution of 0.88% to the GDP of the Member States in 2021 (with a range from 0.16% to 2.7%) as figure 27 above shows. When you consider that EIB and EIF financing generates an added value of 40% and that it is accompanied by other financing five times greater, the impact and effectiveness of these financial arms is clear.

On this last point, the EIB intervenes only as a last resort and as a complement to the traditional banking and financial system. It finances projects that must be viable (there is no question of supporting lame ducks) up to a maximum of 20%, acting as a back-up. It's a question of additionality, of responding to a partial market failure, but also of economic viability. It makes it possible to carry out projects that would not otherwise see the light of day. *It widens the circle of reasonable possibilities.* The approach is anything but utopian. The EIB has a catalytic and multiplier role. It also has a counter-cyclical role, since it will have to intervene to a greater extent in economic downturns.

In a nutshell, the EIB is an improved Keynesian policy instrument from several points of view: less public intervention, since it operates on the sidelines,[391] with a limited impact on competition,[392] financed in large part by the financial markets, including those of third countries. In this respect, we return to the role of the financial operator, which can be likened to an exporting company,[393] attracting more and more financial resources to the EU from the rest of the world. This money is not used for current consumption, but rather for investments that will increase Europe's economic strength in the long term. The multiplier effect is therefore normally higher and longer-lasting than that resulting from

391 And, consequently, respectful of the principle of an open economy based on free competition.

392 It does not affect competition in the financing sector since it finances what is not financed by it. Any distortions will concern the market in which the financed project operates. However, other operators in this market are free to apply for EIB financing, which is granted on the basis of objective criteria. Furthermore, the projects financed by the EIB pursue European objectives in one way or another.

393 On this question, *see* above, Title I, Ch. 1, B, 3.

an increase in purchasing power under a classic Keynesian policy. It is all the more so because many of the projects financed by the EIB are initiated by the private sector and all are financed mainly by the traditional financial sector. We can expect the former to have higher expectations of profitability than the public sector, and the latter to be concerned about the viability of projects.

It is worth noting in passing that the EIB's involvement is now compatible with the principle of an open economy with free competition. It has also become a standard, a must.

Since 1957, the EIB has developed considerable and varied expertise in assessing the viability of projects and developing innovative financial instruments and financing techniques in line with EU objectives and priorities.

For example, it extends to sustainable and eco-responsible finance. As one of its vice-presidents reminded politicians who wanted to create a green public bank in Europe, it already exists and is called the EIB.[394] It was the world's first issuer of green bonds in 2007, i.e. bonds whose entire proceeds are allocated to eco-responsible projects. Today, it remains the market leader.

One constant in its activities is the contribution it makes to the economic, social and, today, territorial cohesion of the EU.

Not only does the EIB lend, but it also provides advisory services (based on its long experience and the expertise it has gradually built up), with a view to enhancing the impact of its financing operations. This second important activity is another way in which the public sector intervenes in the economy, with a view to making life easier for economic operators.

394 A. Fayolle, "Une banque européenne du climat ? Oui, mais elle existe déjà !", *Les Echos*, 11 January 2019.

The European objectives pursued by the EIB evolve in line with the EU's political priorities. Currently, the EIB is investing heavily in energy transition and efficiency[395] as well as in urban renewal.

The EIB also has a vision of the European economy as a whole, through all its activities. The analyses of its macroeconomic department deserve to be given more attention and should be taken into greater consideration by the political world. The EIB's 2022–2023 report on investment, published at the end of February 2023, points to the lack of investment in Europe and calls for action to meet the structural challenges following the example of this essay.

The EIB's return on investment is significant.

The EIB is a jewel of the EU. It is probably the fruit of its financial responsibility, its systematic risk management, its subsidiarity and complementarity with the traditional financial sector, and the development of new intervention techniques. It is also the result of in-depth work and the coming together of extremely diverse knowledge, cultures, profiles and backgrounds. In addition to lawyers and economists, the EIB is home to engineers, doctors… and many others. It is home to a very rich human community.

Financial responsibility, concern for economic viability, added value and multiplier effect, additionality in relation to the market, avoidance of distortions of competition, pursuit of European objectives, technical expertise and rigour, emergence of a specifically European approach irreducible to a national conception, working with economic operators and national and subnational public authorities. These ideas and guidelines should inspire European initiatives in general.

395 For example, 25% of the EIB's portfolio consists of climate-friendly projects. This proportion is set to double in the coming years (European Green Deal, section 2.2.1, "Pursuing green finance and investment and ensuring a just transition").

In passing, it should be noted that the EIB is not a standard-setting institution. It collects money and allocates it to projects, investing it in the European economy. In a pragmatic way, it is gradually developing standards of management and social and environmental responsibility. We need to ask ourselves whether the EU should do more of this in the future. I will come back to this at a later stage.[396]

C. The European Investment Fund (EIF)

Since 1994, the EIB has had a subsidiary, the EIF, which specialises in riskier investments such as guarantees for SMEs and private equity (taking stakes in unlisted companies).

The EIF, which mainly manages third-party funds, currently has around €100 billion invested in these products, alongside private investors. Given that the EIF always takes a minority stake (as it does in EIB financing), the multiplier effect is considerable. Thanks to its unique expertise in due diligence and analysis of the viability of promising companies, the EIF is able to bring together public and private investors.[397] In recognition of its key role and effectiveness, its capital was increased by 70% in early 2021.

The EIF's reduction in the asymmetry of information between investors and the issuer (the company in which the investment is made) is noteworthy. Once again, this is typical of a structural/modern supply-side policy. Through its analysis, the EIF fills an information gap and facilitates the matching of capital supply and demand. It provides investors with enough reliable information to help them decide to "jump into cold water".

---

396 *See* below under D and the conclusions of the essay.

397 In this respect, the EIF is a supply-side policy mechanism that respects the market economy.

Overcoming this asymmetry of information is all the more crucial in Europe, where the average size of economic operators and their comparability are much lower than in the United States.[398]

To a certain extent, the imperfections of the internal market and in particular the small size of the vast majority of companies make bodies such as the EIB and the EIF, public finance companies at national level and, in the private sector, collective investment vehicles all the more important. While the latter make it possible to attract retail investors, the EIB, the EIF and the public investment companies, in particular, make up for the lack of private financing for companies.

D. The Juncker Plan, InvestEU, the EIB and the EIF

The Juncker Plan is one of the major success stories of recent years. With just €21 billion, including €16 billion in guarantees, the EU, via the EIB and the EIF, has raised more than €500 billion,[399] 70% of which in private investment, as figure 28 below shows.[400] The initial, albeit ambitious, target of €315 billion has therefore been well exceeded. The leverage effect is 25, instead of the expected 15.

398 *See* above, Title I, Ch. 1, A.

399 According to the March 2022 figures, the total is €524.3 billion.

400 Taken from the European Commission website, under the tab relating to the Investment Plan results.

Figure 28.

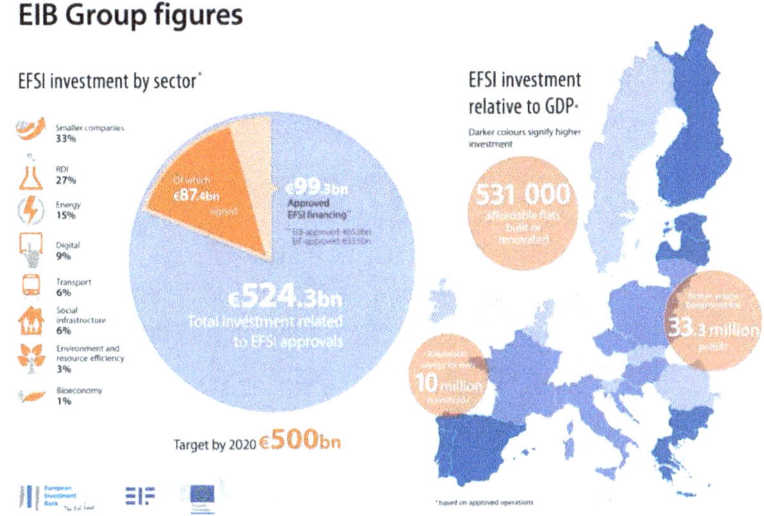

This is a remarkable example of additionality and proportionality: the public authorities have provided just what was needed (small amounts, simple guarantees instead of loans or even subsidies) to generate momentum, financed for the most part by the private sector. Public intervention was adjusted to the level of default, or more precisely the level of investor reluctance.

This reduces the cost to the community. What is more, the impact is far greater than that of a grant or even a loan. In this respect, in addition to the leverage effect, the viability requirements of the projects to be financed by the EIB and the EIF and the predominantly private financing may have led to more successful investments than public subsidies.

Once again, such an initiative has been taken at a time when public finances are in dire straits,[401] following the banking crisis and then

401 As in 1957, when the European Economic Community was created, it was decided to set up the EIB as a bank rather than a fund.

the budget crisis. For this initiative alone, the former president of the European Commission, Jean-Claude Juncker, should enter the annals of history.

In addition, this approach has reduced the distortions of competition that would have resulted from granting subsidies to individual companies.

There is now a second Juncker Plan with a section devoted more to venture capital, research and innovation, the InvestEU Programme, which has already been discussed.[402] Given the higher-risk level of the projects to be financed, the expected leverage effect has been limited to 14 and the initial objective is to mobilise €650 billion of private investment.[403]

This "Juncker Plan II" is an essential element: we need to be able to reduce Europe's investment deficit. Four sectors have been targeted in the first instance: (i) R&D&I, an area in which the EU is falling behind;[404] (ii) infrastructure and digitalisation; (iii) SMEs; and (iv) social investment and talent. As has already been mentioned, the Recovery Plan has added €31 billion in guarantees for strategic sectors. However, as a reminder, this should not detract from the potential of deepening the internal market.

Towards a Strengthening of the EU's Financial Action Rather Than Its Budgetary Capacity?

The successes of the EIB, the EIF and the Juncker Plan raise questions about the best ways for the EU to intervene. Contributing to productive investment in the European economy and society, largely financed by the markets, is a role that the Union, acting through the EIB and the EIF,[405] plays well and could assume on a larger scale.

---

402 *See* above, Title I, Ch. 1, B, 1, on R&D&I and Title I, Ch. 2, D, on the European Recovery Plan.

403 If the leverage of 15 is maintained, the target should be raised to €1,125 billion, taking into account the increase in the initial public stake to €75 billion following the European Recovery Plan.

404 *See* above, Title I, Ch. 1, B, 1.

405 Who are looking to further improve their performance, in particular by digitalising and speeding up their decision-making processes.

The European budget is small compared with that of the Member States and the US federal state. It is equivalent to 1 or 1.2% of European GDP, or €150–160 billion, representing around €300 per inhabitant per year. In passing, let's wring the neck of this duck:[406] Europe is not expensive, a fraction of the average smoker's annual cigarette budget (€2,555).

Member States' budgets range from 30% to 60% of national GNP, with an average of almost 50% (or even more after the pandemic and with the war in Ukraine). To give an idea, before the pandemic, France's budget was 57%, while Germany's was 42%. The US federal budget is equivalent to 30% of US GDP, and the Swiss federal budget is equivalent to 17% of Swiss GDP. The EU budget is therefore small, since it is equivalent to half the revenue of the French state.

However, to this must be added €60 billion in loans per year from the EIB, bearing in mind that €555 billion is currently lent by it – an amount roughly comparable to almost four times the EU budget – and the €100 billion invested by the EIF.

Should this type of action not be stepped up? Following Brexit, several Member States sought to increase their stake in the EIB: Romania, Poland and Luxembourg. They have understood the leverage offered by the EIB.

I also put forward the idea that the Structural Funds could disappear in favour of an increase in the responsibilities and financial resources of the EIB Group, given the greater return on investment of the latter.[407]

In view of the leverage role that the construction of Europe is intended to fulfil, the maximum added value that each of its initiatives must present, and the fact that the EU is a light superstructure with low

406 *See* above, Introduction.

407 *See* above, A.

operating costs, it is essential that the European institutions and bodies (such as the EIB and the EIF) are able to make a maximum of productive investments and financing. Alongside perfecting the internal market (Chapter 1 of Title I) and helping to improve public action (Chapter 2 of Title II), this activity of investing, financing and catalysing private investment is a third driver of European growth.

The public authorities in Europe have little room for manoeuvre, even though the level of national debt was falling before the pandemic (around 80% of GDP; since then, it has risen above 90% and will fall back to 85% by the end of 2022). Additional public funding for EU action in the broad sense (including the EIB and the EIF) is not realistic in the immediate future. What's more, with Brexit, EU revenues have been reduced by around 15%. Not to mention the impact of the pandemic and the war in Ukraine.

It would therefore be conceivable to make greater use of private finance to modernise the European economy, in particular through the EIB and the EIF.

E. The Potential of Economic, Social and Territorial Cohesion Policy

Economic, social and territorial cohesion is rich in potential. The scope of this policy could evolve and be enriched.

Towards a More Structured Europe?

This is still centred on the states and regions, with the idea of a benchmark between them. But can the EU's economic, social and territorial cohesion not go beyond this horizontal relationship between the various parts of the EU?

Given that the EU is a large internal market where the factors of production are freely allocated, and even a growing union of the populations of the Member States, does cohesion policy not imply interconnections, coordination, perhaps even integration? As well as reducing disparities between Member States, which is relatively abstract because it is arithmetical, should cohesion not be a feature of the large economic entity that the Member States and the EU constitute? Does it not presuppose a certain articulation between its different components, interactions, exchange mechanisms, an organisation, consistency and substance of its own?

Certain lessons could be drawn from this in terms of European regional planning. Does an infrastructure project such as the Rhine-Saône Canal, whose rationality can be questioned in a strictly French context, not make more sense at a European level?[408] Should we not be pushing for cross-border, joint projects that are truly European, such as a gas pipeline from the Iberian Peninsula to Germany? Should truly European or global "champions" not be created?

Towards Greater Coordination Between Member States?

Cohesion policy could have implications in terms of support, development aid, distribution and even coordination of centres of excellence across the EU. A Marshallese district is a centre, a critical mass in a field, which generates external economies of scale.[409] Examples include Silicon Valley, the City of London, the Toulouse-Bordeaux axis in aeronautics, Milan and the surrounding area in fashion and design, and the Ruhr in steel and heavy industry.

408 *See* above, Title I, Ch. 1, B, 6.

409 Defraigne and Nouveau, 3rd ed., p. 18.

We could imagine a degree of specialisation between Member States, with regions, centres and Marshallese districts complementing rather than competing with each other, as part of cohesion policy.

Towards Strengthening Each Member State

That being said, this Community interest must not be pursued at the expense of the interests of the Member States. As has been pointed out, a Member State remains a state in its own right, with all the responsibilities that implies, particularly in budgetary terms.[410] In order to assume these responsibilities, a Member State must have the means to do so.

Europe must make each Member State stronger or, more precisely, enable it to become stronger. Otherwise, it will be reduced to a board of certain states, a protectorate of the other Member States. With the risk of certain Member States leaving the club, Europe must represent added value for all the Member States. This may involve the opportunity to become a centre of excellence in a particular activity.

Greater account should also be taken of the differences in objective situations between Member States and the challenges facing some of them. As already mentioned, one example is the disappearance of major domestic economic players in certain states, especially the small and medium-sized states[411] and the new members from Central and Eastern Europe. The main companies in the latter have gone under foreign flags, most often from larger western Member States. The only company from one of these countries in the top 500 of the world's largest companies is Polish, PKN Orlen.[412]

As a result, the prosperity of these countries depends to a greater extent on their ability to attract direct investment from operators in

410 *See* Title I, Ch. 2, A.

411 Belgium, Austria, Ireland, Portugal and Greece, in particular. *See* Defraigne and Nouveau, 3rd ed., p. 97.

412 Ibid., p. 451.

other Member States or even third countries. To this end, the levers on which these states can act are more limited: wage moderation, attractive taxation, hosting low-cost production.

Their lower labour productivity (due in particular to technological backwardness – there are fewer patents and royalties per capita, for example) is offset by a significant wage differential, less social protection, longer working hours and tax competition. If we want to give them the – legitimate – opportunity to loosen this tourniquet and move up the production ladder (as Hungary, Slovenia and Estonia are doing, with figures for patents and royalties comparable to those of the leading Member States) and salaries, the question arises as to what the EU can do to help them do so. In other words, these countries differ from the other Member States not only in terms of their lower economic level, but also in terms of the macroeconomic characteristics that need to be taken into account in any cohesion policy.

In this respect, it should be noted that the budgetary discipline imposed by European integration can, paradoxically, be an advantage. In the long term, it can free up room for manoeuvre so that these states can lay down the conditions for the development of new activities or even investments. It is often overlooked that a Member State can act as a long-term market economy investor, for example via public holding companies investing for the long term.

Finally, these considerations once again argue in favour of a larger internal market, and therefore greater opportunities for growth for SMEs in all Member States.

F. Conclusion

A cohesion policy that places greater emphasis on financial instruments within the Structural Funds (or even following a transfer of responsibilities in this area to the EIB-EIF group) and a second, even more ambitious Juncker Plan (InvestEU) should be able to generate 2% more GDP in the EU, or an additional €320 billion per year.

In total, the reform proposals set out in Title I and Chapter 1 of Title II should, based on a cautious approach, generate a surplus of 12.5% of GDP in the EU27, or almost €2,000 billion.

This should make it possible to combat social insecurity, make it easier to manage two careers within families with more children, decarbonise the European economy and make it cleaner overall, including agriculture, increase our energy autonomy, strengthen our common defence, increase our generosity towards developing countries and assume greater responsibility for a better state of the world, as we shall see in the following chapters and titles. In other words, this increased prosperity should enable Europe to begin the second half of its work, devoted to qualitative non-economic policies.

Chapter 2

Social Europe, Social Justice, Social Democracy

Why Is There So Much Social Disillusionment With, and Even Distrust of, Europe?

Some sections of the population feel that they have nothing to gain from European integration, and sometimes even losing out.[413] They feel insecure, downgraded and even disrespected.[414] There are growing objections to the distribution of the benefits of Europe.

The 2008 financial crisis deepened the wound. The loss was severe for some social categories. Those responsible for the crisis have not been identified and punished. Hence the feeling of frustration and injustice.

Since the launch of European integration, three fundamental trends have contributed to a decline in the relative position of a number of workers.

413 These include workers, SME owners and residents of regions that are losing ground.

414 On the importance of leaders respecting the people, *see* G. Da Empoli, "Les cinq erreurs de Matteo Renzi qu'Emmanuel Macron devrait méditer", *Le Monde*, 21 January 2020.

First of all, the Communist bloc has disappeared. It was partly to ward off the spread of the ideas of this bloc to the West that the common market was created: the productivity gains of the common market would make it possible to pay employees well.[415] The Communist world also gave way to an external pressure in the opposite direction, exerting downward impact on wages: globalisation. Countries that had moved to a market economy represented competition for European workers. This is also the background to the EU's eastward enlargement. This has made it possible to keep lower-cost production within the EU.

Secondly, wage moderation has been all the more marked because globalisation has been accompanied by a loss of competitiveness in the European economy and a slide down the technological ladder. As a result, a number of jobs created in Europe recently are paid less in relative terms than in the past. This partly explains the lack of enthusiasm for the almost halving of unemployment in Europe between 2013 and 2019. This has not put an end to job insecurity. This brings us back to the question of productivity.[416]

Finally, the increasingly financial nature of the economy and the liberalisation of trade have increased the production of wealth, but have widened the gaps within the European population.

Europe's Social Responsibility

Europe is softening the blow of this fundamental change in conditions, not least because most of our economic trade takes place within the EU.[417] However, this is insufficient consolation given the worrying social situation in Europe.

415 *See* above, Foreword.

416 *See* above, Introduction, "A Balance Sheet in Jeopardy?"

417 At the same time, the shock-absorbing mattress that is Europe can contribute to drowsiness and a loss of responsiveness. As the consequences of certain global trends are reduced or deferred, European society is slow to address its structural vulnerabilities.

It is striking that 21.6%[418] of the population remain at risk of poverty (with a peak of 24.8% in 2012[419]) despite the 45% fall in unemployment in the EU between 2013 and 2019; 5.8% remain below the poverty line[420] (compared with 8.5% in 2008, when the banking crisis was triggered – a reduction of 30%). Youth unemployment is more than double the average rate. In addition, more than a quarter of the population is at risk of poverty or social exclusion in almost a quarter of Member States: Bulgaria (32.8%), Romania (32.5%),[421] Greece (31.8%), Latvia (28.4%), Italy (27.3%) and Spain (26.1%). The fertility rate is falling (1.5% while the population renewal rate is 2.1).

The comparison of two figures is worth what it's worth, but it does raise questions. While the Juncker Plan has exceeded its investment targets by 50%, only 40% of the objective of lifting 20 million Europeans out of the risk of poverty by 2020 has been achieved![422] While growth and even the beginnings of structural progress have led to an improvement in the social situation, this still remains insufficient.

The EU's mission is the well-being of its people. It must work for the sustainable development of Europe, based in particular on a highly competitive SOCIAL market economy: aiming at full employment and social progress; combating social exclusion and discrimination, promoting social justice and protection; contributing to a high level of employment, quality education, development of human capital, social protection, etc.

418 That is to say, at least one of the following three situations: at risk of poverty after social transfers (monetary poverty), in a situation of severe material deprivation or living in households with very low work intensity (figures for 2020, *Key figures on Europe*, 2023, p. 27).

419 Social transfers reduce the at-risk-of-poverty rate to 17%.

420 More specifically, severe material deprivation: their living conditions are limited by a lack of resources, such as not being able to pay their bills, heat their home properly or take a week's holiday away from home.

421 Even though these two countries have seen the sharpest fall in at-risk-of-poverty rates.

422 Or even less (*see* the interview with O. de Schutter in the *EDB* 12477 of 30 April 2020).

It is welcome that the current Commissioner for Employment and Social Rights, Nicolas Schmit, wants to restore the importance of this axis of European integration,[423] in particular the social market economy.

Europe also has a clear interest in tackling social issues. In the face of the current changes, it is being used as a scapegoat. It is up to Europe to demonstrate the added value it can bring in the face of growing social unrest. Once again, the impact of its action will be vital. It must be able to help its people grow.

Given this fundamental change in background, we need to think about how to preserve and strengthen social justice, the social market economy, social democracy and, ultimately, our democracy. Without jeopardising the prosperity of the people of Europe as a whole.

Solutions?

In our view, a new situation calls for new solutions. We need to distinguish between the objective of social justice and the means of achieving it. A number of systems and mechanisms need to be adjusted, or even new ones created. At the same time, we need to take into account the EU's strengths and limitations.

A Structural/Modern and Comprehensive Supply Policy?

The recommendations put forward in this essay should help to increase both the employment rate and pay levels: mutual recognition and deepening of the internal market, a proactive employment policy, particularly through the European Semester,[424] a move up the value-

423 *EDB* 12428, 19 February 2020.

424 *See* above, Title I, Ch. 2.

added ladder and greater efforts in R&D&I, reindustrialisation, efforts in the areas of training and employability, and an increase in purchasing power through structural measures.

The idea has also been to launch a dynamic on a virtuous triangle, i.e. a self-supporting growth having to be both clean and inclusive. In particular, the single market was created to safeguard the competitiveness of Member States' economies *in the interest of the whole population.* If the single market makes it possible to generate greater prosperity, this should not be confined to certain sections of society.[425]

Various financial mechanisms have also been implemented to help vulnerable workers in the face of economic change or exceptional events. These include the European Social Fund (ESF), the European Social Fund Plus (ESF+), the European Globalisation Adjustment Fund for Displaced Workers (EGF) and, as part of the fight against Covid-19, the SURE instrument.[426]

Let us assume, however, that structural policies are not sufficient to raise the level of earned income, at least for a significant proportion of the population. Let us also assume that the surplus in economic activity, coupled with improved management of public finances and more investment, does not allow Member States to reduce the tax burden on earned incomes; that the cost of living is not sufficiently reduced by certain measures in favour of consumers (ban on roaming, reduction in the cost of energy, proactive competition policy, etc.).

425 "Income inequality within EU countries has increased in recent decades, despite the mitigating impact of redistribution policies. Real EU GDP per capita has grown by 45% since 1995. However, the pre-tax income of the bottom 50% has grown by only 16%, while that of the top 1% has grown by 50%... Meanwhile, wealth inequality, which is much higher than income inequality, remains a driver of future income inequality through returns on assets such as real estate and equity." (*EIB Investment Report 2019/2020*, p. 13).

426 European temporary support instrument to mitigate the risk of unemployment in emergency situations caused by the spread of Covid-19, created in 2020.

Towards More Proactive, Even More Invasive and Authoritarian Measures?

What other type of measures should be taken? The question needs to be asked, given the critical social situation in Europe and the time it takes for structural/modern supply-side policy measures to take effect.

As a result, we need to be able to envisage more restrictive measures with a more direct impact.[427]

(i) Towards the introduction of a Minimum Hourly Wage?

Given the wide variation in the standard of living from one Member State to another, such a wage cannot be uniform. Indeed, some Member States need low labour costs in order to survive with the hope of gradually moving upmarket. Imposing a minimum hourly wage on Romania and Bulgaria, or even other Central European countries, identical to that in Western Europe would condemn them to poverty.

In addition, in order not to penalise economic development, the minimum wage must be set taking into account labour productivity in the state in question.

The proposal put forward by the current European Commissioner for Employment and Social Rights, Nicolas Schmit, seems to take these constraints into account. It is based on the observation that there is a gap of one to six between minimum wages in the EU, whereas the differences in productivity only range from one to three.[428] It therefore aims to bring them more into line with the level of labour productivity observed in the Member State concerned.[429]

427 This does not exclude private financing initiatives, such as social impact bonds, i.e. the subscription by private investors of bonds to "finance innovative projects aimed at making a measurable contribution to solving problems whose social cost is known" (P. Hermant, "Le potentiel négligé des 'social impact bonds' pour sortir de la crise", *L'Echo*, 23 January 2021, p. 19 (in French)).

428 On the inadequacy of the minimum wage in certain Member States, *see EDB* 12413 of 29 January 2020, p. 17.

429 *See EDB* 12386 of 10 December 2019 and 12499 of 5 June 2020.

It should be pointed out that the desirability of a minimum wage is a matter of debate and that this issue is approached very differently from one country to another. While Luxembourg has such a wage, which is very high compared with that set in other Member States, Switzerland, which is comparable in some respects, has no such mechanism. Its justification is that it is too dependent on the state of the world (Switzerland exports a huge amount, as much as France in terms of value with a population one eighth the size, both to the EU and to third countries).

The disparity in national approaches explains why the directive finally adopted on 19 October 2022 only requires the establishment of adequate minimum wages and the promotion of collective bargaining. It is, however, a first step.

(ii) Towards a Compensatory Allowance for Low-Productivity Workers?

One counterproductive effect of a minimum hourly wage (especially when it is badly calibrated) is to keep people whose productivity is insufficient out of work.

Another approach would be, in the absence of a minimum hourly wage or where the employer cannot pay it, to allow the market to operate at company level and for the difference between the wage and the minimum or virtual hourly wage to be paid by the state. One variant would be a negative tax for these workers. Such a measure has the dual advantage of providing initial access to the world of work and enabling a series of activities of some utility to be undertaken. However, it can be very costly for the public authorities and, ultimately, for taxpayers.

(iii) Social Responsibility of Companies and Public Authorities?

Given the greater potential given to companies by the internal market, especially the larger ones, and even the (relative) disengagement of the Member States, the social responsibility of companies could be increased.

Since European integration has given more scope to companies, or at least to some of them, is it not conceivable that they should be more concerned about the positive impacts of their actions? Can we encourage them, or even require them, to mobilise their financial, human or operational resources for certain actions with a societal impact in addition to their economic activity?

From an economic point of view, there would also be a certain rationality in proceeding in this way. Generally speaking, activities with a strong social impact are not sufficiently profitable economically. If they benefit from free or almost free assistance in terms of infrastructure, logistics and material resources, their costs fall and they can break even. In addition, public subsidies are saved.

This would be a form of contribution in kind by companies, which would cost them nothing, in theory. Economically, it could be justified by the fact that the single market and the measures taken to facilitate economic activity have enabled them to increase their capital stock, in particular their infrastructure. However, in the current state of European construction, this approach is only true for large companies.[430] Why would it be unthinkable to make this available outside production hours? It would be "collectivised", becoming a common asset in hours that would in any case be lost to the company.

430 On the reason for this reservation, *see* the imperfections of the single market for SMEs, above, Title I, Ch. 1.

Of course, it is a long way from idea to realisation. It may be a vision, a utopia or even a pipe dream. I am not underestimating the difficulties in terms of surveillance, insurance, and the risks of damaging or jeopardising the confidentiality of data.

But it is worth thinking about this: is there not a way for companies to make resources available at no cost for causes that have an undeniable social benefit?[431]

The same applies to public infrastructures (which are generally closed earlier than companies). Are they not part of the common heritage?

This would reduce the obstacles to the development of social, cultural and philanthropic activities by lowering or removing barriers to access.

A less radical measure is the current ESG (Environment, Social and Governance) movement. The idea is twofold. On the one hand, companies must integrate the impact of these aspects, especially environmental risk, into the evaluation of their activities and investments. On the other hand, they must be vigilant to ensure that their actions, investments and supply chain comply with environmental, soci(et)al, good governance and human rights factors (proposal for a "vigilance" directive). The idea is to contribute not only to making the economy greener, but also to making it more inclusive[432] and even more ethical.

(iv) A Tax on Wealth?

Insofar as the relative share of GDP accounted for by labour is declining in favour of that of capital, we might also consider a moderate wealth tax, to be paid as soon as a minimum threshold of wealth is reached. However, it is likely that objections to an additional tax will

431 Or in exchange for a responsible contribution to costs (cleaning, etc.). Free service often leads to a lack of respect and the impression that everything is due. I have seen this in my own practice, where the most shameless customers are those who have been given a gift of one kind or another.

432 The social dimension is taken into account in the European Green Deal (section 1 in particular).

be raised in some Member States about the current quality of public management. Hence the usefulness of a more proactive approach by the EU to improving the quality of public management, as advocated above.[433] A wealth tax is accepted in Switzerland: on the one hand, tax deductions are moderate; on the other hand, the services provided to the population by the public sector are of high quality. Can the same be said of all EU Member States?

(v) Shareholder or Bondholder in the EU Company?

The idea of securities calculated on the wealth produced by the European economy, of which every citizen would receive a theoretically reduced fraction, seems to me more realistic and less disconnected from economic reality than that of a universal income. The principle that every citizen is a shareholder or bondholder in the European economy and as such has a minimum right should be developed further. Those with other incomes would not be entitled (unless they were below certain thresholds, in which case they would be entitled on a pro rata basis).

We could also think of a banking and/or insurance product. Every European citizen would be given an account at birth with a capital sum. This account would be funded by their own contributions, or even by certain public contributions, in order to cover certain risks. This account could be used as a guarantee for financing, and even to a certain extent for withdrawals.

Another idea would be for any European citizen to finance a project, for example an entrepreneurial project, up to a certain amount.

With increasing life expectancy, more discontinuous lives, changes in activity, breaks, migration, the need for regular upgrades and adaptations, the social consequences of digitalisation and artificial

433 *See* above, Title I, Ch. 2.

intelligence or other new technologies, insurance and social cover products could be rethought. The EU probably has a role to play in supporting the Member States or providing a minimum foundation.

So, once again, we need to think in terms of today's reality and invent new mechanisms.

(vi) Social Mobility

Another important point is the social ladder. Is having a job enough? Given the level of salaries and the comparative level of certain durable goods such as housing, this is doubtful. Thirty years ago, a family on a single good income could support itself. Today, two salaries are probably necessary. But are they enough? Of course, people consume more and are encouraged to do so. Leaving this aside, is it still possible for the middle classes, and even more so the modest classes, to improve their living conditions and those of their children?

Social mobility should be monitored. In a democracy, it is essential for the population to have prospects for advancement. A functioning social ladder and a sufficiently high or even high birth rate are signs of a healthy society.[434]

(vii) Birth Rate and Family Policy

As explained in the introduction, the European population is shrinking, with women having an average of 1.5 children, whereas the population maintenance rate is 2.1.

Even today, it is difficult for women to reconcile work and having a family. Tremendous resourcefulness is required to ensure that both members of the couple can continue to work while having at least two children, can look after them and have a fulfilling private life.

---

434 However, it would seem that the figures belie the impression that the social ladder has broken down.

This is a project that needs to be launched without delay: how can we reconcile work and family life for both men and women? How can we enable all couples who want to have at least three children to continue working full-time without risking exhaustion or a nervous breakdown?

As well as improving the quality of life and creating a younger, more optimistic society, this would be a fantastic policy for increasing European growth in a sustainable way, making it easier to meet ecological, soci(et)al and military challenges.

TITLE III

EUROPE AND ECO-RESPONSIBILITY

Chapter 1

Protection of the Environment – Combating Climate Warming

Global warming, resulting from the saturation of the environment by carbon dioxide emissions, is prompting us to take a closer look at the state of the planet and our ecosystem. The technological developments of the last few centuries, the activity they have made possible and the galloping demographic growth of humankind are jeopardising the survival of life on earth.[435] Preserving what remains, regaining lost biodiversity and a healthy environment are now priorities.

The efforts made in the 1970s and 1980s to combat acid rain, river pollution and the ozone hole at the poles are grounds for reasonable

435 In particular, the coronavirus pandemic raises questions about the extent to which pressure from human communities on pockets of wild animal life exposes the former to new perils (regardless of the exact cause of this particular pandemic).

optimism. If we want to, we can. We have, or can acquire in the short or medium term, the technological means to improve the situation. We need to be determined, systematic, disciplined and remain calm and pragmatic. The situation does not lend itself to hysteria, sectarianism or manipulation.

Review of European Action

One point needs to be re-established. Europe has not been inactive in this area. For years, it has been taking measures as part of a European environmental policy: 20-20-20 and now 30-30-30 objectives in the energy field, and even more, REACH nomenclature for chemical products, quality of bathing water. More than 76% of glass used is recycled.[436] The European Investment Bank (EIB) gives priority to financing projects that promote the environment and energy efficiency. This dimension is also present in Structural Fund programmes. All this may be rather elusive and technical, but it is real and has a significant impact.

A few figures are worth noting:

- Total greenhouse gas emissions in the European Union have fallen by 23% in less than 30 years, while the economy has grown by 61% (from 1990 to 2018),[437, 438] as figure 29 below shows;

436 *See* the most recent figures of the FEVE (the European Container Glass Federation).

437 *See* the European Green Deal, section 2.1.1. 'Increasing the EU's climate ambition for 2030 and 2050'.

438 This performance needs to be qualified by the fact that some production activities have been "relocated" to third countries.

Figure 29.

Figure 1.24. Greenhouse gas emission decrease should speed up, particularly in transport

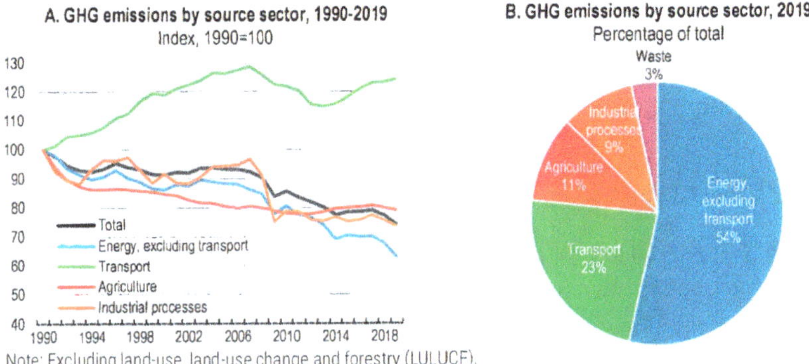

Note: Excluding land-use, land-use change and forestry (LULUCF).

Source: Eurostat (2020), "Greenhouse gas emissions by source sector", Eurostat Database; European Environment Agency.

- In 2019, energy-related CO_2 emissions fell by 5% in the European Union (down 160 million tonnes);[439, 440]
- The development of renewable energies in the EU is said to have reduced the main pressures on the environment;[441]
- Europe has reached its target of producing 20% renewable energy by 2019.

But Now It's Time to Shift into Overdrive

Even more significant improvements[442] and faster must be made, as long as and insofar as the environmental situation requires.

439 International Energy Agency (IEA) announcement of 11 February 2020, *EDB* 12424 of 13 February 2020, p. 21.

440 Total emissions from industry, the power sector and aviation fell by 8.7% in 2019, and those from power stations and industrial installations by 9% (*EDB* 12479 of 5 May 2020). Coal production fell by 24% in the same year (*EDB* 12419 of 6 February 2020, pp. 18–19).

441 On the climate, terrestrial acidification, eutrophication of spring waters and the formation of particles, according to the European Environment Agency (*EDB* 12638 of 19 January 2021).

442 For example, climate neutrality by 2050 (*see* the European Green Deal, section 2.1.1 'Increasing the EU's climate ambition for 2030 and 2050').

In this respect, it should be noted that the compactness of the European territory both enables Europeans and encourages them to make further progress. On the one hand, we need less energy and resources than others to produce, consume and move around. On the other hand, our higher population density requires an ecosystem in better condition than other regions.

(i) One Priority: Technical Progress

One point will be fundamental: scientific and technical progress. Without it, the making the economy greener is a mirage. We need to have the necessary technology and the substantial financial margins that only this can provide in the long term and on a sustainable basis. Otherwise, there will be considerable social disruption. As will the loss of quality of life: are our populations ready to accept this? Probably not.

A first step would be to switch to the most efficient existing technologies. We are still in the past.[443]

We must also ensure that we produce cleaner technologies that are efficient, attractive and likely to become world standards. On the one hand, it is only if this is done that the European effort will make an effective contribution to improving the environment. On the other hand, not only will the use of excessively expensive clean technologies by Europeans alone fail to achieve its goal, but it will also set Europe back definitively.

(ii) For a Global, Systematic and Graduated Approach

Environmental imperatives must be integrated into the various European policies, as they are beginning to be (making the economy greener is becoming a cross-cutting objective) and give rise to an overall strategy.

443 *See* Piccard, in particular pp. 52–57.

This must also combine the environmental dimension with economic efficiency and social considerations (the latter having been lost sight of in France with the increase in diesel taxes that sparked the Gilets jaunes movement). A virtuous triangle must be established in which priority will be given to measures that contribute to an improvement in these three dimensions simultaneously, or at least to pro-environmental measures that have the least negative economic and/or social consequences.[444]

In this respect, timing and sequencing are essential. Several parameters need to be taken into account: the economic cost/environmental effectiveness ratio of greening, the relationship between the urgency of climate change and the pace of technical progress likely to reduce the economic cost of greening.[445]

A key question is whether, by embarking (prematurely?) on greening at too high a cost, Europe is not shooting itself in the foot in vain. Firstly, to what extent can 6% of the world's population change the climate if they are not sufficiently supported? Secondly, is there not a risk that Europe will be weakened economically, with the risk of not being able to implement greening later on, having exhausted its financial margins? Why rush when the environmental situation may still allow a little time, and when technical solutions that are both more effective and less costly will be available in a few years' time? Momentum and rhythm in disruptive innovation are essential. Ultimately, the emphasis must be on the deadline by which we must have the technological and financial resources to reverse the trend and win the challenge.

(iii) A Pragmatic, Eclectic and Holistic Approach

Such an approach presupposes a cool capacity for calculation, imagination, diversity, the absence of dogmatism, serenity and the contribution of everyone according to their means.

---

444 *See* above, Title I, Ch. 1.

445 Even if there are unknowns in this rhythm.

A principle of neutrality and openness must be adopted: whatever technologies are used, the essential criterion is their impact or effect on the ecosystem (taking costs into account too, at least to some extent). Its respect is all the more important in the current transition period, where we do not know what the outcome will be, or what technologies will be used.

Consequently, if the internal combustion engine makes progress in terms of efficiency (the most modern engines today exceed the 40% barrier), if hybrid technology is perfected and makes it possible to do without the very heavy and expensive batteries (currently) of 100% electric cars (which also exposes us to a dependence on supplies of rare materials), if alternative fuels to petrol can see the light of day, why deprive ourselves of them? In this respect, it was a mistake to plan for the death of the internal combustion engine by 2035 in the European Commission's initial proposal.

The pro-environmental strategy involves a range of structural measures to reduce emissions: modernising technologies in all areas (air conditioning systems, lighting, dry car washes, cold dishwashers, etc.), promoting inland waterway, rail and multimodal transport, integrating eco-responsible techniques into construction, increasing renewable energy production, developing the green hydrogen and battery industries, using remote technologies, digital technologies such as artificial intelligence, 5G, cloud computing, edge computing and the Internet of Things,[446] maintaining or even developing nuclear power, osmotic energy, roof bleaching, etc. It would be "reasonable to envisage carbon neutrality from 2040 onwards, since we could then produce half of our needs from renewable energies and the other half could be saved thanks to efficient technologies".[447]

446 *See* the European Green Deal, section 2.1.3. "Mobilising industry for a clean and circular economy".

447 Piccard, p. 101 (in French).

In the same way that small streams make large rivers, the multiplication of progress, however small, will lead to a substantial overall improvement. The label launched by Bertrand Piccard to identify 1,000 inventions that improve the environmental balance sheet is a fine example of this, as it has now been used to certify nearly 1,500 new production processes.[448]

At the same time, we need to increase the capacity to absorb and compensate for emissions. This raises the question of reforestation, both in terms of quality and quantity,[449] in Europe and neighbouring regions, especially around the Mediterranean, and the adaptation of flora. Can you imagine a *Europa* tree that consumes little water and is resistant to fire, parasites and disease? Are reforestation programmes, possibly involving the local population, conceivable? The EU's biodiversity strategy of 20 May 2020[450] envisages the planting of three billion trees by 2030. There is also talk of making cities greener.

(iv) Towards a Carbon Tax?

To ensure that economic operators, public authorities and private individuals realise the impact of their activity on carbon dioxide emissions, there is increasing talk of making them pay for the estimated cost of their emissions to the environment.

Today, the average European emits 5.5 t of CO_2 per year (i.e. almost two times less than an American).

The idea would be to use a tax of €50 per tonne as an incentive to reduce emissions, averaging €275 per year, or slightly less than the

448 Ibid., p. 149.

449 *See* the European Green Deal, section 2.1.7. "Preserving and restoring ecosystems and biodiversity".

450 Communication from the Commission, "EU Biodiversity Strategy for 2030: Bringing nature back into our lives", COM(2020) 380 final, 20 May 2020.

EU budget per capita. For a population of 445 million, this would amount to a total of €122 billion, or less than 0,8% of the current GDP of the 27 Member States.

In view of the GDP gains that should be achieved by deepening the internal market, improving public management and increasing productive investment, this effort would be bearable.

(v) General Mobilisation!

The environmental and climate challenge also invites all the different players in society, insofar as they all contribute to pollution: energy producers, industry, transport (around 15–20%), agriculture, the residential sector (which accounts for 40% of energy consumption[451] and 36% of emissions), the tertiary sector and the civil service. As a result, national emission reduction plans, to be drawn up under the control at European level, must improve everyone's performance. For example, the annual rate of renovation of all buildings varies from 0.4 to 1.2% in the Member States. This rate will have to at least double if Europe is to meet its energy efficiency and climate targets.[452]

Empowering the various components of society is essential. It involves raising awareness, disseminating best practice and, once again, education. Beyond that, it implies the encouragement, and even the obligation, to carry out an annual assessment of the situation, to set up a scorecard and to record progress on an ongoing basis, in accordance with the capacities and responsibilities of each individual. It may also include measures to help improve performance in this area, such as... distributing hens to reduce household waste. Involving the various components of European society and levels

451 *See* the European Green Deal, section 2.1.4. "Building and renovating in an energy and resource efficient way".

452 Ibid.

of government in the pursuit of a common goal is also a way of reclaiming Europe and understanding the major directions and changes taken in this area.

Scientists need to be more closely involved in the design of policies (good intentions are not enough), and governments need to be more involved in land-use planning (we need to act in an orderly fashion: for example, "uncontrolled" reforestation will have perverse or even counterproductive effects, such as an increase in fires).

Efforts must be reasonable and adapted to the capacities of each individual, company and Member State. In this respect, some Member States remain more dependent on hydrocarbons and coal (e.g. Poland following the authoritarian decisions of the USSR). Hence, in particular, the Just Transition Fund,[453] already mentioned.[454]

For a Resource Management Society

In addition to improving the efficiency of trans-European transport and lowering the cost of energy, a resource management policy is needed. How can we produce the most added value from the fewest resources, by recovering as much as possible, recycling or reconverting[455] (idea of the circular economy), and reducing waste, including food waste?[456] We need to think globally.[457] In particular, this dimension should be integrated into the European Semester.

The ratio between GDP and primary energy consumption (primary energy intensity; energy productivity) measures the quantity of energy

453 *EDB* 12495 of 29 May 2020, pp. 7–8.

454 *See* above, Title I, Ch. 2.

455 This includes energy recovery, as 100% recycling is not (always) possible. On this issue, *see* J.-L. Chaussade, "Engageons-nous dans une transition environnementale réaliste", *Les Echos*, 4–5 September 2020, p. 15.

456 One fifth of the food produced is said to be wasted (*EDB* 12508 of 18 June 2020; in the same vein, Piccard, p. 58 and sources cited).

457 In this sense, *see* the European Green Deal, in particular section 2.1.3. "Mobilising industry for a clean and circular economy".

and raw materials needed to produce wealth. The energy intensity indicator will become increasingly important as natural resources become scarcer and the world's population grows. As in other areas, the Nordic countries and Switzerland are the champions of energy productivity.[458]

Europe has a great deal to offer in this respect, given its concentrated territory,[459] the size of its urban population and its greater ecological awareness than in other parts of the world.[460] But we can do much better.

458 Other countries seem to be making spectacular progress too. In the 25 years between 1990 and 2015, Germany reduced its energy consumption by more than 15%, while growing its GDP by more than 40% (source: *Alternatives économiques*).

459 *See* above, Title I, Ch. 1, "Introduction".

460 In particular, residents of the European Union are the largest issuers of green bonds.

Chapter 2

The Common Agricultural Policy (CAP)

CAP: An Engine That Is Rapidly Overpowered or Even Oversized From the Outset

The initial aim of the CAP was to ensure that Europe was self-sufficient in food. In 1957, the Europe of 6 was "only" able to meet 85% of its needs. It is questionable whether the allocation of 75% of the European budget was required to cover the remaining 15%.

In fact, by the end of the 1980s, i.e. more than 30 years ago, agricultural production covered 120% of Europe's food requirements.[461] Not to mention stocks and the destruction of surpluses. So the CAP had already achieved its objective by 233%!

Europe has also become the world's second-largest exporter of agricultural products, with a net surplus in relation to agricultural imports.

461 Defraigne and Nouveau, 3rd ed., p. 420.

Although the CAP now accounts for only 30% of the European budget, or €50 billion, it remains the largest item. Is this justified? Is the CAP not still too powerful a driving force for its primary objective?

The CAP: Some Perplexing Findings

It is incoherent that an economic integration such as the EU, founded on the idea of a large market and an open economy, should have as its main budget line a policy of subsidies, and conventional ones at that. In fact, these subsidies are mainly operating aids. In short, they are a kind of doping agent that distorts competition, hampers innovation and ultimately weakens farms, and whose allocation is not sufficiently dependent on the achievement of certain results.[462]

The fact that subsidies are paid on the basis of the quantities produced or the areas concerned, rather than the financial situation of the farmers, also raises questions. For a long time at least, the CAP budget benefited farms that were not in need.

What's more, the Common Agricultural Policy is not subject to any impact analysis or control of its effectiveness and cost-benefit ratio. As if it were a sacred cow. The CAP shows that the EU is not immune to lobbies and the capture of public funds by certain socio-professional groups.

And is our diet better than that of the rest of the world? Do we suffer fewer diet-related illnesses? Is our ecosystem in better condition, a question that is all the more crucial given the compactness of our territory and the density of our populations? These two particularities may mean that intensive farming using fertilisers and other chemical products can cause proportionately more damage in Europe than in the rest of the world.

---

462 We must not lose sight of the fact that, historically, the CAP has been a kind of compensation given to France. The conception of this policy must change today.

The increasing mortality of bees, the disappearance of small game, the reduction in wildlife and a series of pollutants are also prompting calls for an audit of the European ecosystem. For example, biodiversity is declining in France, with more than a quarter of the 5,000 species assessed by scientists at risk of disappearing from the country.[463] Let us be clear: the agricultural and agri-food sector is not the only, or even the main, culprit in this situation.

A subsidy to ensure self-sufficiency and quality food is conceivable, under certain conditions, as we shall see. It is much harder to justify subsidies to artificially win foreign markets at taxpayers' expense.

Agricultural subsidies[464] are strongly criticised by third countries and weaken us in international negotiations, particularly trade negotiations. As a result, they prevent us from concluding free trade agreements that could be of overall benefit to the European economy.

Would European society not have a clear interest in winning export market share by playing on the quality of European agricultural products, which would in future be produced in an (even) healthier way? We should ask ourselves about the cost-benefit ratio of subsidising European agricultural exports.[465]

The CAP is therefore open to a number of criticisms, in terms of the objectives pursued, the confiscation of the public debate by certain links in the agri-food chain, the means used, the results achieved and the collateral damage.

At the same time, the farming world is suffering, as the wave of suicides in France attests. Literature (*Sérotonine* by Michel Houellebecq) and

463 *Les Echos*, 10 January 2019, p. 2.

464 But that is not all: European indications of origin would be an asset (*EDB* 12477 of 30 April 2020).

465 That said, we must respect the legitimate interests of farmers. If their industry has become an export sector and can remain so on the basis of their merits, it would be counterproductive to try to "make them pay" for any past abuses. All we need to do is adjust the system, and there is no need to top this healthy momentum in its tracks.

the cinema (*Au nom de la terre*, starring Guillaume Canet) echo this. Nor should we lose sight of the importance of the CAP to the income of some farmers (44% in 2016).[466]

The infrastructure, production capacity and know-how we have acquired must not be thrown away, whatever reservations we may have about the CAP's past mistakes. These are assets and strengths. What's more, it is not certain that purely small-scale farming will be able to feed the entire population, even if only in Europe.

We need to go back to the drawing board, respecting the legitimate interests of all parties. It will require an in-depth debate, in a constructive spirit, without taboos, negative judgments, sweeping statements or extreme ideas. We need to develop a policy for an essential sector. This sector must be treated with the respect it deserves (particularly in view of its considerable workload and even arduousness). At the same time, it must incorporate certain requirements that have become essential in our society, particularly given the state of the planet, resources and the European ecosystem. In this respect, agriculture is an industry like any other.

Some Areas for Improvement?

Agricultural priorities probably need to be redefined and improved in the direction of healthier, more environmentally-friendly production.[467] Other legitimate interests need to be taken into account in addition to the economic interests of farmers: environmental protection, the health of the rural population, the health of consumers and affordable quality food for as many people as possible.[468]

466 *EDB* 12154 of 7 December 2018, p. 28.

467 *See* the European Parliament's approval of EU rules for the safe reuse of wastewater for agricultural irrigation (*EDB* 12485 of 13 May 2020).

468 Communication from the Commission, "A Farm to Fork Strategy for a fair, healthy and environmentally-friendly food system", COM(2020) 381 final, 20 May 2020.

We therefore need to clearly redefine the objectives and priorities of the CAP and ensure that they are effectively implemented. The various stakeholders in agriculture need to have their say, and correspondingly assume certain responsibilities.

We need to develop a more systematic approach across the board: universities (agronomy, medical schools, etc.), research and development policy, farmer education, national and European land-use planning, new technologies, agricultural clusters, assistance for farmers and their families, who are the first victims of chemicals, intermediaries (who are all too often criticised), organisations from the farmer to the consumer (cooperatives, mutual societies, vertical integration), and a return to fairs and markets.

As in other areas, it is probably wise to leave room for diversity, multipolar agriculture and technical neutrality. Let us take a sober, objective look at the advantages and disadvantages of different types of agricultural production, without bias, prejudice or fanciful ideas.

Where appropriate, it might be conceivable for certain European agencies to work towards the development of Marshallese districts in the agricultural sector.

This raises questions about the development of the comparative advantages of the Member States (this reflection is in line with a suggestion made earlier about economic, social and territorial cohesion[469]), about a more integrated Europe and about the stimulus that could be given by the EU to this end, in the general interest of course.

If we combine this consideration with the need for less costly and more eco-responsible agriculture, a special effort should be made to exploit black soils (chernozem), which are found particularly in Romania, Bulgaria, Poland and Hungary. "This type of soil is particularly

469 *See* above, Title I, Ch. 2, E.

suitable for farming, especially as its natural properties mean that it does not require large quantities of fertilisers and additives. This is a significant advantage in the context of a new CAP enriched by stricter environmental standards and which provides financial incentives for the limited use of chemical inputs."[470]

Why not have an agricultural agency in one of these countries, aimed at developing cutting-edge, environmentally-friendly techniques?

Be that as it may, awareness of the need to work on the various links in the chain is emerging from the new European "Farm to Fork" strategy, incorporating the objectives of sustainable agriculture (environmental protection[471]), healthy food at affordable prices, and the fight against waste (another aspect of the quest for efficiency).

The traceability of inputs and of the entire production and distribution chain should contribute to an improvement. This more demanding approach is not specific to agriculture, but will apply to all sectors of the economy, in an approach comparable to that relating to ESG,[472] as the proposed "vigilance" directive[473] seems to suggest.

Mechanisms should also be introduced to improve the efficiency of agricultural production in terms of both quality and cost management, as is the case for services of general economic interest (SGEIs).[474]

The comparison should be taken further. Farming is essential for the population. Insofar as a policy aimed at food self-sufficiency is being pursued (and has been achieved), the question of whether subsidies are still necessary is worth asking. One possible answer is to ensure that part of the population has access to quality food at affordable

---

470 Defraigne and Nouveau, 3rd ed., p. 427 (in French).

471 This includes a drastic reduction in the use of pesticides, fertilisers, antibiotics and additives.

472 Integration of environmental, social and good governance parameters, currently limited to part of the financial sector and to large companies.

473 Proposal for a Directive on Corporate Sustainability Due Diligence, COM(2022) 71 final, 23 February 2022.

474 *See* Title I, Ch. 2, E.

prices.[475] This issue is as pertinent as ever, and even more so given the large percentage of the European population at risk of poverty.[476] There is also the issue of ensuring adequate remuneration for a section of the farming community that really needs public support.

If the objective is a high level of quality in the broad sense (environmental and public health requirements), it is conceivable that the cost of these public service obligations should continue to be borne by the public authorities.[477] However, the exact scope and conditions (specifications) and the costs to farmers must be determined. Overcompensation must be avoided.

Controls should be more effective, entrusted to more independent authorities, with the possibility of greater penalties. There have been too many food scandals in recent years (Bastogne in Belgium, South-West France, etc.).[478]

We must also be aware that, at a European level, other policies are important and should receive more funding. The FITNESS principle (doing better with less) must prevail in agriculture too.

That being said, the ecological transition in agriculture will probably require aid, even if it will have to be calibrated; more by using the carrot than the stick.[479] It is worth noting that this is perfectly in line with the ideas put forward above concerning measures to accompany transitions.[480] Here, the disruption is not caused by market mechanisms but by a change in public interest priorities (consumer and farmer health, and even more so environmental protection and regeneration).

475 With 20–25% of the population threatened by insecurity, the debate is a topical one, especially in these times of high inflation.

476 *See* above, Title II, Ch. 2.

477 As a general rule, the "polluter pays" principle prevails. However, it is possible that the potentially lower productivity of certain crops, or even certain types of farms, may justify a departure from this principle.

478 The fight against fraud is one of the objectives of the new "Farm to Fork" strategy.

479 *EDB* 12499 of 5 June 2020.

480 *See* above, Title I, Ch. 2, F (iv).

Evolution will require farmers to take responsibility, but also consumers who aspire to (higher) quality food and who have the means to pay for it. We need to realise that we are the generation in the history of mankind who, on average, spend the smallest proportion of our income on food (the economically vulnerable part of the population should be taken into account, especially in times of high inflation).

In light of this, can we not promote agricultural sectors in the form of producer-consumer cooperatives, where consumers who so wish pay for healthier, higher quality products? A bit like healthcare, where more sophisticated services or those that include greater comfort for the patient mean paying a higher price. If we were to draw a comparison, we could think of subsidised farmers and non-subsidised farmers selling products at free price. The level of subsidy would vary.

Financial techniques could also be used. Once again, we can think of investment funds or even the creation of a labelled fund that could contribute to the greening of agriculture. The money raised could only be invested in farms that comply with eco-responsible specifications. Investors could receive interest or dividends in kind.

TITLE IV

EUROPE, GREATER FREEDOMS AND DEMOCRACY

Chapter 1

Europe, a Tool to Protect Values, the Rule of Law and Freedoms

The EU is also useful in helping to resolve conflicts between the various communities within a Member State and in safeguarding democracy and the rule of law.

Europe, the Protection of Minorities and the Cohabitation of Communities

Peace in Northern Ireland has been facilitated by the joint membership of the UK and Ireland in the EU. It has avoided a hard border between Northern Ireland and Ireland, the spectre of which haunts Brexit.[481] Will Scotland be part of the UK for long after Brexit? Belgium's membership of the EU has enabled Dutch speakers and French speakers to continue to live together in the same country. European

481 Since these lines were written, troubles have broken out in Northern Ireland in late March/early April 2021.

membership has eliminated the risk of dictatorship in Greece, Portugal and Spain. The attempted putsch in Spain, which I witnessed almost live, was one of the most striking political events of my youth.

It is yet another paradox: presented as technocratic, undemocratic and remote from the people, Europe[482] is an element of ethnic pacification. It strengthens democracy. It is a guarantee against tensions between communities and discrimination against minorities that a national democracy is not always able to contain.

Europe and Democracy

Europe was created as a reaction to the failure of democracies in the 1930s. It should not be forgotten that the three major founding Member States saw dictators come to power by democratic means.[483]

Europe, the Rule of Law, and Freedoms

Europe also plays an important role in maintaining and even strengthening the rule of law. The courageous fight by the outgoing Vice-President of the European Commission, Mr Timmermans, against attacks on the rule of law, and in particular on the separation of powers, in Poland and Hungary, the firm stance taken by the Court of Justice of the European Union (CJEU) on Polish policy, and the fact that the benefits of the European Recovery Plan are conditional on respect for the rule of law are all worthy of note.

Let us not be carried away by euphoria. However, when we see how Europe is containing certain poisons to democracy and the damage that President Trump has done to American institutions, there is, at the very least, something to be proud of. Today, Europe is perhaps in

482 To which we must add the Council of Europe, with the European Convention for the Protection of Human Rights and Fundamental Freedoms and the European Court of Human Rights, based in Strasbourg.

483 With the support in France of a movement that has been virtually deified in the collective memory, the Front Populaire; by comparison, the three small founding Member States have not experienced the same excesses.

better democratic health than the United States.[484] We can see how far both have come since the 1930s and 1940s. Not least thanks to the construction of Europe.

Europe[485] also provides citizens with additional protection against arbitrary action and excessive interference by authorities, primarily public authorities. In this respect, fundamental rights, enshrined as general principles of European law and by the EU Charter of Fundamental Rights,[486] constitute additional rights and guarantees for citizens. They are better protected against discrimination and unjustified interference by public authorities. They also benefit from greater guarantees of fair treatment by the administration and the courts. In so doing, Europe has helped not only its citizens but also its States to grow by demanding higher standards of behaviour from them.

In my view, we must be adamant about our essential values, at least within the EU. As much as I call for social and environmental considerations to be integrated as far as possible into economic policies and, conversely, for economic considerations to be integrated into predominantly social and ecological policies, I do not see how we can reconcile our democratic values, our freedoms and the rule of law against other considerations in the EU.

Europe: A Counterweight, a Force for Moderation and Questioning

In political terms, Europe is a force for moderation in the face of excess. Alongside the arithmetic of voting, it raises questions about the quality or, at the very least, the acceptability of a majority's proposals. It puts an end to the cynical principle that, in a democracy,

484 These lines were written before the invasion of the Capitol on 6 January 2021.

485 To which we must add the European Convention on Human Rights and the Court, located in Strasbourg, which ensures that it is respected.

486 Inspired by the European Convention on Human Rights and national constitutional traditions.

the majority is always right. No, it is not the majority that is right, but the power. Europe is an outside viewpoint that can weigh up and question the excesses of national sovereignty, reopening or even elevating the debate.

In a similar vein, the EU plays another valuable role in a world as complex, unstable and changing as ours: it ensures that several structures embody the general interest. The state no longer has a monopoly. No level of public authority is infallible. The plurality of public authorities means that the quality of each can be put into perspective. They are no longer taken at their word. They will only be credible in the long term on the basis of the quality of their work (assuming that public opinion is relatively enlightened and not given over to the darkness of conspiracy), once again on the basis of their added value. The management of the pandemic in the various Member States, with widely varying degrees of success, is a good illustration of this.

At the end of the day, there is room for rational debate with the prospect that the best solution will triumph. In this respect, Europe's political weakness is, paradoxically, an opportunity.[487] It leaves more room for a free debate, unencumbered by an (overly) dominant political conception.

This kind of distancing applies, and should also apply, to the Union. Like the states and regions, it can make mistakes. The management of the pandemic, especially the ordering of vaccines, is a case in point. Different or even antagonistic points of view on the part of the Member States can lead it to improve its views. To voice well-founded criticism of a particular European project is not to be anti-European. Europe will only be accepted if it is effective and based on a culture of results.

487 In a similar vein, P. Sloterdijk, *Réflexes primitifs : considérations psychopolitiques sur les inquiétudes européennes* (transl. O. Mannoni), Paris, Payot, 2019.

Towards Additional Contributions to Freedom and Democracy?

Europe continues to contribute to the protection of our freedoms and the preservation and enhancement of the rule of law and our democracies.

Under the influence of the Nordic countries, administrative transparency, especially access to public authority documents, has been considerably strengthened. As a lawyer, I can assure you that this system is likely to dissuade administrations from taking liberties with the law. The European regulation on the protection of personal data can be seen as a bulwark for our privacy.

Europe is also working to combat the manipulation of public opinion through social media, much of which is the work of Russia (since before the invasion of Ukraine), and to ensure that democratic institutions operate with integrity. The risks of conflicts of interest are being identified. Lobbying the European institutions is regulated… even if there are still holes in the rules.

In accordance with the principle of openness, the EU seeks to encourage public participation in defining European action. In addition to access to the documents already mentioned, European citizens are given a number of prerogatives: the possibility of submitting petitions and, through them, of requesting certain European initiatives, and recourse to the European Ombudsman.

The area of freedom, security and justice also makes it possible to take a series of initiatives to improve judicial protection for the people of Europe and the operation of national courts.

However, the question arises as to whether the EU could do more to modernise and improve our democratic systems.

The vote that led to Brexit highlighted the disaffection of young people, who are put off by the slow pace and relative inefficiency of public procedures. We need to realise that the efficiency of the private sector in new technologies, whether for communications or distance commerce, makes public and political institutions appear obsolete for young consumers. The slowness of decision-making risks disqualifying the very idea of debate. The challenge is to preserve the fundamental elements of our liberal systems and improve the efficiency of our institutions.

Chapter 2

Where is the European Political Society (at)?

A European Political Society Is Still Missing

European citizens enjoy many rights and freedoms in the European Union. One of the characteristics of European integration is that it has improved the status of the citizen compared to that of a nation state.

Firstly, the territory in which citizens can exercise most of their rights and freedoms has increased by a factor of 27 on average. Secondly, they derive rights directly from the EU. In part, the EU was set up to protect citizens against abuses by states and, in general, by public authorities.[488] The people of Europe are also politically represented by the European Parliament.

So the EU is not just an association of states. Its citizens are full members. The states and the people are the two pillars, the two categories of shareholders in Europe Ltd.

---

488 *See* above, Title IV, Ch. 1.

However, a political society is not limited to public institutions such as the European Parliament, the Council and the Commission. Public life and public debate must accompany these constituted bodies.

They are, however, lacking at European level. There is no European public opinion, no media that are truly European[489]. The population continues to be informed via national or local newspapers and television channels. European issues are still viewed through national lenses. Most of us remain profoundly shaped by national space, ways of thinking, practices and networks.

As a result, the European sphere is not subject to vigilant and informed scrutiny by the press and the public.

For example, no country, apart from the United Kingdom, has intervened intervene in the Brexit debate. There are no European societal debates.

European issues are often presented by the national media as differences or even opposing interests between Member States. The crucial point is often whether the viewer's country "won or lost". Rarely is the decision analysed from the perspective of the general European interest. It is never indicated that it represents a win-win for everyone. Journalists are not the only ones responsible. National politicians also bear their share of the responsibility.

Causes of the Absence of a European Political Society

A European political society is sadly absent partly because of the objective difficulties associated with the plurality of languages:[490] in part, because of a lack of interest on the part of the population and because of the complexity, even the aridity, of the issues; partly due to the deliberate policy of governments, which do not want to see the

489 However, the ARTE television channel is gradually becoming one, with some of its programs subtitled in a growing number of Member State languages.

490 Which becomes surmountable with applications (*see* above, Title I, Ch. 1).

emergence of a new power source that they fear could displace them. This brings us back to the Anastasia-Drizella versus Cinderella-Europe syndrome mentioned in the introduction to this essay.

There is, in fact, a paralysing ambiguity about the purpose of European integration. To put the debate, the dilemma, in traditional terms (I think we need to reconsider the approach here): Is Europe a federal construction in the making that will eventually constitute a state and whose current members will be reduced to the status of cantons, regions or Länder? Or is it a confederal construction, in which the main players are and will remain the states?

The fear of being sidelined explains the growing, even obsessive, control that states seek to exert over the construction of Europe. The Member States remain the masters of the Treaties. Their leaders have no desire to share power with those at the head of the European institutions.

What's more, the confusion of roles is perpetuated by political staff. A number of members of the European Parliament (MEPs) are disappointed with national politics. Not to mention the Eurosceptics who – and this is yet another paradox – have gained an income and a platform in Strasbourg that they did not have in their beloved nation state, like the Le Pen family, father and daughter, or Nigel Farage. They come to Strasbourg and Brussels in the hope of returning to the "forefront" of national politics, if not as senior members seeking early retirement from national politics. Some political staff enter the European institutions with a state or sub-state background and tend to approach European issues through these lenses.

Towards Better Identification of the Respective Roles of the Member States and the European Union

The situation can only be resolved if the respective roles of the Member States and the EU are clearly defined and are seen to be complementary rather than competing. We need to think about what Europe can do and what the Member States cannot do., for example in view of Europe's size, competences and the specific instruments and expertise it has developed. This brings us back to subsidiarity and to the more rigorous approach that could be applied in this area.[491]

A more marked differentiation of responsibilities and courses of action could contribute to conciliation and greater efficiency, with better identification of the EU's specific features and its added value to the action of the Member States. It should focus in particular on the way in which European public action can be carried out. For example, should we be thinking in terms of means of action that differ from those of the Member States?[492]

Europe must do certain things that the Member States cannot do or do less well.[493] This requires a certain imagination. We must stop "reasoning" with concepts developed in the framework of nation states, which are now one or two centuries old and vary from one country to another.

Europe is not the projection or extension of the states. It is an addition to, a complement to, an additional and distinct asset. In particular, it gives back to the Member States a fragment of sovereignty that has become illusory in today's world if it is exercised at their level (think of the European regulation on the protection of personal data, which is becoming the benchmark regime in the world). Nor should it be a cumbersome and ineffective duplication that reinforces bureaucracy and obscure regulation as an end in itself.

As long as the various levels of power do not fear being on the verge of being supplanted by another, we can reasonably hope for a better

491 *See* above, Title I, Ch. 1, C, 2.

492 *See* above, Title II, Ch. 1, on the financing, particularly private, catalysed by the EIB and the EIF and in the conclusions of the essay.

493 This does not preclude combined interventions by the EU and the Member States, such as the European Recovery Plan (*see* above, Title I, Ch. 2).

overall performance. The Member States should then be less reticent about developing a European political society and regional political societies. These different strata, these different affiliations are not in conflict but complementary.

Over time, there will also be greater cooperation between European and national or subnational levels of government. This is already tangible, for example, in the area of state aid and calls for European structural funds. The relationship become less and less one of controlling and being controlled, and more between partners involved in the judicious and orderly use of national and European public funds.

I do not believe in or call for the break-up of the Member States. Some of these structures are thousands of years old (France, Spain, Austria). They fundamentally shape the vision and behaviour of their populations. Rather than breaking them up, let us build on them. Let us ensure that the different levels of power are less in sterile or even counterproductive rivalry and more in synergy.

Some Proposals for the Emergence of a European Political Society

European democratic society must in fact be built. It is not enough to merely place a stamp on it and then simply project national democracies onto it. We need to think about forging elements of a truly European democracy, operating alongside and in harmony with national democracies.

For example, the differences between the Member States and the EU could be reflected and extended by particular conditions of eligibility for the European Parliament. Candidates should have a profile that demonstrates openness to other Member States and to the European level.

We could also envisage representation for European citizens who have exercised their freedom of movement, in the form of a fraction of the number of MEPs (for example, the equivalent of one additional Member State).[494] Citizens who have made use of their freedom of movement often find themselves between two chairs politically. De facto, they are deprived of an effective chance of being elected. They constitute an inaudible minority. This is yet another paradox: the people in Europe who experience Europe and Community integration the most, because every day they experience life in another Member State, are politically non-existent at European level. Understand who can! Once again, the state's projection is excessive and abusive.

For the same reason, I am in favour of greater decoupling between national and European political life. The European elections must not be a punishment for the national politicians in place.

The gradual emergence of a European political society in the broadest sense could be assisted by the development of specifically European media and information.

For example, as a practitioner of European law, I subscribe to a daily information sheet, the *Europe Daily Bulletin*. It is factual and can teach European citizens a great deal. I was pleased to read that bathing water quality has never been so good in Europe – a direct result of European initiatives. I learned that, at the beginning of 2020, the public debt of the Member States had fallen by almost 10 percentage points since the 2008 financial crisis. Thanks in part to the European Semester and the Stability Pact. This decline has given Member States more resources to pursue policies of general interest and to invest. It made it easier to overcome the pandemic. The *Bulletin* also taught me that most of the Member States in Central Europe and the Baltic have much smaller public debts than the Western Member States.

494 If I am not mistaken, that's about the only suggestion made in this essay, which would require a change to the European treaties.

A publication of this style should be distributed more widely, and at a lower cost, to the general public.

Broad and regular dissemination of the main indicators of the state of the Union (the Union's health report) and the main objectives would also be welcome, in the interests of readability and support.

A European audiovisual press is also important.

We should encourage the creation of blogs and discussion forums, the injection of intra-Community elements into television programmes… I have fond memories of *Jeux sans frontières* and another programme hosted by presenters from different countries, *Le Francophonissime*. It is striking that this openness has been lost. There is rarely a political programme on which foreign observers and/or journalists are invited.

Language applications and artificial intelligence should be able to overcome the obstacle of linguistic diversity and enable people to follow European news more closely.

There should be more European, and therefore cross-border, associations able to take part in the European debate. In this respect, it is interesting to note that the EU has done more to give consumer associations the right to take legal action than to promote European citizens' movements is a matter of concern.

The public should also take an interest in European integration. This is part of citizenship, of belonging to the community of destiny that is the EU. School training (education, once again!) should be adapted.

There is therefore a great deal of work to do on the emergence of a specifically European interest, which cannot be reduced to that of the Member States, as well as on the reflex to think "European".

TITLE V

EUROPE AND ITS NEIGHBOURS: GENEROSITY, STABILITY AND SECURITY

Chapter 1

Development and Migration Policies

A. Development Aid Policy

As mentioned in the introduction, the EU and its Member States are the most generous bloc in the world, accounting for 47% of global development aid.

However, the results are mixed, since the biggest beneficiaries of this policy are the countries and regions of the world that have developed least over the last half-century.

For some years now, there has been a concern for greater efficiency in this policy, which represents €67 billion of the European budget over 7 years. In particular, the EU is seeking to avoid duplication and overlap with Member State initiatives. As in the case of cohesion policy, it is advocating the use of investment techniques alongside traditional subsidies. This trend is likely to grow stronger.

One might wonder about the multiplicity of objectives pursued alongside the priority objective of eradicating poverty: promotion of human rights, gender equality, rule of law, freedoms.

Just as we must be uncompromising about respect for our fundamental values on our own territory (and more so than we are today), we could be more neutral or at least more granular about the choices made by third countries in their own territories. We could give more assistance to countries that share our values, but neither condemn nor exclude the others.

The European Neighbourhood Policy towards countries on the EU's eastern and southern borders is gaining in importance. This is being increasingly linked to migration policy (B).

B. Migration Policy

Preliminary remark: if the EU did not exist, its Member States, especially those on its southern and eastern borders, would continue to be exposed to migration issues. The source of the problems is not the EU. They stem from geography and geopolitics.

Secondly, the EU has only recently been given powers in this area. Moreover, given the – legitimate – sensitivity of the issues for the Member States, the exercise of these powers remains largely dependent on them.

Migration policy must respect certain values with regard to migrants, fairness between Member States and the sustainability of the reception effort (idea of contributive capacity), in particular in order to preserve the foundations of European society (democracy, rule of law, freedoms, pluralism, respect for women) and avoid its destabilisation.

Emergency reception is a question of humanity towards migrants.

For longer stays, a system of priorities could be established, based on integration, to be assessed from the point of view of employability and cultural criteria, as well as the Member States' capacity/willingness to receive immigrants.

As far as this last point is concerned, we can accept that the Member States are not in comparable situations (do they have a colonial debt or not? This is not the case for most Central European countries). If an effort of solidarity is required, it must be reasonable and gradual.

Development aid from non-EU countries (see A above), especially those in the EU belt, is also part of the package.

Chapter 2

Defence Policy

Another area where the European Union could play an essential role, especially at this time of geopolitical tension, is that of defence. Brexit is a godsend in some respects, as the UK has always opposed the move to majority decision-making in this area. On the other hand, it means the loss of one of the only armies that counts in Europe, as well as being one of the two European Member States to possess nuclear weapons.

Europe suffers from the fragmentation of its military policies. It has twice as many types of military equipment as the United States for half the budget and twice as many management personnel. Its operational effectiveness is virtually nil. It would also save money by pooling the purchases of Member States. There are, however, persistent tensions between national industries. Recent evidence of this is the disagreements over the European fighter.[495]

A gradual convergence of military policies is recommended (we can think of multi-year programmes), as well as the promotion as a priority of profiles with a European outlook (dual nationals, "mixed" marriages, experience abroad, knowledge of languages, etc.).

495 *L'Echo*, 20 March 2021, p. 11.

Given the geopolitical tensions (Russia has been testing the air defences of the Baltic and Nordic countries for years[496, 497] in particular, and its manoeuvres on its western border are increasing every year) and the loosening of transatlantic ties, particularly but not only under the Trump presidency, Europe needs to take more responsibility for itself. There is a renewed need for European leadership and an awareness of Europe's own interests.

However, this does not imply distancing ourselves from NATO. However, it is conceivable that there could be more cooperation between Member States within the framework of their commitments within the transatlantic organisation.[498]

We also need to develop a European military industry with very high value-added technology. Examples from abroad should give us food for thought. Many GAFAs and Israeli technological companies have been encouraged or even nurtured by support programmes with primarily military objectives.[499] A military Keynesianism has been put in place: public authorities contribute to the development of the economy through R&D for dual-use goods and services, both military and civilian. The emergence of a military Europe should be independently of defence and geopolitical considerations, an opportunity for European research and industry.

We could also envisage a European civil and military protection force, capable of internal and external intervention (which would go beyond RescEU, mentioned in the European Recovery Plan).[500] In addition to acquiring know-how that would prove invaluable, this force would give the EU an identity that it lacks and would mean

496 Norway, Finland and Sweden recently decided to step up their military cooperation.

497 This was written long before Russia invaded Ukraine.

498 And in situations where NATO is not involved and the EU may be called upon to act (*L'Echo*, 27 February 2021, p. 11).

499 On the United States, *see* Defraigne and Nouveau, 3rd ed., in particular p. 104.

500 *See* above, Title I, Ch. 2.

that the community of Member States is not just limited to being the Switzerland of the world but is operationally capable of influencing the course of certain elements. After its failure to play a role during the war in the former Yugoslavia and the debacle at the start of the Covid vaccination campaign, it would help to correct the image of Europe of being a soft touch in the Wild West of today's world.

CONCLUSIONS

Europe: A Gentle Way of Life…

After two world wars that devastated the Old Continent, European integration offered a lifeline. To avoid repeating those mistakes, it was conceived as an *Archimedean lever* in more ways than one: a booster of prosperity, social justice, democracy and freedoms, and a guarantee of peace. For example, the single market has made it possible to produce more, better and more cheaply, to increase purchasing power and to accumulate wealth. Citizens have been given many additional rights (freedom of movement, protection against abuse by public authorities, etc.) in a larger area.

Today, the balance sheet is still encouraging. The EU is a good place to live, compared with other parts of the world, even rich ones. Think of the balance between private and professional life (in which other economically developed countries can we take so many holidays and have such a long life expectancy in good shape?), the health and social protection systems. Democratic changeovers take place peacefully and the rule of law is generally acceptable.

Moreover, the gains in prosperity (between 9 and 12.5% of GDP) and living space (x 27) have left national features untouched. As a good lever, European integration has built on national foundations and institutions rather than destroying or replacing them. Diversity is protected at various levels (languages, politics, socio-economic organisation, etc.). Each state continues to determine the size of its public services. The level of social benefits and taxes remains highly variable, depending on the preferences of the population and the attractiveness of the country. Europe contributes a lot without taking anything back, at a modest cost (the European budget barely exceeds 1% of the GDP of the 27). Its leverage effect, its multiplier coefficient, is therefore substantial (9 to 12).

A balance has thus been struck between (i) the principles of a large entity (single market, freedom of movement, open social market economy with free and undistorted competition, prohibition in principle of State aid, obligation of sustainable public finances, budgetary responsibility of the Member States, the EU and companies, protection of fundamental rights, etc.); (ii) certain solidarity measures (economic, social and territorial cohesion policy, European Recovery Plan, etc.); (iii) the autonomy of the Member States (in fiscal, economic, soci(et)al and territorial matters).

... Threatened

Although still among the world leaders, Europe is in danger of falling behind. It is lagging behind technologically, economically, financially and even educationally. It has become complacent, has not invested or innovated enough, and has been living on credit for the past 25 years.

Around 2010, it relinquished leadership of GDP to the USA, which then had a 40% smaller population! Today, the GDP of the 27 has stagnated at €15,500-16,000 billion, compared with just over €24,000 billion in the USA (with 25% fewer people). The US is leaving us behind, with China hot on our heels. We are absent from cutting-edge fields, the latest being artificial intelligence. We are slipping in the rankings of the world's largest companies and market capitalisations. The euro is in the low band against the dollar. Our demographics are bleak.

This global decline threatens our quality of life, our prosperity, our social cohesion, our systems of democracy and freedom, and the future of our children. The current environmental and geopolitical challenges only exacerbate our vulnerabilities.

A Sign of Our Loss of Speed: Productivity at Half Mast

One indicator crystallises this "sluggishness": our *productivity*, i.e. the wealth we produce in one hour of work with a given piece of equipment, is now 35% lower than in the United States. And the gap is widening.

The overall productivity of factors of production is one of the keys to economic health. It also has important social, societal and human implications.

Wages are a direct function of labour productivity, as an employer cannot pay a worker more than the value he or she produces. High productivity therefore increases the circle of possibilities, with direct implications for the quality of life of workers and their families, and the balance between professional and private life (shorter working hours, part-time work, etc.). Finally, it often goes hand in hand with a stimulating activity, a supportive or even innovative environment, and an overall quality of life. Happy countries often have high productivity.

A Gentle Way of Life That Can Nevertheless Be Saved and Strengthened

Do we want to preserve our quality of life and the quality of life for our children? To improve it in a more inclusive, greener and safer society?

In this respect, the EU has untapped potential, which can take us a long way on the path to the future, without having to make any major sacrifices, without increasing its competences or even its financial resources.

A. A Major Asset to Be Exploited to the Full: The Domestic Market

The EU's internal market is the largest of the developed countries and the smallest of all: 450 million inhabitants in an area less than half the size of the United States, which has a population of just 330 million. In other words, a market three to four times more compact. A godsend at a time when energy and raw materials are becoming increasingly scarce!

Yet intra-EU trade is 40% lower than trade between US states... *The same*, or even worse, *applies* to GDP per capita (in 2021, the difference was 44%). Many obstacles to trade and to exploiting the potential of the single market therefore remain. They are even getting worse, as the services market has not been completed, even though services now account for 75% of the economy. As a result, our service companies are lagging behind technologically and – once again – have alarming productivity deficits. What's more, Member States have increased their restrictions on trade since the 2008 banking crisis, and the Commission has not been tough enough in cracking down on them.

The negative spiral threatening European society is largely as a result of this failure (another black spot being the state of public finances in certain Member States): an incomplete and shrinking single market, protectionism, sluggish productivity, deficiencies in research and development and innovation (R&D&I) and therefore in technical progress. The soci(et)al consequences are falling living standards, job insecurity, pessimism and a shrinking population.

Towards Generalised Mutual Recognition of Goods and Services

A simple, radical, rapid and inexpensive measure would be to introduce[501] mutual recognition of goods and services legally produced in a Member State, whether or not there is European harmonisation in this area. From then on, they could be freely marketed in other Member States.

The rapid result will be clear growth in the GDP of the 27, and more varied, more innovative, cheaper and better quality products and services in greater quantity. A stronger European economy. A discreet but lasting and powerful groundswell: the perspective changes diametrically when, instead of 1, 10, 30, 80 million potential consumers, we can reach 445 of them. Entrepreneurial vocations should flourish.

SMEs in all Member States, Get Up!

Mutual recognition will have all the more impact because it will be of particular benefit to SMEs. Do we realise that they make up the vast majority (99.2%) of businesses and that the *average European company employs 5.6 people*? SMEs will finally be able to take part in intra-Community trade, from which 85% are still absent today, grow, improve their productivity, pay their staff better (which will help to reduce the social divide), finance themselves, invest in R&D&I, attract external investors, become unicorns and have access to the financial markets. In this respect, the EU will truly become a more open society.

Where will Europe be if, on average, SMEs double in size, triple its sales and increase its margins over the next few years? The result will be a peaceful Copernican revolution. Gradually, Europe's

501 By a regulation of the European Parliament and the Council or by a ruling of the Court of Justice of the European Union.

23 million businesses will become stronger, more productive, more innovative, richer and more dynamic. We need to get away from the "small is beautiful" image. There is and will be room for companies with one to five employees, given the removal of obstacles and technological progress. But production quality and well-being at work are not incompatible with companies of 500 to 3,000 people or more.

For a Minimum Organisational Base Common to All Companies

A complementary measure to mutual recognition could be a minimum set of requirements for access to and exercise of economic activities. Properly designed (i.e. supportive and not unnecessarily cumbersome), this would help to improve the organisation of businesses, especially the smallest, their production and productivity, prepare them for change and increase their clarity. The latter is important to overcome the reluctance of banks (which are often too conservative) and investors to finance them.

More Public Education on the Single Market

In order for entrepreneurs and consumers to take advantage of the single market, they should be more familiar with how it works, and with its benefits and risks (e.g. in the case of remote ordering). It is essential to adapt the education of Europe's populations to the single market rather than protecting them with a paternalistic straitjacket that differs from one Member State to another, thereby reinforcing the barriers to trade.

Educating the population about the potential and challenges of today and tomorrow is a common thread running through this essay.

Towards a Recalibration and Moderation of the EU's Standard-Setting Activity

The positive spiral enabled by mutual recognition will be strengthened if, especially initially, the European legislator for standards revises his requirements downwards, taking into account the fact that the average operator is not the big company of his dreams but an SME. The best compromise between freeing up production potential, quality requirements, eco-responsibility, the cost and the burden of regulation must be worked out with this in mind. Today, it is mainly the American and Chinese behemoths that can cope with the burden of European standards, having grown up sheltered from them. Rather than liberating and lightening the load, Europe has tended to pour a second slab of regulation on top in recent years. In this respect, the departure of the United Kingdom, which moderated the regulatory ardour of the European institutions, is a great loss.

In particular, the European Parliament must avoid taking itself for an omnipotent legislator pursuing all sorts of legitimate objectives. Its primary mission is to ensure Europe's inclusive (social market economy) and sustainable prosperity. The idea of repealing three or even five rules before adopting a new one is worth pursuing.

Other Urgent Measures

The priority is to unleash the business potential of the Europe of 27, to break down existing barriers to trade between Member States (liberalising sectors that are not yet liberalised, such as ports, giving a boost to technologies that overcome language and application barriers, etc.), to fight much harder against protectionist measures and the failure to transpose directives (for example by providing for a regime that will apply in the absence of timely national implementation).

At the Same Time, a Supportive Framework

To reverse the trend in the long term and make a success of the environmental transition in particular, there is more that needs to be done. Alongside the completion of the internal market and moderated regulatory activity, it is up to the EU to develop an enabling framework by working on the fundamentals. In short, it needs to develop what is sometimes called a structural/modern supply-side policy (although this is very different from the policy of reducing the tax burden on companies and high earners), which is also likely to increase consumer purchasing power in a sustainable way.

Certain vectors of economic activity, which are currently deficient in Europe, are in particular need of improvement.

(i) R&D&I Efforts

Technical Progress Is Vital for Europe

The first is technical progress. The most innovative cars are American, Japanese and South Korean, and new technologies are dominated by these three countries. There is no European GAFA, and we are absent from cutting-edge sectors such as artificial intelligence. We are paying a high price for over 20 years of under-investment in R&D&I, due to the incomplete single market and unhealthy public finances.

Without science, there can be no sustainable growth, no social justice, no green economy, no energy autonomy, no European defence. As the advertisement for a famous car brand puts it: "*Vorsprung durch Technik*", progress through technology. The knock-on effect of technical progress, which is another positive spiral and a common thread running through this essay, is considerable: higher productivity, better pay, greater job satisfaction, a more inclusive, dynamic and confident society.

Technical progress must be a transversal priority in European action, on a par with the greening of the economy, if not more so. It will be more effective for the state of the planet and less damaging for our economy if Europe produces eco-responsible technologies that can be used throughout the world, rather than being the only one to use them. In this respect, the Green Deal is naive: 6% of the world's population alone will not save the planet. The von der Leyen Commission has its thinking completely the wrong way round.

For a Substantial Reduction in the Cost of Patents

To better translate the results of scientific research, which remains excellent in the EU, into European products and services, we need to immediately and drastically reduce patent registration costs (these are four times higher than in the USA for a much less optimal internal market). As a first step, these costs need to be divided by 10 (and by 20 for patents relating to clean technologies). The EU now accounts for just 20% of patents filed worldwide, compared with 30% 10 years ago, a fall of 33%. The reduction in registration costs should benefit SMEs in particular.

More Incentives to Innovate

In view of the success of the Nordic approach in this area, Member States could be recommended to lower taxation on intellectual property income, again with a particular focus on patents relating to clean technologies.

Towards More Investment in R&D&I

Given the deficit accumulated since 2000, the level of investment in R&D&I must exceed the target of 3% of GDP set at the time and temporarily rise to 4 or even 5%, i.e. an additional effort of 2–3%.

The deepening of the internal market advocated above will provide a partial solution to the problem in the long term. Our R&D&I

deficit is due in particular to the fact that private investment is lower in Europe than in the United States and Asia, due to imperfections in the internal market that make it less profitable. Public authorities also need to invest more. We need to make up the shortfall in private sector investment while the proposed structural measures take effect.

Public seed investments in R&D&I aimed at catalysing a maximum of private funding could be envisaged, along the lines of the Juncker Plan and its successor InvestEU. We can also speed up the catching-up process in R&D&I by developing attractive frameworks, for example through collective R&D&I investment vehicles. Better support from the financial system for the growth of unicorns after their first few years of existence is also crucial. Too many promising European companies are being taken over by companies from third countries.

Following the example of the Maastricht criteria for public finances, binding targets could be set for Member States in terms of the percentage of GDP allocated to investment in R&D&I (even if part of this comes from the private sector). Or, at the very least, during the annual examination of national budgets (European Semester), particular attention should be paid to the levels of public and private investment in R&D&I and the measures envisaged by the state to raise them.

Investment, particularly in R&D&I, is another common thread running through the essay.

Other Measures to Promote Research

The promotion of an entrepreneurial spirit among researchers, better links between the worlds of research and business, greater awareness of science and technology… Once again, an education adapted to the challenges of today.

A European Research Area (ERA) is also a priority. Certain areas need to have more of a European dimension, which is another of the main thrusts of this essay. Such is the case with research. Just look at how Switzerland and the UK are scrambling not to be excluded from this area and from European funding programmes. The idea is not to break national frames of reference in this area, but to transcend and integrate them into a larger, more fruitful whole.

(ii) Reindustrialising Europe

A third vector for improvement is reindustrialisation in the broadest sense.

Industry offers a number of advantages over a service economy. Firstly, it generally pays better, due to higher productivity. It also generates greater R&D&I activity, which brings us back to technical progress. Finally, it generates twice as many jobs, both direct and indirect, which strengthens and diversifies the economy.

No Turning Back (i): Eco-Responsible Reindustrialisation

This industrial redeployment must include the environmental dimension. It is up to our researchers, industrialists and public authorities to rise to this challenge. Industry and growth must be more qualitative and efficient.

No blaming of industry in the name of a religion of ecology. A company, even in the industrial sector, can be clean. In this respect, a discreet revolution is underway, especially in countries where an eco-liberal/conservative movement has the wind in its sails. The emphasis must be on technological neutrality and performance-based standards, with no a priori exclusion of one technology or another. Once again, a breadcrumb trail highlighted in the course of this essay…

No Turning Back (ii): An Industrial Policy That Respects a Market Economy Where Competition Is Free and Innovative

The EU's mission is to develop the most favourable framework possible for the European economy in order to guarantee its competitiveness while respecting the principle of an open economy with free competition.

As a result, the industrial policy implemented by the EU in recent years to encourage strategic initiatives and remedy market shortcomings is to be encouraged. The initial results are promising (semiconductor industry, alliances in the fields of batteries and green hydrogen).

There is nothing to prevent the EU from creating the general conditions conducive to industrial activity, provided that it maintains competition between several European operators, if only for the sake of risk diversification. We must also avoid subsidising certain companies and returning to the industrial policy of the 1970s.

Innovative approaches to industrial policy, more respectful of the single market and an open social market economy where factors of production can be freely allocated, are to be encouraged. Europe can be at the forefront of winning combinations between the market economy and public economic initiative. This is another focus of this essay.

(iii) A Financial Sector That Is Healthy, Liberated, Complete and Innovative All at the Same Time

As a fourth positive spiral, Europe's financial sector must (re)become an effective complementary engine for the economy, including for its energy and environmental transition and its rise in R&D&I. Europe's response to the 2008 crisis was off the mark in several respects.

The Unchecked Cancer of Bad Bank Debt

Firstly, it did not deal quickly enough with doubtful bank loans (or non-performing loans[502]), which amount to several hundred billion euros 15 years later. Instead of taking targeted, forceful measures, too many regulations and controls were imposed indiscriminately on operators who did not present any particular risks, along with a paralysing compliance culture. The result is clear: on the one hand, banks that are still vulnerable and unable to provide sufficient financing for the EU economy, which is 70% dependent on them; on the other, European operators have plummeted in the world rankings of the largest banking, financial and insurance companies. With it, a reduced capacity to attract capital from the rest of the world and to finance the European economy.

The Unsuccessful and Poorly Adapted Attempt of Shift to Market Finance

Secondly, European policy is wrong to weaken the banks and want to REPLACE them with Anglo-Saxon-style market finance, known as disintermediation because it brings together "directly" the providers of funds and the seekers of funds. It is important to develop the latter IN ADDITION to, and not at the expense of, the former. Two engines are better than one, especially when it comes to meeting ecological and military challenges.

Furthermore, the CMU project is naive. A culture of financial markets cannot be decreed. Europe is different from the United States, given the incomplete single market and the much smaller size of its companies, as already mentioned. The latter are prevented from accessing the financial markets, in particular because of the lack of reliable information. Strengthening market finance will take time, as it presupposes the full completion of the internal market and a change in mentality.

---

502 That is, in default of payment 90 days after the due date.

For a Multipolar Financial System

It would be wiser to develop a multipolar financial system, broader than the bank-financial market pairing. This also means promoting self-financing (which should be facilitated by the proposed deepening of the internal market),[503] the fund industry, insurance and pension funds.

The fund industry is the greatest success of European financial services policy, because it represents a middle way between banking and financial markets. It is therefore more in tune with the current state of the single market and the mentality of European investors.[504] Its potential is not exhausted. In particular, funds with an R&D&I label could be considered, as well as funds promoting more eco-responsible agriculture.

Insurance accounts for a significant proportion of private savings. With the (unfortunate) ageing of the European population, their importance is likely to remain or even grow. It would be a good idea to allow them to invest more in venture capital. Pension funds have a fundamental role to play in Member States whose pension systems are inadequate. They are useful everywhere because of the supplementary pensions they provide, the solidarity they maintain between pensioners and the state of the economy, both upwards and downwards, unlike a pure pay-as-you-go pension scheme, and the very long-term investments they make.

We also need to ensure that the European financial sector is able to attract money from the rest of the world.

---

503 *See* above, Title I, Ch. 1, A.

504 An open-ended fund is obliged to redeem its units if an investor wishes to exit, rather like a bank, although the value of the units may fluctuate. Secondly, the fund management company selects the investments and relieves the investor of this task, acting as a financial intermediary. Lastly, funds are generally distributed by banks, for whom they are convenient products because, through the diversification they guarantee, they are considered less complex and easier to evaluate and recommend than direct investments in a company.

For an Innovative Financial System and More Financial Education

We will also need to work on the elements that our financial system lacks if it is to evolve towards a more innovative, re-industrialised and eco-responsible economy. This raises the question of the range of banking and financial services to be offered and the expertise needed to provide them. Greater emphasis must also be placed on financial innovation.

By the same token, rather than being excluded from the most lucrative investments, Europeans, including retail customers, must be properly prepared for them through financial education. This will also contribute to the success of the Capital Markets Union in the longer term. Again, education. It should be emphasised that, in this area, it contributes to equal opportunities, to an open society where, regardless of social origin, people have a real chance to rise financially.

(iv) People Mobility and Human Capital Development

Mobility, training and the development of human capital are also essential factors for sustainable growth, particularly in a society that places greater emphasis on technical progress and reindustrialisation.

Mobility Initiatives

While very positive initiatives such as Erasmus and EURES, the little-known European job portal, are to be welcomed, they need to be expanded. The mobility of people is a solution to national unemployment and a route to a more rewarding life. We could think about facilitating expatriation, making it compulsory to follow up job offers in neighbouring regions, encouraging the matching of job offers and applications from all over Europe, via applications, better interconnections between national offices, etc.

Training and Human Capital Development

The EU can help to make up for the shortfall in training, particularly continuing training, in order to adapt to modern technologies.

The issue of human capital is fundamental, particularly in order to increase the employability of the population and labour productivity. There are so many developments in technical fields, but also in soft skills and human development. Promoting the teaching of music and the visual arts, education aimed at developing self-confidence (Finnish approach), etc. would be fertile ground for progress.

More broadly, EU training and human development initiatives are likely to help EU residents grow and make better use of their talents. Once again, the education factor.

Towards a Better Work-Life Balance

A priority in human development should be the 2 + 3 objective. Today, it is still difficult for a couple to lead two careers and bring up several children. This is an obstacle to personal development, particularly for women who aspire to a fulfilling private and professional life. That is the potential for happiness, activity and jobs that needs to emerge. Not to mention its contribution to demographics, where the trend in Europe is worrying, with 1.5 children per woman when the fertility rate required to maintain the population is 2.1.

Europe must make a firm commitment to this project, which has potential at every level. With one stone, we can achieve three or four moves.

(v) Transport

Europe must take advantage of being a microcontinent and a large, compact market. This compactness enables it to produce and circulate goods and services fluidly, using less energy (energy intensity rate) and polluting less. However, this major advantage remains largely unexploited.

The trans-European transport network must therefore be completed as a priority, and may need to be extended.

The fragmentation of competences in this area between the Member States poses a problem. Rail freight is losing ground to road freight, despite all the solemn declarations in favour of the former, and the train between two European capitals, Brussels and Luxembourg, is slower today than it was 30 years ago! Is there not a need for European regional planning in parallel with the legitimate powers of the Member States in this area? A project such as the Rhine-Rhône Canal may not be economically rational on a purely French scale, but on an EU scale. Europe itself needs to grow in this area, as it does in research.

The environmental dimension must be duly integrated, given the contribution of transport to greenhouse gas emissions (around 20%). Alongside the promotion of technologies that save on physical journeys or rationalise them (5G, digitalisation, remote communication techniques, smart cities, etc.), our infrastructures and means of transport must therefore be made cleaner. In this respect, the future probably lies in the complementarity of modes of transport, with the emphasis on those that are the most eco-responsible (e.g. train-road, train-boat, rail motorways). As things stand at present, greater use should be made of sea/river and rail.

There should be no dogmatic or exclusive preconceptions, however. The principle of technological neutrality, another key element of this essay, is important. Road and air transport have their uses, and could provide a positive surprise. The principle of banning the internal combustion engine by 2035 was ill-advised in this respect, as the technical progress likely to be made between now and then could make it an alternative to electric cars (think of biofuels: it's not the internal combustion engine that pollutes, but certain fuels!) Europe should only set targets, not decide how to achieve them. Let researchers and entrepreneurs come up with winning solutions.

(vi) Energy Policy

Europe needs to become more self-sufficient in energy, to diversify and secure its external supplies, to have sufficient energy at a low cost, while integrating environmental requirements. Do we realise the extent to which our companies pay more for energy than their American competitors do?

As with transport, a non-dogmatic, pragmatic and flexible approach must prevail. At least when it comes to energy transition, it is best not to close any doors and to be versatile. Reality will be the test bed. The energy or energies that best achieve the objectives set out above will emerge. In the meantime, we cannot avoid debates on nuclear power.

Emphasis must also be placed on storage, interconnection, distribution, conservation (and therefore information, awareness and even education, once again) and efficiency in order to reduce energy losses and wastage as much as possible.

At least two key indicators should receive more attention: the rate of energy dependence, especially on third countries, and the rate of productivity or energy intensity, which measures the quantity and cost of energy required to produce added value. It is vital to reduce the former given that our energy supply is much more dependent on external sources than the United States. On the other hand, our energy productivity is 33% better than that of the Americans. Given the compactness of our territory and our acute sensitivity to environmental issues, we can still significantly improve it.

As in the fields of transport research in particular, the Europe of Energies has yet to be achieved. We still do not think European enough in these sectors. Europe needs to be more than just a juxtaposition of national networks, with its own rational planning in this area. It too must be able to grow.

Preferred Methods and Instruments for Establishing a Supportive Framework

To make the single market "viable", particularly in these six areas, the specific characteristics of the EU (limited budget, competences, powers and administration, greater possibility of working in the medium and longer-term horizons than national governments) militate in favour of certain approaches, generally distinct from those used by the states. These can also be applied to other areas of EU action.

(i) A Structural/Modern Supply Policy

The EU must prioritise the development of a quality framework and improve the general conditions for economic activity.

It must not take the place of economic players or the general public, or relieve them of their responsibilities, but rather facilitate their initiatives and even help to maximise their effects. It must not undermine the supply and demand mechanism. The EU must be an ally, an enhancer to the market economy, to businesses, to people, including users and consumers. It must help these categories of players to grow. In short, it must develop a structural/modern supply-side policy, tackling the missing factors first. It should be emphasised that the sustainable improvement of purchasing does not overlook the need to improve purchasing power in the long term. The Member States should draw inspiration from this approach when they take action in the areas covered by European integration.

(ii) A Systematic Search for Added Value

The principle of subsidiarity should be assessed more rigorously. Irrespective of the inadequacy of national responses, a European initiative must provide significant added value of its own, particularly in economic terms. We might consider requiring a multiplier coefficient or at least a systematic assessment of the contribution to prosperity of the initiatives envisaged.

Combined with respect for the principle of an open economy with free competition, the principle of subsidiarity strengthened in this way would mean that, where it is competent, the EU would have to demonstrate four things (i) market failure, (ii) the inadequacy of action by the Member States and (iii) the intrinsic and substantial added value and (iv) the proportionality of its intervention. The European institutions and bodies must be more demanding in this respect. The EU itself must grow.

This is crucial because, today, prosperity must be able to finance not only an inclusive society, but also one that is eco-responsible and militarily robust.

(iii) Towards a Virtuous Triangle of the Eco-Responsible Social Market Economy

In this respect, the more economically buoyant the framework, the more ambitious the social and environmental objectives can be. It will then be possible for companies to support more demanding soci(et)al and environmental standards. Far from leading to social or environmental dumping – another common misconception – a large, efficient market allows quality requirements to be raised (consumer protection, health, environmental protection, etc.). Think of product safety, especially for toys, the ban on roaming, bank deposit guarantees of up to €100,000 per saver, and requirements for the chemical composition of goods (REACH).

(iv) Towards the Development of More Standards

European products and services can become international standards. We do not realise the extent to which certain European "designations of origin" for some of our goods and services have prestige throughout the world. Through the combined force of product quality and a well-developed legal framework (once again, a synergy between the market and public authorities). A kind of soft power. Much more positive than the extraterritorial *diktats* of certain third countries. The European institutions should develop more frameworks such as UCITS,[505] REACH,[506] VAT,[507] and GDPR.[508]

An Improved Single Market: Added Value in Figures

An improved single market of this kind, coupled with a tried and tested but still perfectible competition policy and an astute trade policy (seeking free trade agreements with third countries that are socially compatible with the European model, safeguarding international trade, as the Europe of 27 is a net exporter of goods and services), should generate appreciable growth gains.

In the light of the various studies in the field, *the proposals developed above are, taking a conservative approach, likely to generate additional growth of at least 7% of GDP*.

The idea is not to increase prosperity in order to consume more and further deplete our environment. On the contrary, I am in favour of more qualitative and efficient sustainable growth.[509] Quite simply, Europe's sound economic health is essential to the ecological transition

505 Undertakings for collective investment in transferable securities.

506 Registration, Evaluation, Authorisation and Restriction of Chemicals. European Regulation concerning the Registration, Evaluation, Authorisation and Restriction of Chemicals.

507 Value-added tax.

508 General Data Protection Regulation.

509 On qualitative growth, *see* Piccard, pp. 83–103.

(more than 1.5% of the annual GDP of the 27), to a more socially just society (more than 20% of the population is threatened by poverty), to the agricultural transition and the defence effort (2% of GDP), to catch up with our technological lag (4 to 5% of GDP at least over the next few years instead of the current 2%), and to complete the European transport network, developing energy interconnections, showing greater solidarity with developing countries (0.7% of GDP instead of 0.47%), bearing in mind that, for a number of Member States, there is the burden of debt and deficit.

B. The EU: A Booster for Public Management

Another part of our society that Europe can improve is more unexpected: the public sector. Given that the public sector represents on average half of the GDP of the 27 Member States today, any improvement, however moderate, in its performance in the broad sense (which is not just economic) will have a considerable effect on the well-being and prosperity of the population. Conversely, if the public sector continues to lag behind, it will frustrate and reduce the progress of businesses and citizens alike.

The construction of Europe contains many seeds for progress in public management. The time has come to nurture them. The EU can also be a lever for modernising public action, making it an effective driving force that complements the single market.

A source of hope, Member States should be more receptive to these ideas today. Given the fall in unemployment in the EU, they no longer need to maintain "fictitious jobs". On the other hand, given the scale of the challenges outlined above, the public sector also needs to make productivity gains.

Member States and the EU are therefore faced with an extremely stimulating and rewarding task: the Union of Public Sectors. How can we raise the average level of public management in the EU? The EU can play various roles here.

(i) Guaranteeing the Key Balances

The Sustainability of Public Finances

Firstly, the EU can act as a guarantor of the major budgetary balances, through various channels (the 3% and 60% rules, the European Semester, control of State aid and economic services of general interest, etc.).

Contrary to popular belief, the health of public finances is improving in Europe. For example, for the first time, no eurozone Member State had an excessive deficit in 2019. Public debt in the EU had fallen by an average of 5% in 6–7 years, making it easier to cope with the pandemic and the war in Ukraine. Between 2021 and 2022, Greek public debt fell from 195 to 171% and continues to fall.[510]

It would be a good idea if the remaining Member States that are reluctant to balance their budgets nevertheless improved their management. Their behaviour weakens or even undermines the EU27, especially at a time of rising interest rates and when so many challenges require public authorities to have financial room for manoeuvre.

The effectiveness of the rules on financial equilibrium must be strengthened, as must the penalties (loss of access to the Structural Funds, loss of eligibility for European programmes, etc.). Stricter control of the rules on state aid and services of general economic interest (SGEIs), and even a tightening of the rules in this area (efficiency requirement), are also likely to reduce public deficits. To give an order

510 At the end of the first quarter of 2023: 168%.

of magnitude, SGEIs represent 6% of the GDP of the 27 Member States and, based on my practice, I can attest that proper application of the European rules can reduce the cost by 20% without compromising the generosity or quality of the public services offered to the population.

Sustainable public finances make it easier for Member States to cope with unforeseen difficulties, to pursue policies of general interest rather than debt servicing, to implement counter-cyclical policies wisely, to be more generous towards the world's poorest countries, and to leave more savings available for private entrepreneurs. As a result, they often go hand in hand with a dynamic economy, more innovation and productivity, and less unemployment.

Price Stability

The second major balance to be preserved is that of price stability, which is the primary mandate of the European Central Bank (ECB). It is a way of protecting people's purchasing power and providing the necessary security for long-term investment.

Since the 2008 crisis, the ECB has been overly tempted to favour a monetary stimulus policy in the form of excessively low interest rates (negative rates in real or nominal terms), in particular so as not to add too much to the debt servicing costs of over-indebted Member States. The result has been to impoverish pensioners, distort the bond market, keep zombie companies alive (which is undermining European productivity), and invest too little in long-term production. While the eurozone is free of exchange rate risks, its economic performance is worse than that of the other EU Member States!

The ECB needs to put the pedal to the metal on cyclical measures, which are by definition temporary and exceptional, and ensure that there is less distortion of supply and demand in a number of segments of the capital market.

Monitoring Macroeconomic, Social and Environmental Balances

Europe can also monitor certain fundamental macroeconomic, social and environmental balances. To this end, it has the European Semester, an annual procedure for examining draft national budgets, national committees set up within this framework, such as the productivity committee, and the multilateral surveillance mechanism. Criteria as essential to prosperity and social peace as the level of investment in R&D&I, the unemployment rate, productivity trends, etc. are regularly examined within these frameworks.

(ii) Towards More Proactive and Effective Public Action

Beyond Balances: A Contribution to a More Proactive Approach

The EU can also improve and boost certain policies.

A first tool, which could be very fruitful, is the European Semester in which the European Commission and the Council examine the draft budgets of the Member States. The Member States remain responsible for their national budgets, while respecting their competences, their diversity and their political preferences; they are, however, invited to put their work back on track, to integrate certain priorities of common general interest.

A first area of success is the systematic promotion of an active employment policy by the Member States. The results have been spectacular: a 45% fall in unemployment between 2013 and 2019 (from 12 to 6.2%) and almost 50% by the end of 2022, despite the pandemic and the war in Ukraine! Productivity, the key to our prosperity, social peace and quality of life, has been under scrutiny since 2016. The eco-responsibility of public budgets is set to play an increasingly important role.

In the current circumstances, it would be a good idea to give more space in the European Semester to a series of key energy parameters and to the vitality of the European economy in terms of patents and R&D&I.

State aid law is designed to improve government intervention in the economy. Firstly, it encourages governments to favour measures of general scope in order to create a favourable biotope for companies operating on their territory, without discrimination (this brings us back to a structural/modern supply-side policy). Secondly, when they intervene in relation to specific businesses or economic sectors, they should pay close attention to the profitability of the projects they plan to support. Finally, intervention in favour of unprofitable projects is subject to a series of conditions.

The contribution of *State aid control* to the quality of public action could be further optimised, for example by insisting on more stringent requirements regarding the positive impact of aid (e.g. by requiring a multiplier coefficient).

Beyond Balances (ii): Structural Improvements in Public Management

The various instruments put in place (European Semester, Stability Pact, broad economic policy guidelines, control of State aid and SGEIs, etc.) could lead to greater ambition in public management and a renewed vision of public economic action.

Consider in particular:

(i) the generalisation of best national budgetary practices (techniques for drawing up and executing the budget);

(ii) the prohibition of the financing of public services and the pension system through debt (it is not up to future generations to pay for these current expenses);

(iii) the measurement of the productivity of public action (BARS curve) and of public investment (requirement for a multiplier coefficient?);

(iv) the size and composition of public spending;

(v) the possible introduction of a dose of competition in certain public service systems (health, education, etc.);

(vi) control of the percentage of managerial posts;

(vii) the conditions imposed on the recruitment of new civil servants, synonymous with the creation of an additional perpetual debt, etc.

With regard to the composition of the budget (above under iv), the question arises as to the place, alongside transfer and redistribution expenditure (benefits, social security, health policy, etc.), of sovereign responsibilities (internal security, justice, defence, civil protection, etc.), protection of the ecosystem, the strategic state and investment. Social democracy is precious. However, it must not overshadow the other responsibilities of the public authorities, nor should it put them to sleep. Member States' capacity to invest, innovate, adapt and respond to current and future challenges must not be compromised.

(viii) Cooperation (exchange of best practices, etc.) or even coordination in the management of the respective public debts of the Member States could also be envisaged. Responsibility, particularly financial responsibility, is essential in the construction of Europe and applies equally to the EU (which cannot have debts), the Member States (only the population of a Member State is responsible for the policy decisions it has chosen) and companies. Temporary and conditional solidarity mechanisms between Member States are, however, conceivable as long as they do not remove responsibility from those who benefit from them, add value to the whole and do not (excessively) prejudice the other Member States and the EU.

We could envisage a partial and functional "mutualisation" of the debt of those Member States that show progress in their management through a collective refinancing system... as long as this progress continues.

Greater Respect for the Principle of a Market Economy

Europe would benefit from a more effective application of the principle of a market economy in which competition is free and resources can be allocated efficiently. *At European level*, this principle means that EU intervention is only triggered if there is a market failure.

However, this principle is also binding *on Member States* when they act in areas of interest to the Community as a whole. Greater respect for this principle should lead to public action that is more mature, more proportionate, more based on the driving forces of the economy and society, less costly for public finances and less counterproductive.

European society would benefit from Member States regulating only where necessary and giving priority to the development of general frameworks that are likely to increase initiative and productivity, without distorting competition. All it would take is for the Court of Justice of the European Union to give this principle the scope it deserves.

Far from preventing public intervention, the principle of respecting an open market economy would make it easier to distinguish the good from the bad and to aim for greater granularity in public policies.

EU: An Opportunity to Renew Private-Public Interaction

In a similar vein, another area for progress is for the EU to promote better synergies between the market and public action. This can help to transcend the traditional and, in my view, outdated opposition between private initiative and public interventionism. Public economic action can be an additional driving force, provided that it complements the market and interacts positively with it.

Some Private-Public Synergies

Several types of synergies between the public and private sectors have already been mentioned:

- regulatory standards which provide an additional quality label for European products and services and facilitate their export to the rest of the world (UCITS, etc.);
- modern industrial policy;
- public seed investment (Juncker Plan, InvestEU, etc.) or back-up investment (EIB, EIF);
- the development of public expertise that the market does not generate and which contributes to a better functioning of the market (EURES portal, reduction of information asymmetry between SMEs seeking financing and investors via the EIF, etc.).

What these achievements have in common is that the public sphere makes a contribution that, for various reasons, the market cannot provide.

Added Value of Financial Instruments in the Pursuit of General Interests

The EIB, the EU's development bank owned by the Member States, is able to raise €60 billion worldwide every year, which it then makes available to the European economy, both public and private, in the form of loans and guarantees. Today, the EIB's outstanding financing amounts to €550 billion, or more than 3% of the GDP of the 27 Member States, three to four times the EU's annual budget!

The EIB finances the European economy without distorting competition, acting as a last resort to support the traditional banking sector when the latter is unwilling to lend the full amount (market failure). It does not risk undue exposure since it invests up to a maximum of 20%, and only in viable projects. A fine example of how public action can complement the market economy. It is also a fine example of financial accountability, since the EIB has to balance its books without a public budget.

The EIF, which takes equity stakes in SMEs and provides them with guarantees, also manages €100 billion entrusted to it by third parties, generally public authorities. Once again, on the basis of its efficiency.

The successes of the EIB and the EIF raise the question of whether, rather than increasing the Community budget and pursuing a policy of traditional subsidies, it would not be more appropriate to increase the capital of these two organisations. The multiplier effect (once again, this notion) of their interventions is, in fact, much greater.

More generally, the EIB and the EIF raise questions about what are the most appropriate instruments (particularly financial) for achieving European objectives of general interest. Their successes argue in favour of adapting *economic, social and territorial cohesion policy*. This policy should be more about development and less about transfers. In recent years, the Structural Funds have begun to use loans or equity investments rather than subsidies, with the advantage that the former are not non-repayable. This trend needs to be extended.

It is interesting that the EU's development aid policy is opening up to such financial instruments in order to improve its effectiveness.

Public guarantees are also a way of facilitating the switch to an eco-responsible economy: without a helping hand from the public authorities, a number of economic operators, even public ones, will be reluctant to make a long-term commitment (20, 30, 40, 50 years) for a complex transition.

Member States would be well advised to take inspiration from these European cases as well.

Improving Public Action in the EU: Forecast Results

Still taking a conservative approach, the Union of the public sectors could increase the GDP of the EU27 by 3.5% and, combined with the completion and perfecting of the internal market, lead to a 10.5% increase in GDP.

C. Priority for Investment

To safeguard European society, meet the challenges it faces and give it a lasting fresh impetus, it is not enough to improve the internal market and the overall efficiency of public action. We need to look further into the future and invest more.

In this respect, the EU has a substantial advantage. Its operating costs are low (much lower than those of the Member States, contrary to popular belief). The European budget in the proper sense of the word (€170 billion, or just over 1% of the GDP of the 27) can therefore be allocated first and foremost to productive investment in order to safeguard tomorrow's growth and prosperity. Add to this the firepower of the EIB and the EIF, mentioned above.

Priority areas could be some of those mentioned above, i.e. R&D&I, technologies of the future, transport, energy, defence, resource management, with a growing concern for a more environmentally friendly economy (energy efficiency, concern for efficiency, circular economy). It may be time to reduce the share of the Common Agricultural Policy in the Community budget, which still consumes a third of it.

A structural/modern supply-side policy will also aim to encourage private investment, particularly from public start-ups. The most obvious example is that of the Juncker Plan where, with €21 "small" billion from the European budget, including €16 billion in the form of guarantees, more than €500 billion of investment has been generated.

The key words will be the synergy between private investment and public intervention, the complementarity of the latter and its strict correlation with the identified market failure, an idea already mentioned in relation to public action in general.

Greater emphasis should also be placed on financial innovation to facilitate investment. For example, the design of frameworks and private investment vehicles benefiting from a favourable regime as long as they pursue a long-term policy, or even European objectives (in particular R&D&I efforts, and all the more so in eco-responsible R&D&I), is an avenue to be explored.

Target Figures

Based on a conservative estimate, these recommended investments should generate an increase in GDP for the EU27 of at least 2%.

With a windfall of 12.5% more GDP each year (7% for improving the internal market, 3.5% for improving public action, 2% for investment), the Member States and the EU should be able to tackle the challenges of a social Europe, eco-responsibility and common defence, as suggested by figure 30 below.

Figure 30.

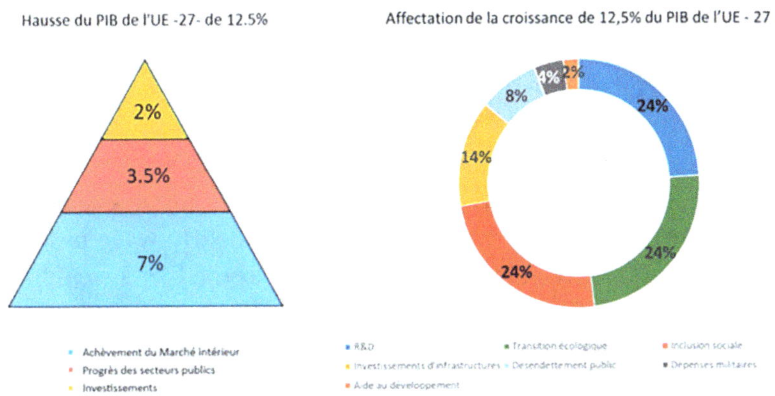

In the light of other more optimistic projections, supported less by concrete proposals, the estimate of this windfall is cautious. For example, the European Parliament has put the cost of non-Europe between 2019 and 2024 at more than €2.2 trillion a year, putting the margin for growth at more than 15%.

D. For a More Inclusive Society

The Contribution of a Comprehensive Structural Policy to Social Justice

The proposals put forward above should lead to (i) more jobs and (ii) better paid jobs. The population could also (iii) be taxed less, given the progress in public management and the higher employment rate which would reduce social security costs. Purchasing power should be (iv) further increased by a competition policy and a monetary policy more focused on price stability. Finally, (v) better quality public services should be provided at constant or even decreasing prices.

If the Structural Policy Is Inadequate, a More Proactive Approach Is Needed

If the structural policy outlined above is not enough to guarantee a higher level of social justice, more proactive and far-reaching measures will have to be considered, at least initially, particularly in view of the time required for a structural/modern supply-side policy to bear fruit. We might consider a minimum hourly wage based on labour productivity in the Member State concerned, or a wealth tax. It would also make sense for those companies that receive a larger and more favourable playing field from the EU to take on more social responsibilities.

E. The Environmental Challenge: Fundamental but Not the Most Difficult for Europe

All things considered, the environmental challenge is more affordable for Europe than for other regions of the world. Indeed, as already mentioned, Europe can count on a considerable asset, its compactness: it is the largest market in the world in the smallest area, comparatively speaking. Our energy productivity is a third better than that of the United States. What is more, we can improve it substantially, as our population is receptive to environmental issues. That said, Europe's small size requires a healthier ecosystem.

The work on the fundamentals recommended above should lead to technical progress and better planning of our common space, likely to improve the ecological balance sheet. It will also free up the financial resources to make the investments needed to turn our economy and society green. Greater emphasis needs to be given to Europe's capacity to design and produce eco-responsible technologies that can be exported worldwide (rather than being the sole user).

This effort must be systematic in European initiatives as well as in the actions of governments, businesses and individuals. For example, patents and other intellectual property rights relating to clean technologies should be subject to lower registration costs and more attractive taxation. Aid for clean R&D&I should benefit from a more liberal regime. The same goes for investment funds labelled as clean R&D&I. There could also be a more favourable depreciation policy when a polluting technology is replaced by a cleaner device.

The sum total of (small) steps on energy and environmental issues should pay off. This project is also likely to contribute to the cohesion of European society.

F. Democracy and Freedoms: Precious Assets to Be Preserved and Strengthened

Our system of democracy and freedoms is a jewel. We must be uncompromising in our defence of it on European territory, against both internal and external adversaries. Not only is it the foundation of European society, it is also an unprecedented force in the pursuit of the general interest objectives mentioned above.

The EU is important for maintaining the rule of law, the separation of powers, the freedoms of tolerance and pluralism, the hallmarks of an open society where everyone has the chance to develop and grow in respect for each other.

After all, is this not the area in which the EU, despite being accused of not being democratic enough, has been most successful and most consistent? Set up as a reaction to the errors of the German, French and Italian democracies of the 1930s (the three major founding Member States), it has contributed to the peaceful coexistence of different ethnic and linguistic groups within the Member States, and to the strengthening of fundamental rights and the rule of law. Today, it is fighting tooth and nail against the slide towards totalitarianism in Member States that have just emerged from Soviet dictatorship. Not to mention its support for Ukraine.

However, we must work to improve our democracies. We must not be complacent. Progress is possible in this area too.

Europe can contribute to this process and help democracies flourish. These can be enhanced in particular by greater participation – provided it is of high quality – of the population in decision-making.

Citizens must also be better educated to fight against manipulation and destabilisation, for example via social media, particularly those orchestrated by third countries. Democracy cannot pride itself on being the worst system of all. These other systems can be perfected, even in their corrupt state.

It is also important that, alongside local, regional and national political societies, a new political society develops around the EU. European political life could be integrated into the lives of European citizens through various channels (specifically European media, scoreboards, citizen involvement in certain European policies such as making the economy greener, applications to overcome the language barrier, education, etc.). Such participation, in turn, is likely to provide an additional stimulus to the effectiveness of European action, through the increased scrutiny it would bring.

G. Foreign Policy

With stronger economic, social and democratic foundations, Europe will also be able to take up the challenge of its common defence, within the wider framework of NATO. In particular, the 27 will be in a position to assume the cost of a greater contribution to their defence.

The EU will also be able to give itself the means to pursue a foreign policy without imperialist pretensions, starting with its relations with its immediate neighbours, for whom it will be a pole of stability and development. More broadly, it will ensure the development of international economic exchanges and the reduction of poverty in the world.

H. The European Union: A Booster and a Lever

The EU enhances prosperity, openness, inclusiveness, freedoms and the rule of law. The extra wealth and social peace it can generate is also a lever for more social and ecological development and greater external security.

It must pursue these objectives for the people and businesses of Europe, as well as for the Member States, who have entrusted these objectives to the EU and remain the masters of the construction process with their citizens. This requires an open and free society and economy, a framework conducive to activity, initiative, innovation and human development, individual responsibility at every level of government, conditional solidarity mechanisms, and an EU that is more assertive in certain areas (regional planning, research, transport, energy and even education, etc.).

The EU can do most of this within the current legal framework, without revising the Treaties, without acquiring new powers, and without new financial resources. It must play its complementary role in conjunction with the Member States. The EU is neither a state nor a superstate, but a supranational organisation, with a light, inexpensive administration, relieved of day-to-day management, dedicated to defining enabling frameworks, concerned with preserving and improving fundamental aspects in a series of key areas.

EU action can, and indeed must, take different forms from that of the Member States. It has specific advantages (such as its helicopter vision, its ability to give major impetus and to work over the longer term, the capacity to catalyse private investment via its financial arms, the EIB and the EIF). At the same time, it has limitations and weaknesses that are distinct from those of the Member States (limited budget, administration by design, no taxing power, inability to contract debts).

The EU must ensure that each of its initiatives brings significant added value in the pursuit of its objectives. This requires thorough groundwork, the gradual development of specific expertise and the systematic pursuit of efficiency and regulatory and administrative restraint.

Concentrating on its core responsibilities should improve its relations with the Member States, which fear – wrongly – that they will be marginalised and replaced by the EU. Greater efficiency combined with better communication on its achievements should attract more public support from the populations who actually enjoy many rights and interests as a result of it.

In this way, the conditions for the birth and development of a genuine European political society, which would complement the national political societies and not replace them or threaten them, would be brought together.

One of the guiding principles of this essay is to seek to make the most of the EU27, a community rich in talent and diversity, including the coexistence of the private and public sectors, in a small area, and to help its various components to grow by placing them in a favourable context. The margins generated will enable Member States to pursue policies in the general interest, in line with the preferences of their populations, and to move towards a cleaner economy in a more inclusive and safer society.

I. Targets for 2030

The prospects outlined above should enable the EU to achieve, by 2030, at least:

- Increase average worker income by 10% and GDP by 12.5%;
- Reduce unemployment by 15%, poverty by 20% and the risk of social exclusion by 25%;
- Improve our productivity and energy efficiency by 30%.

Prosperous, serene, dynamic and alert, Europe will also be able to play a stabilising role and contribute to the development of neighbouring regions and populations.

Looking beyond these numbers, it is a question of helping the population, businesses, Member States and the EU to grow with a view to increasing the opportunities and the quality of life of its peoples.[511] It is about reinjecting dynamism, progress and hope.

We have a fine instrument at our disposal. Let us make the most of it and make the most of its potential. The challenges of today

511 Hence the subtitle of this essay, *A Europe That Will Make Us Grow*, suggested to me by Isabelle Lebbe, Investment Management Partner at Arendt & Medernach and recent holder of a master's degree in Change Management from INSEAD.

and tomorrow require us all to raise our game. In this respect, we can be optimistic. The Capitol is not far from the Tarpeian Rock, especially when, like Europe, we are halfway or three quarters of the way there.

Appendix: Practical Recommendations

1. Deepening and completing the internal market. Priority to radical, immediate and inexpensive measures, such as:
   - A general mutual recognition of goods and services legally produced in a Member State, whether or not there is European harmonisation;
   - A common minimum foundation for companies;
   - A much more determined fight against protectionism (with, in particular, a system applying by default to Member States that have not transposed the directives in time);
   - The promotion of language applications;
   - Liberalisation measures.
2. Educate consumers, savers, investors and workers rather than resorting to old-fashioned patronage, restrictions and bans, etc., so that they can take full advantage of the single market and play an active part in technological and economic developments.
3. Regulatory streamlining adapted to the modest average size of companies (5.6 employees per company); regulatory streamlining: “3 to 5 out; 1 in”.
4. Refocusing the EU on its core competences: priority to economic prosperity and a highly competitive and innovative social market economy.
5. Positive spiral between this cluster and the social and environmental clusters, a European measure designed to generate added value in these three areas.
6. Greater emphasis on the added value of any European intervention (multiplier requirement), particularly in terms of economic, social and territorial cohesion.
7. Greater respect by the EU and the Member States for the principle of an open market economy where free competition prevails in order to ensure an efficient allocation of resources.
8. Principles of technological and energy neutrality.

9. Priority to public investment and guarantees, rather than subsidies, and encouraging private investment.
10. Strengthening the EIB and EIF or at least the use of their financing instruments.
11. Creation of labelled funds for innovation (with a more favourable regime for clean innovation) and for the greening of agriculture.
12. A 10-fold reduction in the cost of registering patents and a 20-fold reduction in the cost of "own" patents.
13. Investment in R&D&I of 5% of the GDP of the 27 instead of 2% to make up for the shortfall in this area. - Binding RDI investment targets for member states, the EU, the EIB and the EIF.
14. Systematic promotion of clean technologies (e.g. patents, but also aid and labelled collective investment vehicles, more favourable depreciation rules in the event of replacement by cleaner technologies).
15. CAP budget cut to benefit more investments.
16. Clean, competitive reindustrialisation.
17. Towards a multipolar financial system (banks, markets, funds, pension funds, insurance, self-financing) and not just the bank-financial market pairing, reorganised, partially liberated and once again innovative.
18. Investing in lifelong learning and adapting to a changing world.
19. Strict approach to public intervention and standard-setting initiatives, to limit them to what is necessary and guarantee their effectiveness and efficiency:
    - Market failure;
    - Insufficient national solution;
    - Intrinsic European added value;
    - Working on what is missing;
    - Concern for the multiplier effect of public measures;
    - Public intervention as a last resort, conditional, proportionate, temporary, monitored, reviewed;
    - Contribution to essential economic prosperity, environmental and inclusive added value on a complementary basis, as part of a positive dynamic;
    - Impact assessment by independent economic centres;

- The need for brevity;
- Research into the development of standards;
- *Ex post* evaluation.

20. In favour of a European semester and multilateral surveillance with greater emphasis on monitoring productivity, innovation and certain fundamental energy parameters.

21. For a monetary policy that is more respectful of its mission of price stability and the principle of an open market economy with free competition.

22. More stringent accounting requirements for SGEIs and even a higher multiplier for State aid – more enforcement of the rules on state aid and SGEIs.

23. Modernising public management: towards greater effectiveness and efficiency:
    - Sustainability of public finances;
    - Temporary solidarity mechanism that does not remove responsibility: refinancing national debt with a net positive balance;
    - Improving public management on key issues (unemployment, productivity, innovation, energy policy and performance, drafting and execution of national budgets, procedures for hiring new civil servants (compared with permanent contracts); BARS curve, productivity of public investment, methods of financing different public policies, etc.).
    - Greater integration of the European dimension (in national recovery plans);
    - Reduction in the percentage of managerial posts, reflection on the reallocation of financial and human resources in the public sector following reforms and in particular liberalisation and Europeanisation, which make certain national public managers less necessary or at least militate in favour of their “downsizing”;
    - Open market economy with free competition;
    - Better combination of policy and structural measures-contracyclicality;
    - Principle of responsibility;

24. More investment, including military investment.

25. For more qualitative and efficient growth and agriculture.

26. For the emergence of a greater European dimension in research, economic, social and territorial cohesion policy, transport, energy, recovery plans, agriculture, independent economic centres, political society, the media, spatial planning (the idea of addition rather than substitution), etc.
27. Reconciling full-time work for both members of a couple with a large family (objective 2 + 3).
28. Concern for the interests of each state: possibility of regaining control of the national economy, one Marshallese district per Member State.
29. Audit of European policies: internal market, structural funds, CAP, energy, transport.
30. Wealth tax, minimum hourly wage, compensatory allowance or negative tax on low-productivity jobs, etc.
31. Agricultural SGEI, agricultural investment funds, a European agricultural agency in the East, a sector with education, European regional planning.
32. On the environmental front, systematic promotion of clean technologies (aid, innovation, investment funds, etc.), and a carbon tax.
33. Democracy: combating misinformation and manipulation, limiting the size of proposals and texts for European regulations and directives.
34. A 28th "State": population of EU civil servants and expats, etc.

TABLE OF CONTENTS

Concurrences Review

Concurrences is a print and online quarterly peer reviewed journal dedicated to EU and national competitions laws. It has been launched in 2004 as the flagship of the Institute of Competition Law in order to provide a forum for academics, practitioners and enforcers. Concurrences' influence and expertise has garnered contributions or interviews with such figures as Christine Lagarde, Bill Kovacic, Emmanuel Macron, Antonin Scalia and Magrethe Vestager.

Contents

More than 15,000 articles, print and/or online. Quarterly issues provide current coverage with contributions from the EU or national or foreign countries thanks to more than 2,500 authors in Europe and abroad.

Format

In order to balance academic contributions with opinions or legal practice notes, Concurrences provides its insight and analysis in a number of formats:

- Forewords: Opinions by leading academics or enforcers
- Interviews: Interviews of antitrust experts
- On-Topics: 4 to 6 short papers on hot issues
- Law & Economics: Short papers written by economists for a legal audience
- Articles: Long academic papers
- Case Summaries: Case commentary on EU and French case law
- Legal Practice: Short papers for in-house counsels
- International: Medium size papers on international policies
- Books Review: Summaries of recent antitrust books
- Articles Review: Summaries of leading articles published in 45 antitrust journals

Boards

The Scientific Committee is headed by Laurence Idot, Professor at Panthéon Assas University. The International Committee is headed by Frederic Jenny, OECD Competition Comitteee Chairman. Boards members include Douglas Ginsburg, Benoît Cœuré, Howard Shelanski, Richard Whish, Wouter Wils, Joshua Wright, etc.

Online version

Concurrences website provides all articles published since its inception, in addition to selected articles published online only in the electronic supplement.

Write for Concurrences

Concurrences welcome spontaneous contributions. Except in rare circumstances, the journal accepts only unpublished articles, whatever the form and nature of the contribution. The Editorial Board checks the form of the proposals, and then submits these to the Scientific Committee. Selection of the papers is conditional to a peer review by at least two members of the Committee. Within a month, the Committee assesses whether the draft article can be published and notifies the author.

www.ingramcontent.com/pod-product-compliance
Lightning Source LLC
LaVergne TN
LVHW020050110826
845155LV00021B/57